Woodbrooke College
200 26134
D0714495

Richard Norton-Taylor was European Community and Brussels correspondent for the Washington Post and Newsweek between 1967 and 1975, while also contributing to The Economist and the Financial Times. He joined the Guardian in 1975, concentrating on Whitehall, official secrecy, and behind-the-scenes decision-making. His books include: Whose Land Is It Anyway? an investigation into land ownership (1981, Turnstone Press); The Ponting Affair (1985, Cecil Woolf); Blacklist, The Inside Story of Political Vetting (with Mark Hollingsworth, 1988, The Hogarth Press); In Defence Of The Realm: The Case for Accountable Security and Intelligence Services (1990, Civil Liberties Trust); A Conflict of Loyalties, GCHQ 1984-1991 (with Hugh Lanning, 1991, New Clarion Press).

He is a trustee of the Civil Liberties Trust and of London Action Trust. He won the 1986 Freedom of Information Campaign award, and the same year was prevented by a court injunction from reporting the contents of Spycatcher, the memoirs of the former MI5 agent, Peter Wright. The Government's injunction was dismissed in the High Court by Lord Justice Scott.

Richard Norton-Taylor was one of the few journalists to cover the Scott inquiry from start to finish. His play, Half the Picture, based on the inquiry, received a 1994 Time Out Drama, Comedy and Dance award for its "brave initiative".

Truth Is a Difficult Concept:

Inside the Scott Inquiry

RICHARD NORTON-TAYLOR

WITH MARK LLOYD

A **Guardian Book**

320.4

First Published in Great Britain in 1995 by
Fourth Estate Limited
289 Westbourne Grove
London W11 2QA

Copyright © 1995 by Richard Norton-Taylor

The right of Richard Norton-Taylor to be identified as the author
of this work has been asserted by him in accordance with Copyright,
Designs and Patents Act 1988.

A catalogue record for this book is available from the British Library.

ISBN 1-85702-321-8   20026134

All rights reserved. No part of this publication may be reproduced,
transmitted, or stored in a retrieval system, in any form or by any means,
without permission in writing from Fourth Estate Ltd.

Designed, produced and edited by PD2, *The***Guardian**

Printed in Great Britain by Redwood Books, a division of BPMG Plc

Truth Is a Difficult Concept

"Sunlight is said to be the best of disinfectants;
electric light the most efficient policeman."

Louis Brandeis, former US Supreme Court judge.

"The cover-up is greater than the original sin;
the greatest sin of all is to be found out."

Senior Whitehall official (anon).

Acknowledgments

The Scott inquiry was set up by a beleaguered Government in November 1992. This book is based on its 87 public hearings held between May 1993 and July 1994. Other material was provided by sources who would like to remain anonymous.

The public hearings were often eye-openers. Sometimes, they were frustrating. On occasion, they were (unintentionally) entertaining. They were made more stimulating and enjoyable by my colleagues in the media – Mark Lloyd of Channel 4 News, Michael Dynes of The Times, Sean O'Neill of the Daily Telegraph, Dave Connett, then of The Independent, Gavin Cordon of the Press Association, Jimmy Burns of the Financial Times and Graeme McLagan of the BBC.

Christopher Muttukumaru, the inquiry's secretary, and David Price, its spokesman, were helpful on matters of published – or officially publishable – facts, and otherwise always courteous.

I would like to thank Tony Ageh and Camilla Nicholls of the Guardian for appreciating the significance of the inquiry, and Jane Carr of 4th Estate. Nicolas Kent, artistic director of the Tricycle Theatre in Kilburn, north London, who had the imagination to perform material from the inquiry on the stage. His courage was rewarded by enthusiastic reviews and an appreciative audience.

I would especially like to thank Apala Chowdhury of the Guardian's Product Development Unit for her work in putting the book together; for her suggestions, encouragement, enthusiasm, goading and editing. She was a wonderful collaborator.

And I would like to thank my wife, Anna, who lived through the inquiry, the play, and the book, with someone who for so long appeared distracted and, at times, obsessed.

Contents

Introduction

On the surface, the Matrix Churchill trial caused hardly a stir. Despite the acrid smell of scandal, of a desperate attempt by the Government to conceal a mix of cover-up and conspiracy, media interest was minimal. The slow seepage of disclosures did not encourage either consistent or prominent reporting. MPs, too, were innocently unaware of the worms wriggling under the desks of ministers and mandarins.

The trial's collapse changed all that – for a time. Amid belated parliamentary outcry, Whitehall was thrown into a state of panic as senior civil servants – including John Major's closest advisers – ran around in search of alibis and excuses when they realised the Government was in the dock. In a "tilt" towards Iraq agreed behind Parliament's back, it had secretly given the go-ahead to exports knowing they would be used by Saddam Hussein to make weapons. It then watched as three businessmen were prosecuted for selling arms-related equipment to Iraq in which it had itself connived.

Officials, and later ministers, knew that Paul Henderson, former managing director of Matrix Churchill and chief defendant at the trial, had been supplying information to MI6 about Iraq's weapons programme. Four ministers had put their signatures to documents – Public Interest Immunity certificates – which would have prevented the disclosure of documents crucial to the defence had they not been overruled by the trial judge.

Government lawyers conspired with civil servants to suppress embarrassing and damaging information. When they were found out, civil servants blamed each other, or ministers, while ministers blamed their officials in what became the biggest buck-passing operation in the history of Whitehall.

What started off, from Whitehall's point of view, as a damage-limitation exercise led to the most exhaustive inquiry ever undertaken into Britain's machinery of government – such was the scope John Major gave Lord Justice Scott. The badly-shaken Government hoped the inquiry would give it time to prepare its defence, and deflect awkward questions. Backed by the Speaker, Betty Boothroyd, ministers refused to answer questions about any issue remotely relevant, telling MPs to await the outcome of the inquiry. Ministers and the Commons' Table Office blocked questions even though Lord Justice Scott said in a letter to the Labour backbencher, Llew Smith: "I, for my part, have no objection to government ministers answering parliamentary questions regarding matters within the terms of reference of the inquiry."

Robin Cook, shadow trade and industry secretary, pointed out that MPs were being barred from asking questions on the very issues which were being raised and reported at the inquiry. "I cannot think of a distinction more likely to encourage Parliament to fall into desuetude and disrespect," he said with uncanny echoes of how MPs had been kept in the dark for so many years about the way the Government had helped to arm Saddam Hussein. If MPs wished to complain, they should do so privately, said Betty Boothroyd, whose secretary, by intriguing coincidence, was Nicolas Bevan, a former senior ministry of defence and cabinet office official who was a key witness in both the Iraqi supergun affair and the Matrix Churchill arms-to-Iraq case being investigated by the Scott inquiry.

The Government picked Lord Justice Scott for the job to avoid charges that it had chosen a compliant judge. It hoped, nevertheless, he would conduct a narrow inquiry, that he would give the Government the benefit of the doubt. The Government's gamble did not pay off. The rigorously independent member of the judiciary, with Presiley Baxendale, the sharp-shooting QC at his side, made it clear from the start he had little time for the arrogance of closed government, and the circumlocution of its perpetrators.

The inquiry slowly undressed Whitehall, exposing incompetence, dissembling, dishonesty, a patronising approach to Parliament and – perhaps worst of all – unacceptable interference in a criminal prosecution. Armed with tens of thousands of documents, Scott and

Baxendale frequently knew the answers to questions before they asked them, as some of the more wily witnesses appreciated. Many of the most illuminating insights were provided by unintended humour – the source of some of the best comedy as well as of self-inflicted wounds.

Had the inquiry been televised – as it certainly would have been in the US – it would have attracted wider interest at the time. The judge suggested that television cameras would have trivialised the proceedings. Nevertheless the inquiry was a goldmine for students of the way we are governed, much more enlightening than prepared lectures or textbooks. It was also an eye-opener for MPs, too often the care-worn, cynical, guardians of our parliamentary democracy. Too few MPs, and hardly more than a handful of members of the public turned up to 1 Buckingham Gate, London SW1, to witness such a unique experience. Whitehall will do its utmost to ensure that never again will a judge be given such freedom to conduct a public inquiry into the activities of government.

Chronology

1979　Thatcher becomes Prime Minister

1980　Iran-Iraq war begins

1985　Guidelines restricting exports to Iran and Iraq announced in Parliament

1987　Iraqis take control of Matrix Churchill

1987　November: First MI6 report confirming British machine tool companies selling equipment to Iraqi arms factories

1988　January: Alan Clark meets machine tool exporters

February: Ministers approve first batch of Matrix Churchill exports to Iraq

March: Saddam Hussein's forces attack Kurdish town of Halabja with chemical weapons, killing 5,000 civilians in the first use of such weapons by a state against its own citizens

August: Ceasefire in Iran-Iraq war

September: Paul Henderson says MI6 re-recruits him

December: Ministers agree to secret policy shift relaxing controls on exports to Iraq and Iran

1989　February: Iran announces *fatwa* against Salman Rushdie. Britain limits new, relaxed, export guidelines to Iraq

February: Ministers approve second batch of Matrix Churchill exports to Iraq

September: Observer journalist, Farzad Bazoft, arrested in Baghdad

November: Ministers agree on third batch of Matrix Churchill exports to Iraq

1990　March: Bazoft executed

1990　April: Customs at Teesport seize steel pipes, parts for Iraq's supergun project

June: Matrix Churchill visited by Customs

July 19: Cabinet committee approves more liberal export policy towards Iraq

July 27: Department of Trade and Industry approves final batch of Matrix Churchill exports to Iraq, knowing they are to be used to make shells and missiles

August 2: Iraq invades Kuwait

October: Customs raids Matrix Churchill

November: Charges against two men relating to the supergun affair dropped on the advice of the Attorney-General. Customs furious

1991   February: British land forces engage in Gulf war

February: Henderson and two fellow Matrix Churchill directors arrested

November: The Matrix Churchill 3 committed to trial at the Old Bailey

1992   June-September: Four ministers sign Public Interest Immunity certificates designed to prevent vital evidence from being disclosed at the trial

October: Matrix Churchill trial opens at the Old Bailey

November 9: Trial collapses

November 10: Major sets up the Scott inquiry

1994   May: Conviction against two Euromac directors sentenced in the Iraqi "nuclear triggers" case quashed on appeal

1994   July: Conviction against two men sentenced for trying to sell sub-machine guns to Iraq via Jodan quashed on appeal

The Scott inquiry received written evidence from more than 200 witnesses, sat in public session for over 430 hours, sat in closed session for about 60 hours, gathered over 200,000 pages of documents. Over 60 witnesses were heard in more than 80 days of public hearings.

A further 15 (mainly members of the security and intelligence agencies) gave evidence in secret sessions. The inquiry cost between £2 million and £3 million.

MEMBERS OF THE INQUIRY TEAM/THE INDEPENDENT/GERAINT LEWIS

Dramatis Personae

SIR RICHARD (RASHLEIGH FOLLIOTT) SCOTT: 60-year-old son of a
Gurkha colonel, born in the foothills of the Himalayas, spent his early
days on the north-west frontier before his parents moved to South
Africa where he was educated at Cape Town University. Won
Commonwealth scholarship to Cambridge (where he won a blue for
rugby). Met Rima, his New York-born, Panamanian dancer/teacher
while at Chicago University. Recreations include fox-hunting (Grafton
Hunt, north Oxon), tennis, bridge. Still fit – he often cycled to the
inquiry.

Former chairman of the Bar, became Chancery judge in 1983. A year
later, he found for the Government against the Guardian saying that
documents leaked by FO clerk Sarah Tisdall were government property.
Liberal instincts reflected in 1985 when he granted a group of South
Wales miners an injunction to stop mass NUM picketing. In 1987, found
for the Guardian and the Observer against the Government's attempt to
ban Spycatcher, memoirs of the former MI5 officer, Peter Wright.
Promoted to Court of Appeal and, in 1994, to post of Vice-Chancellor,
head of the High Court's Chancery division – traditionally a stepping
stone to becoming a Law Lord. Followed recent trend of senior judiciary
to promote independent-minded judges. Fully accepted a son and a
daughter's conversion to Islam. Impeccably dressed, polite, but sceptical,
and master of the sharp intervention. Example: "They don't make
lavatory seats in a munitions factory" – to unfortunate Ministry of
Defence official, Alan Barrett.
**Author's note: As Vice-Chancellor, head of the High Court's Chancery
division, he now holds the official title, Sir Richard Scott. I have used the
title he held throughout the public hearings: Lord Justice Scott.**

PRESILEY (LAMORNA) BAXENDALE: 43-year-old convent- and Oxford-educated counsel to the inquiry, once voted to have the most mellifluous name in the Bar. Parents allegedly chose the name after friends saw a silver loving cup engraved: "To my darling Presiley." Father, manufacturer of Turkish Delight; married to Richard FitzGerald, tax barrister. They have two children, Charlie and Felicity. Lives in Nash terrace house near London's Regent's Park. Described by long-term friend as an "unconventional product of boarding school".

Counsel to Jasmine Beckford and Kimberley Carlile child abuse inquiries. Member of ICSTIS where she rejected a plan to ban Dial Mr Dark. "I find it extremely boring," she said. "It makes no reference to chopping up one's mother." Member of chambers of Lord Lester, Liberal Democrat peer and human rights lawyer. Counsel for Whitehall departments in many civil cases where she learned to digest and interpret official documents. Earned £800 a day as chief inquisitor, the sword to Scott's dagger. Examples: "The response is not an answer to the question, is it?" (to FO diplomat, David Gore-Booth); "I have seen no document which supports what you're saying" (to former FO minister, William Waldegrave). Favourite words include "gosh", and once replied "ace" to a witnesses' question. Idiosyncrasy: disarming giggle before putting the boot in.

CHRISTOPHER MUTTUKUMARU, inquiry's secretary and an Oxford University acquaintance of Presiley's. He was Scott's spokesman and minder, indefatigable writer of questionnaires to about 250 witnesses, chasing up recalcitrant Whitehall departments slow to supply documents. From a distinguished Sri Lankan family (his father was an ADC to the Queen, and Sri Lankan ambassador to Iraq and Iran); and a cricket enthusiast. For nine years, barrister in chambers of Dingle Foot, former Labour Solicitor-General, then joined legal secretariat of Attorney-General's chambers where he worked with Sir Nicholas Lyell, a key witness at the inquiry. Specialised in European Community Law there, and later joined the Treasury Solicitor's Department. Chosen because of his knowledge of the way Whitehall works, with the added advantage of being "positively-vetted" (security cleared to read classified documents). Unlikely to be welcomed back at the Treasury Solicitor's Department.

THE INQUIRY TEAM included: Paul Regan (Home Office, later left to take up Fulbright scholarship in the US); Helen Duffy, (Treasury Solicitor's Department – later took time off to work with disadvantaged people in Guatemala); Peter Edwards (Inland Revenue); Peter Hampton (judge's clerk); David Price, press officer (formerly at the Department of Health); Sonia Octave (Home Office); Christopher Stone and Stella Fusco (DTI); Mufasir Mohammed (Department of Environment), Wendy Moore (DTI), Karen Wiseman (Crown Prosecution Service), Velma Bernard (DTI), Julie Bernard (DTI), Debbie Drake (Home Office).

MAIN WITNESSES:

LADY THATCHER, Prime Minister between 1979 and 1990 – throughout the period covered by the export guidelines – told inquiry she knew nothing about how they were operated despite her private secretary (Sir Charles Powell who, though contacted by the inquiry, was never called to give evidence in public) telling Whitehall she should be kept "very closely in touch at every stage and consulted on all relevant decisions". A well-prepared Thatcher replied that only "the big things" came to her. Thatcher's message to Whitehall throughout her administration was that arms sales was a priority. She personally signed the £270 million Jordan Defence Package in 1985 – after Whitehall knew Jordan was being used as a conduit for arms sales to Iraq.

JOHN MAJOR said he knew nothing about the operation of the guidelines when he was Chief Secretary at the Treasury (1987-89), at a time when export credits to Iraq were doubled; Foreign Secretary (1989), when the FO was expressing concern about machine tool exports to Iraq (when he met Tariq Aziz, then Iraqi foreign minister); Chancellor (1989-90) and Prime Minister (from 1990). He insisted he was not involved "in the formulation of the guidelines, consideration of the guidelines, amendment of the guidelines, or interpretation of the guidelines". He said he knew nothing about the Matrix Churchill prosecution and heard about the 1988 secret shift in the guidelines only after the collapse of the trial.

WILLIAM WALDEGRAVE, younger son of an earl, classics scholar and prize fellow of All Souls, Oxford. Entered the Commons in 1979 as member of so-called Blue Chip group. Minister of State at the Foreign Office, 1988-1990, at the time his department expressed increasing concern that Matrix Churchill machine tools were being used in Iraq to make weapons. Responsible for liaising with MI6, whose intelligence, based in part on information provided by Paul Henderson, warned about the use to which the machine tools were being put. Bullied by his ministerial colleagues, Alan Clark and Lord Trefgarne, into approving exports to Iraq. Conceded it turned out to be "a wrong judgment, but that was the judgment we made. Clearly, with hindsight, that was a wrong judgment." Said guidelines were not changed because a change would have had to have been announced in Parliament – an argument Clark described as a "slightly Alice-in-Wonderland suggestion". Doubly unfortunate in that he gave evidence to the inquiry when he was minister responsible for open government. Switched to Minister of Agriculture in mid-1994 reshuffle. A potential victim of the inquiry.

LORD HOWE, Foreign Secretary (1983-89); author of original guidelines on exports to Iraq and Iran announced in Commons in October 1985. Proposed a more liberal policy on exports to Iraq in 1988, but insisted it had to be kept secret because of outcry over gassing of Kurds. Passed the decision-making buck to Waldegrave. Sharply criticised the inquiry's procedures, saying he was speaking on behalf of his "former flock".

SIR NICHOLAS LYELL, Attorney-General, 1992 – , another potential victim of the inquiry. The one man who constitutionally had the authority to stop the Matrix Churchill prosecution. Most damaging charge against him: failed to ensure that the reluctance of his government colleague, Michael Heseltine, to sign Public Interest Immunity certificate ("gagging order") was passed to the court. His claim ministers had a "duty" to sign PII certificates widely challenged.

MICHAEL HESELTINE, president of the Board of Trade since 1992. Had the political nous to say he would be accused of being involved in a "cover-up" if he signed a PII certificate before the Matrix Churchill prosecution. He did so only after being told by Lyell that he had no choice, something he made clear in his evidence. He said that after reading Whitehall documents, it seemed "everybody knew" that British exports were destined for Iraqi arms factories. Warned Major that, to a sceptical public, the phrase "flexible interpretation" to describe the secret 1988 decision – rather than admit to a "change" in the guidelines – would be a distinction without a difference.

KENNETH CLARKE, the Chancellor, who when Home Secretary (1992-1993) signed PII certificates on behalf of MI5 and MI6. Rashly promised to resign if the inquiry found him "at fault" – a hostage to fortune. His certificates suggested that "innocent lives" would be at risk if intelligence documents disclosed. The documents were crucial for Henderson to establish his links with MI6, a fact Alan Moses, chief prosecuting counsel, readily acknowledged. Clarke said he did not know any of the details of the case.

ALAN CLARK, Minister for Trade (1986-89); Minister of State for Defence (1989-92) made no secret in Whitehall about his opposition to controls on arms exports. Told the inquiry he regarded the guidelines as "so imprecise and so obviously drafted with the objective of flexibility, even elasticity, in mind as to make them fair game". Blamed by the Government for the collapse of the Matrix Churchill prosecution – certainly was more frank in Old Bailey witness box than had been in pre-trial witness statements. Admitted at inquiry to have indulged in "dissimilation", "sleight of hand" and sailing "close to the water". Described prosecution as "dotty". Major and Sir Robin Butler and customs prosecutors were told in 1990 that his attitude towards the guidelines was "ambiguous" when alleged that two years later he had given a "nod and a wink" to machine tool exporters, encouraging them to export arms-making equipment to Iraq.

LORD TREFGARNE, Minister of State for Defence (1985-89); Minister for Trade (1989-90). Alan Clark's ally in wanting to promote exports to Iraq. A reluctant witness, suggesting the inquiry was entirely unnecessary. Agreed to attend after assurances he would be treated "with courtesy and consideration". Told inquiry Henderson deceived him about real purpose of machine tool exports. Said ministers were responding "in difficult and changing circumstances to the often conflicting interests of British foreign policy, British trade, and British security".

PAUL HENDERSON, former managing director of Matrix Churchill, Coventry-based machine tool firm when controlled by Iraqis between 1987 and 1990. Says he was approached in 1988 by MI6 (with whom he had earlier been in contact) to provide information about Iraq's arms procurement, and recruit Iraqi directors as spies. MI6 says it did not approach him until 1989, and that he passed on limited information. Denied Trefgarne's claims about assurances that equipment was not going to make weapons. Says MI6 "dumped" him as soon as Customs determined to prosecute. Described by "John Balsom", his MI6 agent-runner, in court as "a very brave man".

SIR ROBIN BUTLER, Cabinet Secretary and head of the Civil Service since 1988; told the inquiry: "It was all happening below my eyesight level", but he is the top Whitehall official responsible for the effective running of the government machine as well as Civil Service ethics. Described "accountability", as in ministerial accountability, to be a "blame-free word". Perfect mandarin – example of mandarin-speak: "It was an accurate but incomplete answer. The purpose of it was to give an answer which in itself was true. It did not give a full picture. It was half an answer." Attacked the media for "distorted", "wild", and "prejudiced" reporting of the inquiry.

DOUGLAS HURD, Foreign Secretary since 1989, who also passed the buck. Told the inquiry: "By definition, ministers are not going to reach down [for information] because they do not know what there is to reach for." Claimed there was no evidence of ministers indulging "in some secret and wicked and wrong conspiracy". Expressed "unease" about not being told of MI6's connections with Henderson.

DAVID GORE-BOOTH, Eton-educated head of Middle East Department in Foreign Office (1989-93) and since British ambassador to Saudi

Arabia. Opposed Matrix Churchill exports to Iraq, not because of intelligence reports, which like so many witnesses he dismissed as unreliable, but on grounds of "common sense". Deeply resented having to give evidence, telling Baxendale that answering questions about the past reminded him of his doctor's retrospectrascope "which you stick into people and it enables you to look backwards". Told the inquiry: "Of course half a picture can be accurate."

IAN MCDONALD, head of Defence Export Services Secretariat at the Ministry of Defence since 1986. Far more loquacious at the inquiry than when MoD spokesman during the Falklands war. Impatient with the export guidelines, did not see vital intelligence reports, explained he was "not a believer in hierarchic management". Asked about how parliamentary questions should be answered, he replied, "Truth is a very difficult concept."

ALAN BARRETT, McDonald's junior at DESS between 1987-1990, now at the ministry's ship-repairing secretariat in Bath. One of the officials who in practice operated the secret 1988 guidelines. He said he forgot about intelligence reports. Also said in an official minute that Thatcher was "involved" in decisions about Iraqi arms procurement. Said he could not say how he knew this, but he "certainly did not make it up".

ERIC BESTON, senior DTI official responsible for export controls in the mid-1980s, now its regional director for the East Midlands. Favoured flexible application of export guidelines, and admitted giving misleading evidence to the Matrix Churchill trial. Told the inquiry: "I think the way in which questions are answered in Parliament tends to be something of an art form rather than a means of communication." Explaining why he spent more time regulating the antiques trade than on defence sales to Iraq, he said, "It sounds a little absurd, but it was an area of licensing which tended to involve large, expensive things owned by rich and powerful people."

TONY STEADMAN, head of the DTI's Export Licensing Unit in the 1980s under Beston. Said he forgot intelligence reports, allowed government lawyers to change his witness statement for the trial. Admitted that the DTI implied to exporters it "did not really mind" whether British machinery was used by Saddam Hussein to make weapons. Said he did not properly read key intelligence reports because he was "extremely busy".

ANDREW LEITHEAD, assistant Treasury Solicitor who changed Tony Steadman's witness statement. Agreed Public Interest Immunity certificates were often used for "administrative convenience", regardless of the contents of the documents. Admitted that certificates were photo-copied in standard form, and argued that ministers had no choice but to sign them.

ALAN MOSES QC, chief prosecution counsel, told the judge in the Matrix Churchill trial that Whitehall documents covered by ministerial PII certificates would not help the defence "in any way". They were to prove crucial to the defence. Moses told the inquiry that he had not seen some key documents – including intelligence reports. If he had seen them, he would have abandoned the case.

LT. COLONEL RICHARD GLAZEBROOK, MoD official responsible for vetting arms exports. His repeated warnings that arms-related exports to Iraq would breach government guidelines were dismissed by MoD defence salesmen and DTI officials. Was not told about sale, after the August 1990 invasion of Kuwait, of over 5,000 Royal Ordnance shells to Jordan – known to be a conduit for arms sales to Iraq.

SIR HAL MILLER, Conservative MP for Bromsgrove until 1992 and business contact of Peter Mitchell, one of the two men charged over the Iraqi supergun affair. Threatened to reveal embarrassing information – including his warnings – apparently ignored by Whitehall, about the likely use of steel pipes seized by Customs – if a trial went ahead. After confronting Sir Patrick Mayhew, then Attorney-General, he claimed Mayhew had responded, "You wouldn't do that, would you?" to which Miller said he replied, "Just watch me." Supergun charges reluctantly dropped by Customs after consultation with Mayhew.

SIR PATRICK MAYHEW, Attorney-General (1987-92) now Northern Ireland Secretary, remembered "a chance encounter" with Miller in the Commons, but insisted it was "inconceivable" for him to have urged Miller or anyone else to withhold evidence that would advantage a defendant.

MI6 AND DEFENCE INTELLIGENCE STAFF OFFICERS (ANONYMOUS) Gave evidence to the inquiry in secret. The DIS privately admitted to the inquiry that it should have done more to ensure its warnings that British equipment was going to Iraqi arms factories got to the right people in Whitehall. MI6 officers said claims by ministers and officials that they had approved export licences at the request of MI6 – to allow it to maintain flow of information – was correct early in 1988. But MI6 suggested thereafter, this was used as an excuse. MI6 officers also privately admitted they did not take note of a key meeting with Paul Henderson.

L-R: ALLEN, HENDERSON, ABRAHAM/PHOTO NEWS SERVICE

1

A Matter of Semantics

"We were in a very frenetic atmosphere." John Major.

November 9, 1992, the day the trial foundered, did not start well for
John Major. As Paul Henderson and his two co-defendants, Peter Allen
and Trevor Abraham, celebrated with champagne outside the Old Bailey,
Sir Robin Butler, the Cabinet Secretary, sent the Prime Minister a most
unwelcome minute.

Butler said an official chronology of events noted against the date
December 1988 that: "Department of Trade and Industry, Ministry of
Defence and Foreign Office ministers agree unpublished relaxation of
the Iran-Iraq guidelines." The message was clear: for nearly four years,
a succession of ministers, including Major, had repeatedly misled MPs.

In what Major later described as "a very frenetic atmosphere" amid
"a great deal of uncertainty", officials in the Cabinet Office and
Whitehall departments worked through the night in a frantic search to
see if they could come up with a plausible denial, or some kind of
explanation that might protect ministers from the serious charge of
having repeatedly deceived Parliament.

Major's advisers knew John Smith, leader of the Opposition, would
seize on repeated assertions by ministers that exports to Iraq had been
strictly controlled by guidelines first announced in the Commons by
Lord Geoffrey Howe, then Foreign Secretary, in October 1985. The
1985 guidelines, ministers had persistently claimed, had been
"scrupulously" followed until the invasion of Kuwait in August 1990.

Butler called a meeting of senior officials, asking them to meet at the
Cabinet Office at 6.30pm. After leaving to attend a dinner for Russia's

SECRET

To:
Secretary of State

From:

M V Coolican
Head OT 2/3
Room 6.31
Kingsgate House
215 8118

14 June 1990

cc: 2. ▓▓▓▓▓▓
3. ▓▓▓▓▓▓
4. ▓▓▓▓▓▓
5. ▓▓▓▓▓▓
6. Mr Nunn
7. File

MATRIX CHURCHILL

Issue

What action to take in respect of a request from Customs &
Excise for our agreement for them to visit Matrix Churchill

Evidence was available in 1987 to the same effect but to
protect sources Ministers took a decision to let the particular
exports by Matrix Churchill go ahead.

Argument

(1) are Ministers willing to have the 1987 and subsequent
decisions exposed and made the subject of courtroom argument?

(2) are Ministers willing to face a worsening in our relations
with Iraq ?

Iraq is already very huffy about recent successful attempts to
break-up their arms procurement activities and a move against
Matrix Churchill which is Iraq owned will only add to the
problem. To the extent that other companies are involved the
current line - that if people break our laws they must expect
punishment and that we are not picking on Iraq - can be
sustained. But UK trade interests in Iraq will no doubt suffer
(and possibly some unfortunate people also).

SECRET

M V COOLICAN

President Yeltsin, Butler returned and worked through until 2.30 the following morning. "People were working feverishly ... The Prime Minister was appearing at Prime Minister's question time the next day," Butler explained to the inquiry later.

On Tuesday, November 10, John Smith rose from the opposition front bench. "Does the Prime Minister," he asked, "recall assuring the House in January 1991 that 'For some considerable time we have not supplied arms to Iraq'? How does the Prime Minister reconcile that assurance with the revelation in the government documents produced at the Matrix Churchill trial that, as late as 27 July 1990, only six days before the invasion of Kuwait, machine tools known to be intended to make fuses for missiles and artillery shells were supplied to Iraq?"

Major replied, "The Right Honourable and learned Gentleman knows that from 1985 until the Iraqi invasion of Kuwait the Government operated under guidelines first set out by the then Foreign Secretary, my noble friend, Lord Howe."

Smith: "Does the Prime Minister understand that there are two aspects of this matter which are causing grave concern to the British public? The first is that equipment was supplied to Iraq which could have been valuable to it in the hostilities against British service personnel; and the second, that the truth about a secret change in policy appears to have been concealed from the House and also from the British public." (Smith called for an immediate inquiry to be set up into "this deeply disturbing matter".)

Major: "Let me say to the Right Honourable and learned Gentleman that there have been some extraordinary stories about this matter and I agree with him that they must be clarified beyond any measure of doubt."

He then told MPs that Sir Nicholas Lyell, the Attorney-General, would tell the Commons that the Government had decided to set up an independent judicial inquiry into the whole affair.

Major told Smith that the original guidelines stayed in operation throughout even though, just the day before, he had been told by Butler that they had been secretly relaxed by ministers in 1988.

Major repeated what he told Smith, making no mention of the 1988 decision, in a letter to Paddy Ashdown, the Liberal Democrat leader, on

November 12. Asked at the Scott inquiry to explain this apparent inconsistency, Major replied that the wording of the Butler minute was "interesting ... It says 'relaxation'. It does not actually say that the guidelines were changed."

When pressed to explain further, Major was rather more circumspect. "One of the points you have to consider, of course," he told Scott, "is whether there was a change in 1988. I had no knowledge of any discussion of the change in 1988. It was on that basis I replied to the question [to John Smith] in the House."

The two crucial issues – whether the secret 1988 decision amounted to a change in the guidelines or not, and who knew about it – were to take up many hours of exchanges at the inquiry. Government witnesses did their best to deflect the inquiry by indulging in an extraordinary exercise in semantics.

But the first priority was to protect the Prime Minister. On November 13, 1992, Stephen Wall – one of his private secretaries, now ambassador to Lisbon – wrote to Major: "The Cabinet Office and other departments will be working through the weekend to produce as comprehensive a chronology as possible on the Matrix Churchill issue ... There are a lot of simple questions, but very few simple answers. It emerges, for example, that the Howe guidelines of 1985 were amended by ministers in December 1988, but the amendment was never announced to Parliament." There was "no evidence", said Wall, that Major had seen Whitehall documents about the 1988 discussions during his brief tenure as Foreign Secretary in the summer of 1989. Major was to explain to the inquiry: "I asked to check what I had actually known and what I had not known in the welter of papers that crossed ministers' desks, and there is the response from the Civil Service that I had not seen the documents."

Major was not out of the woods. In his November 9 minute to Major, Butler pointed to evidence given by John Goulden, a senior FO official – since appointed ambassador to Turkey – to the Commons Trade and Industry Committee in January 1992. Goulden told the committee that the original guidelines had indeed been "amended" in 1988. So, in November 1992, we had ministers denying to Parliament what it had admitted to it seven months earlier.

In his evidence to the inquiry, Major explained that, though he had read Butler's minute, he did not get as far as the reference – somewhere after page 12 – which referred to the Goulden admission.

But there was still a problem. On February 17, 1992, Major had written to Gerald Kaufman, then shadow foreign secretary, telling him that government policy towards Iraq had never changed but had remained the same from 1985 right up to the invasion of Kuwait in August 1990.

(A phrase contained in a draft of Major's letter to Kaufman, stating there had been "minor modifications" to the guidelines had been crossed out. Scott asked Major who had crossed out the tell-tale phrase. "I can't recognise the writing and it is not me," insisted the Prime Minister, as though he had been accused of stealing sweets. It soon transpired that the phrase had been crossed out by Stephen Wall.)

Questioned about the letter to Kaufman in November 1992, at the height of the controversy surrounding the Matrix Churchill trial, Downing Street justified Major's failure to reveal to Kaufman the change in the guidelines by saying there was no need to do so since it had already been admitted by Goulden to the Commons committee.

The trouble was that in his evidence to the Scott inquiry, Major had said he made no reference to the 1988 policy shift towards Iraq in his letter to Kaufman, not because it had already been admitted, but because he was unaware of it.

But as Kaufman pointed out, Downing Street claimed Major omitted to tell him in his letter of the change in the guidelines, not on the grounds that Major did not know that the information was available to him, but on the grounds that the select committee hearing had made the information available to everyone.

The Government's official line was contradicted by one very senior FO official. In the frantic search through the files, Sir Timothy Daunt noted in a classified minute that junior ministers "took a conscious decision not to make an announcement" about the 1988 "tilt" towards Iraq. Papers disclosed at the trial, he added damagingly, "seem to some extent to substantiate [the accusation that] ministers connived in bending the guidelines".

Meanwhile one senior Cabinet Office official took it upon himself to come to the rescue. After rummaging through FO files, Nicolas Bevan came to the conclusion that although ministers did consider changing the policy, they "also subsequently decided not to do so". The 1988 decision, he said, amounted merely to "flexible interpretation" of existing guidelines and not a change in policy.

Pauline Neville-Jones, Bevan's boss in the Cabinet Office – now promoted to the post of political director in the Foreign Office – told Major, "It is absolutely true to say there was no change in the guidelines and, therefore, that the House was not misled."

How do Major's advisers explain the contradiction between Goulden's evidence to the Commons committee and Bevan's conclusions, bearing in mind that Goulden's official briefing for the committee had been approved, not only by the FO, but by the Ministry of Defence and the Department of Trade and Industry as well? In his researches, Bevan had only looked at Foreign Office files, and had managed to come to a conclusion that contradicted that of the FO's own senior officials.

How could Whitehall resolve the contradiction? Easily. Goulden, Butler told the inquiry, had simply "misled himself".

"It is not just him being caused to mislead himself," retorted Presiley Baxendale QC, the inquiry counsel. "It is the FO, the MoD and the DTI all misleading themselves, is it not?"

"Yes, I can imagine it was," responded Butler, adding, "this was all happening below my eyesight level."

Bevan conceded at the inquiry that the "interpretation of flexibility" which the Government was to rely on as an excuse for keeping Parliament in the dark might have amounted to a change in the guidelines. "You may say it is a matter of semantics."

"It was a very convenient way of not having to announce something," suggested Baxendale. "Do what you are going to do, but calling it flexibility of interpretation [means] not having to announce it."

Mr Bevan replied, "That's what ministers decided to do."

To his suggestion that there was no change in the Government's position towards Iraq, but if there had been one, it was not a change in policy because, in practice, the result was negligible, the judge remarked, "It's rather like saying, 'I wasn't there, but if I was I didn't do it'."

Back in November 1992, it was left to Michael Heseltine, president of the Board of Trade, to demonstrate the political acumen he showed throughout the entire arms-to-Iraq affair. He cautioned Major unsuccessfully against trying to argue that the 1988 decision merely amounted to "flexible interpretation" of existing guidelines and not a change in policy. "To a sceptical audience," said Heseltine, "that may seem a distinction without a difference." It would be "extremely disingenuous" to say the agreement did not amount to a "more liberal policy". The whole issue "underlines the unstable nature of the ground beneath ministers' feet", he said. It was a prophetic warning.

LORD JUSTICE SCOTT CYCLING TO THE INQUIRY/THE GUARDIAN/SEAN SMITH

2

The Guidelines

"I would argue they illustrate the — and this is the kind of thing you could say about them — the constructive tension between positivism and ambiguity, a doctoral thesis of Professor Ayer." Alan Clark.

A mark of the panic in Whitehall, and its determination to calm the waters, was the decision – announced by the Attorney-General the day after the collapse of the Matrix Churchill trial – to appoint Lord Justice Scott, of Spycatcher fame, to head the judicial inquiry. Scott was widely known to be one of the most robust and independent members of the senior judicial bench. Six years earlier, he had dismissed with contumely the Thatcher administration's attempt to ban the memoirs of the former MI5 agent, Peter Wright, in a stinging attack on excessive official secrecy. "I found myself unable to escape the reflection that the absolute protection of the Security Service that Sir Robert Armstrong [then Cabinet Secretary] was contending for, could not be achieved this side of the Iron Curtain."

It was widely rumoured that Lord Mackay, the Lord Chancellor, deeply disturbed by what he had learnt about the conduct of the Matrix Churchill trial, wanted a judge who was prepared to expose wrongdoing even at the expense of damaging the reputation of government law officers. Although his advisers denied the suggestion, there is no doubt the judicial hierarchy, led by Lord Taylor, the Lord Chief Justice, was determined to get to the bottom of the Matrix Churchill affair and other related cases to help restore confidence in the courts. All nervous Whitehall officials would say was that Scott was chosen because Major's badly-shaken Government was desperate for "credibility". Despite

Scott's reputation, they hoped he would confine himself to narrow issues, give the Government the benefit of the doubt, and return to the Court of Appeal. It was a triumph of hope over expectation. It was a choice the Government – ministers and civil servants – was to regret.

A week later, Major gave what was to prove to be his second hostage to fortune. He gave Scott potentially enormous scope. He told MPs, "All relevant issues will be covered by Lord Justice Scott's inquiry whose terms of reference will be: 'Having examined the facts in relation to the export from the United Kingdom of defence equipment and dual-use goods to Iraq between December 1984 and August 1990, and the decisions reached on the export licence applications for such goods and the basis for them, to report on whether the relevant departments, agencies, and responsible ministers operated in accordance with the policies of Her Majesty's Government; to examine and report on decisions taken by the prosecuting authority and by those signing Public Interest Immunity certificates in R v Henderson and any other similar cases that he considers relevant to the issues of the inquiry; and to make recommendations'." Major added, "The terms of reference have not been restricted to Matrix Churchill. They include the supergun and other defence and dual-use sales. The terms of reference relate not just to arms questions, but to decisions taken on the prosecution of companies and on public interest immunity. All ministers who are called will give evidence; all civil servants who are called will be instructed to co-operate; all papers that the inquiry calls for will be made available. Lord Justice Scott will be entirely free to decide on the publication of his report and of the evidence he takes. If Lord Justice Scott finds that his powers are in any way insufficient, he can invite the Government to alter the basis of his inquiry and the Government would agree to do so. The inquiry will report to my Right Honourable friend, the president of the Board of Trade."

The announcement sent shivers across Whitehall.

Scott made it clear from the start that he, rather than Whitehall, would lay down the ground rules for the inquiry. On March 31, 1993, at the first – and only – press conference he was to give before the completion of his report, he said he expected testimony of ministers, former ministers and civil servants to be given in public unless there was

an "overriding reason of national security" why it should not. He
released correspondence with Sir Robin Butler in which the Cabinet
Secretary had told the judge that hearings should be held in secret when
witnesses claimed disclosure would be "damaging to the public interest".
Scott replied that he intended to adopt a narrower test, preventing the
disclosure of information only when it would cause "serious injury to
the interests of the nation". He alone would make that decision.

Although Scott heard MI6, MI5, and Defence Intelligence Staff
officers in closed session, intelligence reports – with the identity of
individual agents protected – were read out in public hearings. Scott was
to have running battles with Whitehall over how much should be
published in his final report.

Scott said his principle interest was in "government knowledge of, or
complicity in, exports in breach of the guidelines or export control
legislation". He added, pointedly, "The final catalyst in bringing to a
head public disquiet was the collapse of the prosecution in the Matrix
Churchill case and concern over the manner in which Public Interest
Immunity certificates had been used."

Scott was prevented from asking witnesses to give evidence under
oath by a 19th century law, the 1834 Statutory Declarations Act, which
prohibits administering oaths outside a court of law or an investigation –
unlike Scott's, set up by the 1921 Tribunals of Inquiry (Evidence) Act.
Scott intended to adopt an inquisitorial approach – rather than the
adversarial contests in court trials – without cross-examination by
lawyers representing witnesses. Questioning would be restricted to
himself and Baxendale, although Christopher Muttukumaru, the
inquiry's secretary, also occasionally chipped in. The procedure, the
surest way of getting at the truth, provoked simmering resentment in
Whitehall. It was to erupt into the open when Lord Howe came to give
evidence in January 1994.

Sir Nicholas Lyell, the Attorney-General, gave Scott an undertaking
that witnesses would be immune from prosecution under the Official
Secrets Act and the Perjury Act. Sir Robin Butler – who combines his
role of Cabinet Secretary with that of head of the Civil Service – told
Whitehall departments after pressure from Civil Service unions, that
officials who gave evidence would be protected from the rigours of the

code covering their conditions of service. He said that even though the code insisted their ultimate loyalty was to their departmental ministers, officials would not be disciplined if they revealed ministerial wrongdoing. Despite these unprecedented safeguards, it soon became apparent that they were not enough to encourage all witnesses to come clean.

The export guidelines which were to cause the Government so much anguish were drawn up in 1984, ironically in an attempt to make it easier for ministers to defend their policy in public. "The Iran-Iraq war," William Waldegrave, former minister of state at the Foreign Office, was to tell the inquiry, "was turning out to be a really major war. It was not just an incursion. Persians and Arabs had been squabbling with each other for 8,000 years, but this was turning out to be a really major war with hundreds of thousands of people killed."

They were prompted by Sir Richard Luce, one of Waldegrave's predecessors at the FO, and one of the few members of the Government who expressed real anxiety about selling arms-related goods to Iraq and Iran. He was the only witness at the Scott inquiry who suggested that British policy should involve considerations of morality.

On November 13, 1984, he wrote a memo to Lord Howe, then Foreign Secretary. Headed "Sales of Defence Equipment to Iran and Iraq", it began: "You need no reminding about the amount of time we have devoted to this complicated subject and the difficulties it has presented to both of us, both in conducting our relations with the two sides in the conflict – other Arab States and the Americans – and in presenting a sufficiently clear and robust defence of our policy to Parliament, the press and British public."

What became known as the Howe guidelines were designed to unravel the knots tying up the Government over attempts to draw distinctions between "lethal" and "non-lethal" exports. They stated:
"i. We should maintain our consistent refusal to supply any lethal equipment to either side.
ii. Subject to that overriding consideration, we should attempt to fulfil existing contracts and obligations.
iii. We should not, in future, approve orders for any defence equipment which, in our view, would significantly enhance the capability of either side to prolong or exacerbate the conflict.

iv. In line with this policy, we should continue to scrutinise rigorously all applications for export licences for the supply of defence equipment to Iran and Iraq."

Three weeks later, on December 4, 1984, Howe minuted Lady Thatcher. Echoing Luce, he said the guidelines would make it easier to defend the Government's position "in public and in Parliament". In a phrase which was to provoke hours of debate in Whitehall and yet more hours of exchanges at the Scott inquiry, Howe told the Prime Minister that guideline (iii) "enables us to retain a modicum of flexibility".

Despite the stated purpose of the guidelines – to make it easier publicly to defend government policy – Howe nevertheless told Thatcher, "I do not believe ... that it will be appropriate to seek an opportunity to seek a high-profile announcement of the new arrangements in Parliament. Rather, we should allow the new guidelines to filter out through answers to parliamentary questions and inquiries from the media."

It took ten months before the Government finally decided to publish the guidelines – on October 29, 1985 – in answer to a question from the Liberal Democrat MP, Sir David Steel. "It did trickle out," explained Howe to the inquiry. "David Steel was the recipient of the last gulp of the trickle."

The aim of the Government – which was itself divided – may have been to upset nobody. It eventually ended up by upsetting everybody. British exporters were opposed to any controls; significant elements of domestic parliamentary and public opinion were opposed to trade with both combatants in the Iran-Iraq war; despite, or perhaps because of, the Iran-contra scandal, Washington was officially hostile to Iran as were Saudi Arabia and the Gulf states (Britain's lucrative Arab friends). It was a question of balancing competing political and commercial interests towards two countries, both potentially valuable trading partners, accounting for about £1 billion a year in export trade, in an important and volatile region of the world.

So what did the guidelines amount to? Scott and Baxendale caught out Howe as he tried to downplay their importance. After explaining they constituted an "inhibition" rather than "a prohibition", he was reminded that in a letter to Lord Mottistone in November 1988 – just as the Government was planning to relax controls on exports to Iraq – he said the guidelines "*prohibit* the export to either country [Iraq or Iran] of any equipment which would significantly enhance the capability of either side to prolong or exacerbate the conflict". Howe was also reminded that in July 1986 Peter Collecott of the FO's Middle East Department, wrote in an official minute: "The ministerial guidelines for exports to Iran and Iraq are intended to *stop* the flow of defence-related equipment." And while, on the one hand, Howe minimised the significance of the guidelines, he was also quick to claim that they amounted to "a huge national sacrifice".

Both Howe and his successor, Douglas Hurd, suggested they were just one of many policy tools. Howe spoke of other considerations such as human rights. "Take Chile, for example. Chile is now one of us: newly-elected, democratic president – and all the rest of it," he told the inquiry, "[but] Chile in the bad, old regime, was the reason why a mounting apprehension developed in Government about continuing to licence arms sales ... There was the mounting pattern of civil rights abuse."

Paul Channon, former trade and industry secretary, told the inquiry that, on one occasion, Lady Thatcher prevented the export of refurbished hovercraft to Iran, not because they broke the guidelines, but because the sale would have upset Saudi Arabia, a valuable market for British arms.

And then, of course, there was the Iranian *fatwa* against Salman Rushdie, issued on February 14, 1989. As a result of the *fatwa*, the Government decided to maintain the original, stricter, pre-1988, approach on exports to Iran even though the 1988 relaxation of the guidelines were designed to apply to both Iran and Iraq. This led to the "tilt" towards Iraq, a shift which made nonsense of ministers' repeated assurances to Parliament that it maintained a policy of "neutrality" between the two countries.

The export guidelines were a masterpiece of Whitehall drafting. It was put most graphically by Alan Clark, the former trade and defence minister cast by the Government in the role of scapegoat for the collapse of the Matrix Churchill trial, but one of the star witnesses at the inquiry. He compared the guidelines to a Cheshire Cat, adding, "They were high sounding, combining, it seemed, both moral and practical considerations, and yet imprecise enough to be overridden in exceptional circumstances ... [They] were an extremely useful adjunct to foreign policy offering a form of words elusive of definition."

Clark continued, "I would argue they illustrate the – and this is the kind of thing you could say about them – the constructive tension between positivism and ambiguity, a doctoral thesis of Professor Ayer" – a reference to the philosopher, AJ Ayer, author of Language, Truth and Logic.

Clark added, "The whole of guideline (iii) is magnificent – 'We should not in future sanction any new orders which, in our view, would significantly enhance the capability of either side to prolong or exacerbate the conflict.' It is a brilliant piece of drafting, because it is far from being restrictive. It is open to argument in respect of practically every one of its elements. I regarded the guidelines as being so imprecise and so obviously drafted with the objective of flexibility in either direction – elasticity, shall I say – as to make them fair game."

For Alan Barrett, an official in the MoD's Defence Export Services Secretariat, the guidelines were "a convenient tool. You can use them when you want to, you don't use them when you don't want to, and all the time you can change the guidelines."

"Is that right?" asked Scott

"Yes," replied Barrett.

Channon was equally frank. He told the inquiry, "I think [ministers] changed the rules as they went on ... In reality, if ministers decide to ignore the guidelines, they can be ignored."

Thatcher expressed her view in the following exchange:

Baxendale: "Lady Thatcher, I should like to start with the establishment of the guidelines in December 1984 ... The document is Lord Howe's minute to you of 4th December, 1984."

Thatcher: "I have it."

Baxendale: "Some of the witnesses we have had have described these guidelines as a framework within which they had to work, or as a hurdle which exporters had to cross in addition to other existing constraints on exports. Does that fit in with how you saw the guidelines?"

Thatcher: "They are exactly what they say. Guidelines. They are not law. They are guidelines."
Baxendale: "Did they have to be followed?"
Thatcher: "I beg your pardon?"
Baxendale: "Did they have to be followed?"
Thatcher: "Of course they have to be followed, but they are not strict law. That is why they are guidelines and not law. And of course they have to be applied to the relevant circumstances."

John Major was even more unhelpful. Asked whether he was involved in any discussion about the guidelines when he was Foreign Secretary in mid-1989, he told the judge, "Neither at that stage, nor later, was I involved in the formulation of the guidelines, consideration of the guidelines, amendment of the guidelines, or interpretation of the guidelines."

The guidelines, Thatcher said, had to be followed. But she also emphasised they were not law and had to be applied "to the relevant circumstances". Whitehall seized on the discretion implicit in the guidelines on exports to Iraq and Iran, even though it knew that by doing so, it was misleading Parliament.

Whitehall delights in the freedom provided by discretionary powers. As far as export controls are concerned, it has them in abundance. Scott, in many ways a traditional liberal, was astonished by the absolute powers enjoyed by the Government when it came to controlling exports. In a discussion paper circulated to Whitehall and other interested parties, he pointed out that the Government had "no general common law or constitutional power, in peace time, at least," to prohibit or control the export of goods from Britain. The power to do so resided in statute. The statute was based on the wartime Import, Export and Customs Powers (Defence) Act 1939.

The Act stated it would remain in force until the Privy Council declared the emergency "came to an end". The end of the second world war was not officially recognised until 1990 when, without any opposition, the Act was repealed. It was replaced by the Import and Export Control Act which officially declared the wartime emergency over. But that was all. As Scott noted, "By this means, the emergency powers conferred on the Government by the 1939 Act were made permanent." The Act gives the Board of Trade the power to impose controls without telling Parliament. "It is surprising to me, at least," said the judge, "that the 1990 Act was not, it appears from Hansard, the subject of any real parliamentary debate. The making permanent of the 1939 Act powers was justified by the Minister of Trade [Tim Sainsbury] as 'essentially a technical measure'. It was accepted on that footing by Ms Joyce Quinn on behalf of the Opposition. No other member spoke on the second reading." He described the powers given to the Government by the statute as "totalitarian in concept and in effect".

He questioned whether the Government should use export controls as an instrument of foreign policy. "Is it satisfactory," he asked, "that the refusal of an export licence to a private citizen can be used by Government as an instrument of foreign policy, e.g. to demonstrate outrage over ... Iran's statements regarding Salman Rushdie, or to avoid criticism by, or to court favour with, some foreign government known to be opposed to the export?" Whitehall officials have made clear since that, as far as they are concerned, the answer is a decisive "Yes". They intend to keep their discretionary powers, and continue to use exports controls, just as they use arms sales, as a tool of foreign policy.

Howe told Scott that the decision to make the powers permanent under the 1990 Act was "about right".

Scott: "Notwithstanding the undemocratic features of it?"

Howe: "Well, undemocratic or not, Sir Richard, they had been on the statute book from 1939 ..."

Scott: "1939 was a rather special emergency, was it not?"

Howe: "Yes, but they lasted unchallenged."

ALAN CLARK, FORMER MINISTER FOR TRADE AND FORMER MINISTER OF STATE FOR DEFENCE/PHOTO NEWS SERVICE

3

The View from Whitehall

"The companies should be warned of the falling guillotine, and urged to produce as fast as they can." Ian Blackley, Foreign Office official.

"Mr Clark," said Baxendale, "we asked you to provide a general statement describing your role as a minister at the Department of Trade and Industry and the Ministry of Defence. You say: 'My general understanding, coloured possibly by some personal prejudice, is that it was my duty to promote, facilitate and give impetus to British exports and the industries from which they emanated.'"

Alan Clark was a superb champion both for the DTI and the MoD's Defence Export Services Organisation. Their view of the world is not always appreciated by the rest of Whitehall, even those who had an interest in promoting exports. The inquiry heard how Robin Fellgett, a Treasury official responsible for export finance, minuted Nigel Lawson, then Chancellor, about a proposal – strongly backed by the MoD and DTI – to sell British Aerospace Hawk aircraft to Iraq in July 1989.

"Hawk," warned Fellgett "may well enhance military capability ... And we must avoid any financial implications arising through the involvement of MoD and their wayward arms salesmen." He told a Treasury colleague that the MoD's Defence Export Services Organisation "are gung-ho to support sales of military equipment to Iraq and almost anywhere else".

Baxendale picked up the point with an increasingly nervous and unhappy Alan Barrett. Fellgett's remarks were "totally unjustified", he said. Baxendale reminded him that a Whitehall document showed he had commented on a description from Lieutenant Colonel Richard

Glazebrook of the MoD referring to Alan Clark as being "gung-ho for defence sales!"

Barrett replied that he could not remember using those precise words. "What does 'gung-ho' mean?" he asked.

Scott replied, "I would take it as meaning very, very enthusiastic – perhaps double the 'verys' – very, very enthusiastic."

Barrett agreed, "Yes, very enthusiastic."

After the 1988 Iran-Iraq ceasefire, the guidelines were "otiose", Mr Clark later told the Scott inquiry. Continued references to them, notably by the Foreign Office, were "a confounded nuisance". He said he personally was prepared to announce revised guidelines secretly agreed by ministers in December 1988 to allow more exports to Iraq. Barrett acknowledged that after the Iran-Iraq ceasefire, there was "no MoD interest" in the guidelines.

Yet on January 10, 1989, Clark, then at the DTI, wrote to Waldegrave at the FO, telling him that neither his own department, nor the MoD, felt an announcement of the guidelines to be either necessary or desirable. "Any such announcement," he said, "would trigger a significant number of inquiries from the UK defence industry and the press as well as interested third parties in the Gulf. With so many conflicting interests, any change would be likely to upset someone. We would, therefore, favour the implementation of a more liberal policy without any public announcement."

Howe seized on this as proof that Clark was not as in favour of openness as he made himself out to be. Scott replied that Clark had argued it was the FO which was so adamant about secrecy and that he went along with it as an incentive to the FO to overcome its reluctance to revise the guidelines.

Howe conceded that may be right, adding, "The interesting thing about Alan Clark is that he is in many ways an extremely engaging person. One certainly found oneself dealing with him in that way, because he was an amusing person, much easier to be engaged with and to admire from afar than actually to deal with and work with. That, I think, is the thing that he would recognise about himself. He embodies all the charm and irritating capacities embodied in one individual who is a walking illustration of the word 'reckless'. He couldn't see an apple cart without wanting to overturn it."

The FO was an easy target. Although it was more cautious than other Whitehall departments, it was both schizophrenic and indecisive. David Gore-Booth, former head of the FO's Middle East Department and now ambassador to Saudi Arabia, told the inquiry that the FO had been arguing against exports to Iraq "until it was blue in the face". Rob Young, Gore-Booth's successor, believed that Matrix Churchill machine tools were being used by Iraq to make weapons but DTI and MoD pressure overruled the FO's concerns. David Mellor admitted he did not raise suspicions about Matrix Churchill exports on a visit to Baghdad as FO Minister of State in February 1988 – when he had a seven-hour meeting with Tariq Aziz (Iraq's former foreign minister) and two hours with Saddam Hussein. Mellor said there was "no point in raising something unless you wanted to do something about it". Tim Renton, Mellor's predecessor at the FO, admitted that chemicals which could have been diverted to Iraq for use in weapons were cleared for export to Egypt following DTI pressure and despite opposition from both the FO and the MoD. Defence Intelligence Staff assessors warned there was a "strong possibility" that British chemicals were being passed on to Iraq. British exports to Egypt included parts for ground-to-ground missiles which could be adapted to fire chemical weapons. After the Gulf war, United Nations inspection teams in Iraq discovered missiles of the same type fitted with nerve-gas warheads.

Despite the concerns of some of his colleagues, Ian Blackley, of the FO's Middle East Department, made an astonishing suggestion. He warned them in a memo in January 1988: "If it becomes public knowledge that the tools are to be used to make munitions, deliveries would have to stop at once. The companies should be warned of the falling guillotine, and urged to produce as fast as they can. They must also renounce publicity and lobbying for their own good." It was a memo of which Alan Clark would have been proud.

A year later, Waldegrave's private secretary wrote to Howe's office. "You may wish to show the Secretary of State the attached papers concerning a potentially politically-sensitive export to Iraq. The machinery in question has legitimate civil uses, but could also be employed in munitions manufacture or even uranium enrichment. Mr

Waldegrave's inclination is to support [Stephen Lillie's, an FO official] recommendation that the applications be approved. He has commented that screwdrivers are also required to make hydrogen bombs."

Waldegrave, who later admitted "with hindsight" he made wrong judgments, asked the inquiry if he could say a word about what he called "the extraordinary capacity of people in the Middle East to believe peculiar things about Britain". He went on, "There is a story, which I believe is true, that the Iranians say that if you lift up the beard of the Ayatollah, you find 'Made in England' written underneath because we wanted to get rid of the Shah, because the Shah was to pro-America. It is quite difficult to redress that kind of public opinion."

"Is it something you should try?" asked Scott.

"I think the Foreign Office came to the conclusion it was doomed sometimes," Waldegrave replied.

By giving Saddam Hussein the benefit of the doubt and turning a blind eye to intelligence reports, the Foreign Office was its own worst enemy. At times it appeared to have been sabotaged by MI6. Scott accused the FO of sending Waldegrave into a crucial meeting on November 1, 1989 with Alan Clark and Lord Trefgarne – his opposite numbers in the DTI and the MoD – "armed with a bow and arrow when he should have had a Kalashnikov". A briefing note drawn up by a junior official on the eve of the meeting made no mention of a stream of MI6 reports containing "firm evidence" that Matrix Churchill machine tools were being used by Iraq to make weapons. Instead, the note stated that "our friends" – a reference to MI6 – now believed that the lathes "may not, at any rate initially, be used for the direct manufacture of munitions, or for nuclear applications". MI6, it said, was "inclined to believe" assurances from Dr Safaa al-Habobi, even though he was already known to Whitehall as head of Iraq's Arms Procurement Network. Al-Habobi was director-general of Nassr State Enterprise for Mechanical Industries, one of Iraq's biggest arms plants north of Baghdad, and known by MI6 to be a senior Iraqi intelligence officer. He organised the setting up of TDG, the Iraqi-owned company which bought Matrix Churchill from Tube Investments in 1987. (In 1988, senior ministers approved an entry visa for Al-Habobi to enable the security and intelligence agencies to follow what he was up to. They followed, and did nothing.)

The October 31 note for Waldegrave was drafted by Simon Sherrington, a junior official who had only recently been positively vetted to give him security clearance to see intelligence reports. He told the inquiry he had not seen any of the earlier MI6 reports which contradicted the underlying message of the October 31 report. Sherrington said he drafted the advice after talking to an MI6 officer, identified only as "Mr O", either at a meeting or on the telephone. He said he checked the contents of his draft with Mr O and the FO's scientific department. Mr O told the inquiry in secret written evidence that the draft did not reach him until it was too late. Sherrington insisted that if Mr O had a "serious query" about the contents, he had "every opportunity" to say so. He made no "adverse comment".

The intelligence agencies (see Chapter 7) have a separate agenda from law enforcement bodies – the police and Customs and Excise. Their interest – reflected in many episodes, including the monitoring of terrorists and the BCCI bank scandal – is to maintain surveillance, to keep track of targets in the hope of gathering more and more information. The job of the police and Customs is to pounce whenever they have hard evidence of criminal activity.

When not pleading ignorance, ministers and civil servants insisted throughout the arms-for-Iraq affair that they allowed exports to Iraq, knowing they breached the Government's guidelines, because the intelligence agencies wanted to keep open the channel of information – provided by Paul Henderson. Henderson was promptly dumped by MI6 as soon as Customs made it clear they were determined to pursue the case.. MI6 tried to distance itself from the affair when it became clear that its covert role soon would become public. A memo written by an unidentified MI6 officer claimed that a secret Cabinet Office document drawn up in July 1990, was inaccurate. The document, called, "The Iraq Note", stated that: "Ministers have allowed the supply of some Matrix Churchill machine tools for *ad hoc* reasons of an intelligence nature" – a reference to Henderson.

The MI6 officer told the Cabinet Office that his understanding of the situation was "somewhat different". He claimed that MI6 told Whitehall by the end of 1988 that the Government could take action against Matrix

Churchill exports. This is not borne out by other Whitehall documents. According to these, it was not until August 1989 that MI6 said Whitehall could "draw selectively" on information from intelligence and, even then, a decision to refuse Matrix Churchill export licences "would not be easy". This avoids the question that Henderson himself knew all along about the intelligence obtained by MI6 since he – or his former colleague, Mark Gutteridge – had provided it in the first place. And in early 1988, an anonymous Matrix Churchill employee had separately warned Whitehall about the company's exports to Iraq.

Ian McDonald, head of the MoD's Defence Export Services Secretariat, told the inquiry that MI6's claim that the Iraq Note was inaccurate was "very puzzling". He assumed that MI6 was concerned throughout that stopping Matrix Churchill exports would compromise its source – now known to be Henderson. His assumption may well have been true; it was also convenient.

The MoD was itself divided. Lieutenant Colonel Richard Glazebrook is one of those awkward, obstreperous individuals determined to speak their mind, both in public and in private. He is one of the MoD's most experienced assessors of weapons systems responsible for vetting arms exports. "When you see he is one those attending a meeting, your heart sinks," a minister told the author. In other words, he is not frightened of telling ministers what they would prefer not to hear. Unsurprisingly, he was no friend of the MoD's export salesmen.

Describing how the Government had ignored his opposition to arms-related sales to Iraq, he told the inquiry how he unearthed "a can of worms" when he discovered what was being cleared for export by the DTI and some officials within the MoD. He said, in his view, and that of his military colleagues, Matrix Churchill machine tools were "lethal" and should never have been cleared for exports. Glazebrook was so concerned about the "whittling away" of export controls that, in June 1989, he drew up a report to warn ministers of how "UK Ltd is helping Iraq, often unwillingly, but sometimes not, to set up a major indigenous arms industry". Britain's contribution to Iraq, he said, included setting up a major research and development facility to make weapons, machinery to make gun barrels and shells, and a national electronics manufacturing complex. Taken together, the exports represented "a very significant enhancement to the ability of Iraq to manufacture its own arms and thus to resume the war with Iraq". Export guidelines should be tightened, he said, "from the point of view of both military and security concerns".

Glazebrook concluded his report by warning that "The minister [Lord Trefgarne] should be made aware of this unfolding situation, especially since it could reach the press." Not only did it not reach the press, it did not reach ministers. Ian McDonald admitted to the inquiry that the report was withheld from ministers. Why? The report was "irrelevant or premature". While weapons of mass destruction were "by definition a bad thing", said McDonald, "a conventional arms build-up is not *per se* a bad thing".

Glazebrook described how a British officer expressed horror before the start of the Gulf war when he was told about the sophisticated military equipment the Government sold to Saddam Hussein. The equipment included a modern version of a radar jamming system, made by Plessey, that was sold to Iraq in 1987 despite opposition from the MoD's military advisers. Glazebrook described how, after the Iraqi invasion of Kuwait, he was asked by a Royal Signals officer what sort of equipment the Government had supplied to Baghdad. Glazebrook told him about the Plessey radar system. "Oh, bloody hell," the officer replied, "we've got nothing to touch that." Glazebrook wrote down the comment in a report to his MoD colleagues "to rub salt in the fact that I was opposing [the sale] all the time". Plessey had argued that the equipment was only for training purposes. "It was like saying you're going to buy a shotgun with two barrels, but you're only going to fire one of them," Glazebrook told the inquiry. He disclosed that defence ministers approved the sale to Iraq of an automatic vehicle location system called Terrafix, despite opposition from officials.

Glazebrook also told the inquiry how International Military Services (IMS) – wholly-owned by the MoD – supplied chemical warfare equipment to Jordan despite repeated warnings from the Defence Intelligence Staff that it was likely to be diverted to Iraq in breach of a British government embargo. Although Thatcher was personally told of the deal, it was kept secret from senior officials whose job was to vet all sensitive exports to the Middle East. Defence Intelligence Staff had

LT.COL. RICHARD GLAZEBROOK, MOD OFFICIAL RESPONSIBLE FOR VETTING ARMS EXPORTS/ THE INDEPENDENT/JOHN VOOS

warned as early as 1984 that chemical warfare antidotes supplied to Jordan could end up in Iraq. A year later, Thatcher signed a £270 million Jordan Defence Package, including the sale of NBC (nuclear, biological and chemical) equipment. It included 70,000 syringes and 1,000 chemical warfare training suits. Other defence equipment sold to Jordan without Glazebrook's knowledge included thermal imagery night sights and sophisticated radar. Glazebrook fired off an angry letter to his MoD colleagues: "IMS is attempting to ship chemical warfare defence equipment in defiance of HMG [government] guidelines. IMS should be informed of HMG's displeasure at this attempted evasion."

The inquiry learned that even after Iraq's invasion of Kuwait, the Government approved the export of large quantities of artillery shells, despite being warned by defence intelligence that they were likely to be used by Iraqi forces. The exports – over 5,000 shells produced by Royal Ordnance – were approved without Glazebrook's knowledge.

Ministers and officials combined to cover up the sale to Baghdad of a launch site for Exocet missiles while Iraq was threatening neutral shipping in the Gulf. The inquiry heard the sale went through in 1986 after the intervention of Norman Lamont, then Minister for Defence Procurement. Construction of the site was one of several IMS contracts, including an Iraqi naval base and an Iranian dockyard which the MoD pursued in the mid-1980s despite strong opposition from the Foreign Office. In a reference to the IMS missile-site deal, Lamont told Tim Renton at the FO, "We need to be able to answer any criticism that the participation of this wholly-owned government organisation is improving the Iraqi capability to attack shipping in the Gulf." The IMS role, he argued in his letter, dated February 21, 1986, was only supervisory. It related "only to the construction of the building and the installation in it of the general safety and monitoring equipment ... Test equipment of the weapons will be supplied and installed (after IMS have left) by French contractors. The fact that the missiles are already being monitored and tested in temporary facilities convincingly demonstrates that the proposed IMS work cannot be interpreted as a real enhancement to the Iraqi war effort." Alan Collins, former head of the FO's Middle East Department, told the inquiry this was enough for the FO to drop its opposition. Whitehall then agreed to keep "a low profile" on the IMS contracts with Iraq, while ensuring that "minimal publicity" would be given to the company's deal with Iran.

The fact of the matter was that very few people in Whitehall – civil servants or ministers – cared whether British exports were being used by Iraq to make weapons. Glazebrook cared, senior officials in the FO anguished, Customs – furious about what it regarded as persistent Whitehall attempts to sabotage legally-enforceable export controls – took revenge, as we shall see. But that was about it. Everyone else turned a blind eye.

The widespread view was summed up in a minute sent to Alan Clark in September 1989 by Eric Beston, the senior DTI official responsible for export controls. "Even if machine tools were intended for munitions manufacture, there is no longer sufficient reason under ministerial guidelines to prevent export." This advice came from an official who, three years later, was to appear for the prosecution in a witness box at the Old Bailey where the Matrix Churchill defendants were charged, in effect, with no more than pursuing Whitehall's own covert policy. In the end, Whitehall plotted, while civil servants, according to Mark Higson of the Foreign Office, were "lying to each other".

Arms sales was a top priority for the Government, and Thatcher in particular. She was personally involved in the Jordan Defence Package, and the Malaysian Pergau Dam Aid Package linked, albeit unofficially, to arms exports. She took a close interest in the multi-billion pound Al Yamamah arms deal with Saudi Arabia, and weapons exports to other countries, including Oman and Brunei. "They didn't think they were doing anything wrong," explains a senior Whitehall official, critical of the Government's position. "They believed they had Thatcher's support and they were doing exactly what Thatcher wanted them to do."

Waldegrave – who, unlike Thatcher, supported even the sale of Hawk aircraft to Iraq – put it this way to the inquiry: "There is in this country a certain ambivalence. We are ... the free world's second trader in arms-related goods. People want the jobs they do not always want to think about. Whenever Mrs Thatcher or Mr Major comes back, having batted for Britain and won a great deal, everyone says, 'Hooray!' They are heroes on the front page."

In 1993, Britain exported £6,000 million worth of weapons, a fourfold increase since Thatcher came to power. The figure represents 20 per cent of the world market, second only to the United States. The Ministry of Defence says more than 500,000 jobs are directly or indirectly dependent on the weapons industry. According to The Economist magazine, the British economy relies more on arms production than any other in Europe. Arms sales account for more than half the credits covered by the Export Credit Guarantee Department, mainly to Malaysia and Indonesia. The Ministry of Defence is British industry's biggest single customer. A 1992 Cabinet Office study noted that 44 per cent of government-financed research and development was devoted to the arms business, compared with 40 per cent in France, 13.5 percent in Germany, and 5.5 per cent in Japan.

Arms were paramount in Thatcher's foreign travels "batting for Britain". Arms deals followed British aid, and increased aid followed those countries – including Jordan, Oman, Nigeria, Thailand, Indonesia, and Malaysia – which were far from being the world's most needy. Despite earlier ministerial denials – notably by Mark Lennox-Boyd, a junior FO minister – the Government acknowledged that £234 million in aid to Malaysia's Pergau Dam project was linked, temporarily, to the sale of British weapons to the country. In 1994, the Commons Foreign Affairs Committee's report into the project attacked the Ministry of Defence for its conduct in the affair, but dwelt only on its "reprehensible" failure to consult with the Foreign Office before negotiating an arms deal with Malaysia.

Documents disclosed to the Scott inquiry show that, as early as January 1981, the Cabinet's Overseas and Defence Committee, chaired by Thatcher, discussed how to "exploit Iraq's promising market for arms".

PRESILEY BAXENDALE QC, INQUISITOR AT THE INQUIRY/THE GUARDIAN/SEAN SMITH

4

The Big Prize

"Because something was not announced, it could not have happened." Alan Clark
on William Waldegrave's "Alice-in-Wonderland suggestion".

Baxendale asked Mark Higson to look at a handwritten note by
Waldegrave on a Foreign Office document dated October 6, 1989, a
month after Farzad Bazoft, the Observer journalist, was arrested in
Baghdad for spying. (Bazoft was executed on March 10, 1990.)

She asked, "Could we just look at it for a minute? – 'I doubt if there is
any future market of such a scale anywhere where the UK is potentially
so well-placed – if we play our diplomatic hand correctly – nor can I
think of any major market where the importance of diplomacy is so
great on our commercial position. We must not allow it to go the
French, Germans, Japanese, Koreans etc ... The priority of Iraq in our
policy should be very high: in commercial terms, comparable to South
Africa in my view ... A few more Bazofts or another bout of internal
repression would make this more difficult.'

"What I wanted to ask you about was did those comments of
Mr Waldegrave sum up, so far you were aware, the Foreign Office view
of Iraq at the time?"

Higson: "Yes ... The Iraqi market, after the end of the Iran-Iraq war,
was summed up as being 'the big prize'. However distasteful we
found the Iraqi regime, we could not afford to be left behind in
developing trade links, and we were in prime position, to use a motor-
racing phrase."

Baxendale: "In your statement, you say you were aware of changes to
the guidelines through the discussions between Mr Waldegrave, Lord

Trefgarne, and Mr Clark in 1988.

"The revised guideline reads: 'We should not in future approve orders for any defence equipment which, in our view, would be of direct and significant assistance to either country in the conduct of offensive operations in breach of the ceasefire' – It was a relaxation, was it not?"
Higson: "Yes, and it was not announced – we continued to churn out the same old line."

Shortly after the Iran-Iraq ceasefire, Howe sent Thatcher a document, entitled, "The Economic Consequences of the Peace". In a covering note to the Prime Minister on August 31, 1988, he said: "An important conclusion of the paper is that the post-war reconstruction of Iran and Iraq will create major opportunities for British industry ... Opportunities for sales of defence equipment to Iran and Iraq will be considerable ... we can use discretion within the ministerial guidelines to adopt a phased approach to borderline cases, relaxing control on a growing number of categories as peace takes hold."

Sir Charles Powell, Thatcher's private secretary, responded to Howe's memo, dated September 2, 1988, cited repeatedly during the inquiry, and which goes to the heart of the issue of Thatcher's personal involvement in the arms-to-Iraq affair. The Prime Minister is "generally content", he said in the memo that was circulated by the FO around Whitehall. He added: "The general strategy, however, will obviously require decisions over the next few weeks or months on a number of difficult and sensitive issues, such as the guidelines for defence sales to Iran and Iraq and the pace at which we build up relations with Iran. The Prime Minister will wish to be kept very closely in touch at every stage and consulted on all relevant decisions."

The problem facing the Government in its determination to relax controls on exports to Iraq was the public outcry over Saddam Hussein's treatment of the Kurds. In March 1988, Iraqi planes attacked the Kurdish town of Halabja killing an estimated 5,000 civilians. The Government was slow to acknowledge hard evidence of Saddam Hussein's outrages, but finally conceded that he had indeed used nerve gas against his own citizens.

Howe told his officials to keep quiet about the decision for fear of a public reaction. Terrified of a leak, he said the paper on Economic

Consequences of the Peace must not be circulated. One of his officials noted: "[Howe] is reluctant to put this paper forward and thereby initiate a process whereby it will become known that our line on arms sales to Iraq has been relaxed ... It could look very cynical if, so soon after expressing outrage about the treatment of the Kurds, we adopt a more flexible approach to arms sales."

Howe took what Scott suggested was an even more cynical approach by adopting a more liberal policy to arms sales, but keeping it secret.

Scott: "The memo from your private secretary – it was intended to give officials a green light for a more relaxed approach, but giving them a red light for any publicity to be given to that approach?"

Howe: "Basically, it was encouraging them to get moving down that path."

Scott: "When you say, or your private secretary says, that you feel 'it could look very cynical if, so soon after expressing outrage over the Iraqi treatment of the Kurds, we adopt a more flexible approach to arms sales', does it follow from that that it would, in your view, have been very cynical if, so soon after expressing outrage over treatment of the Kurds, the British Government were to have adopted a more flexible approach to arms sales?"

Howe: "No, I don't think so."

Scott: "You do not think it would have been very cynical?"

Howe: "I do not think so, no. The fact is that, as soon as you are embarked upon the necessary policy, in competition with other nations, of enhancing a commercial position – a commercial position that is more inhibited than other nations' – any attempt to enlarge that base is capable of being criticised by others."

Scott: "Can this not be explained to the public in a manner that the public would understand?"

Howe: "Not easily. Not if you visualise the emotional way in which such debates are conducted in public."

As Sir Robin Butler noted in his minute to Major the day the Matrix Churchill collapsed, William Waldegrave, Alan Clark, and Lord Trefgarne met to discuss revised export guidelines on December 21, 1988. The new guideline (iii), which relaxed controls on exports to Iraq and which was never announced in Parliament, stated: "We should not in future approve

LORD HOWE, FORMER FOREIGN SECRETARY/PA/FIONA HANSON

orders for any defence equipment which, in our view, would be of direct and significant assistance to either country in the conduct of offensive operations in breach of the ceasefire."

Ministerial witnesses to the inquiry – officials were far from sure – insisted the new guidelines were never put to the Cabinet nor, despite Sir Charles Powell's note, to Thatcher personally. Even though the new wording was applied consistently inside Whitehall from the end of 1988 right up to the Iraqi invasion in August 1990, Waldegrave insisted to the inquiry that it was used only on a "trial basis". Howe described the agreement by junior ministers in December 1988 as "ectoplasmic" – a word defined in the dictionary as relating to "substance that supposedly is emitted from the body of a medium during a trance".

On February 7, 1989, Waldegrave's private office told Howe: "I understand that DTO, MoD, and FCO officials have agreed a form, the form of words tabled on 21 December appears after all to meet our joint requirements and should continue to be used on a trial basis for the time being." The note added: "Mr Waldegrave is content for us to implement a more liberal policy on defence sales without any public announcement on the subject. However, there remains a possibility we will be asked a direct question about our policy, either in the House, or by foreign governments. We would propose to answer along the following lines: 'The guidelines on the export of defence equipment to Iran and Iraq are being kept under constant review and are applied in the light of the ceasefire and in developments in the peace negotiations.'" In other words, the Government would not admit to changing the guidelines.

The note continued: "If Mr Clark and Lord Trefgarne are content, Mr Waldegrave proposes we now put this approach to our respective secretaries of state and the Prime Minister."

"Had they stopped being 'ectoplasmic' at that stage?" Baxendale asked Howe.

Howe: "They are still a shade ectoplasmic because they are still on a trial basis, are they not?"

Baxendale: "They are agreed, are they not?"

Howe: "Yes."

In April 1989, Waldegrave told his colleagues, "We should continue to interpret the guidelines more flexibly in respect of Iraq as we have done in practice since the end of last year."

(He also referred to the reversion of "a stricter interpretation for Iran". After the *fatwa* against Salman Rushdie, the Government abandoned its policy of "neutrality" towards Iran and Iraq, although this, too, was withheld from Parliament.)

The inquiry devoted many days debating whether the new guideline (iii) amounted to a change in policy, or merely – as ministers insisted – a modification of existing guidelines; a shift in existing policy. For some witnesses, it was a matter of semantics; in fact, it was crucially important to the Government. Its defence for not telling Parliament about the secret 1988 decision was – and, indeed, continues to be – based on the argument that the decision did not amount to an actual change in policy.

Gore-Booth did his best for the Government by saying he did not see why there should not be "a very vigorous implementation of a flexible interpretation".

But the inquiry learnt that Michael Coolican, a senior official in the DTI's export control department told Heseltine following the collapse of the Matrix Churchill trial that Whitehall documents made it "quite clear that in effect the operation of guidelines differed from public statements".

Ian McDonald claimed there had been no change in policy. His junior, Barrett, had no doubts. "The aim was to release more dual-use goods and also perhaps defence equipment such as air defence radars which could only defend and not be used in attack." Asked by Baxendale whether the new guidelines allowed the export to Iraq of "equipment which would have been caught as defensive, but is no longer caught because it is not offensive"?

Barrett replied, "Yes."

Baxendale: "That is a real change, is it not?"

Barrett: "Yes."

Baxendale: "For Iraq, you are to use the new wording, not the old wording?"

Barrett: "Yes ... there was little choice once ministers decided that there was to be no announcement. There was, therefore, to be no change strictly in the published guidelines. Thus we had no choice but to use the new words as a form of interpretation and to enable the [MoD] Working

Group to go about their job."

Baxendale: "Did you think at the time that this was really just playing with words, because in reality you were going to use the new words for Iraq, were you not?"

Barrett: "We may have been playing with words, but ministers decided what we were going to publish or what we were not going to publish, to be more precise."

Faced with the mountain of evidence contained in Whitehall documents reluctantly handed to the inquiry, Waldegrave too was forced to acknowledge that the new guideline (iii) was used consistently by officials after December 1988. The documents showed that, behind the scenes, he himself adopted the exact words in the new guidelines which he earlier insisted had not been agreed.

Baxendale confronted Waldegrave with his circular argument that the guidelines were never formally changed since they were never formally approved by the Foreign Secretary and the Prime Minister. And they could not be announced without their approval. "Changing the guidelines," he said, "means announcing them."

Waldegrave: "It is perfectly clear the guidelines were never changed."

Scott: "There is a problem about this, which has been keeping me awake at night. The proposition that seems to come from your paper to the inquiry is that the guidelines were announced in 1985. The guidelines could not be changed without the proposal going to senior ministers, the Prime Minister, and without being announced in Parliament. None of these things ever happened. Ergo, the guidelines were never changed."

Waldegrave: "To accept that is the only argument, you have to believe that Whitehall is basically honest, which I do."

Baxendale: "Surely the most important thing is what they are doing?"

Waldegrave: "Absolutely."

Baxendale: "The policy you are operating is not what you say, it is what you do."

Waldegrave: "We kept saying to each other: 'You cannot agree these revised guidelines until they have gone to Number 10 and goodness knows what.'"

The exchange continued:

Baxendale: "You said that, after the *fatwa* [against Rushdie], no one

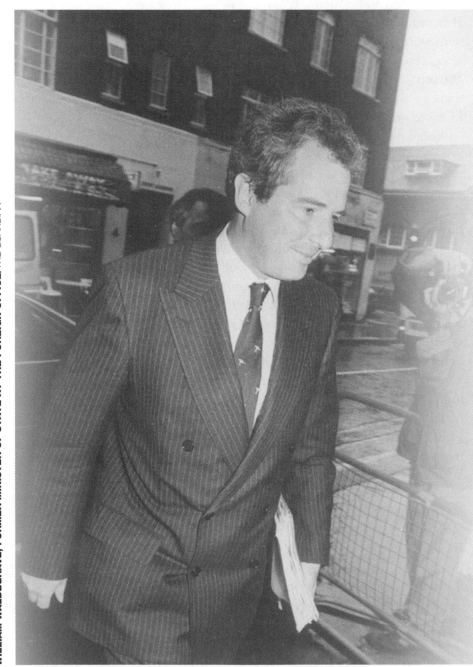

WILLIAM WALDEGRAVE, FORMER MINISTER OF STATE AT THE FOREIGN OFFICE/THE GUARDIAN

referred to the revised wording of the guidelines again."

Waldegrave: "You have clearly shown me from the documents that this is wrong. If you, Sir Richard, have been worrying about this at night, you can imagine that I have, because it is jolly important to me, and I have come to the conclusion that we did not do wrong."

Baxendale: "There was a Ministry of Defence paper from Mr Barrett saying: 'Mr Waldegrave is content for us to implement a more liberal policy on defence sales without any public announcement on the subject'."

Waldegrave: "It is not the most brilliantly-drafted note."

Baxendale: "It fits very nicely."

Waldegrave: "The letter should have said something like: 'Mr Waldegrave is content for us to implement the more liberal *inter   pretation* of the existing guidelines'."

Scott: "Why can you not tell Parliament what [form of words] is being used on a trial basis?"

Waldegrave: "We did not want to stir up a hornet's nest. After the collapse of the Matrix Churchill trial and all this came to the fore, I looked at this and I remember talking to Sir Robin Butler, the Cabinet Secretary, about it at the time, saying I do not remember changing the guidelines. Into the papers we dived and [found] actually that is not what happened."

Baxendale: "You dive into the papers and you find it is not what happened. We have dived into the papers and we have seen that in practice that is what happened."

Scott: "You cannot have a flexible interpretation to amount to a change, can you, and, therefore, avoid the announcement?"

Waldegrave: "Well, that's what all the argument, I guess, is about."

Alan Clark, so much the antithesis to Waldegrave that it is difficult to imagine the two engaged in any constructive debate, told the inquiry, it denied "the ordinary meaning of the English language to say that the guidelines were not changed". Asked by a puzzled Baxendale what he meant when he said in his written statement to the inquiry that it was "a matter of record" that guideline (iii) remained in place, Clark replied, "One is now back to the slightly 'Alice-in-Wonderland suggestion', where

I remember my former colleague, Mr Waldegrave, said, 'because something was not announced, it could not have happened.' He was arguing that because it had not been announced, it could not have happened, a sort of Berkeleyan philosophy. He said there was 'palpably' a more liberal policy in operation."

A well-prepared Thatcher simply side-stepped questions about her views on the 1988 decision by suggesting it was all beneath her. "It seems to me abundantly clear that, when ministers proposed this change, they did not regard it as a change of policy, but a change of circumstance."

Major adopted a different tactic, exuding deference and pleading ignorance. He told the inquiry, "What in practice was happening is not something that I frankly find myself in a position to judge ... There does seem to be some dispute amongst officials and others ... I had no knowledge of those changes ... My opinion, *post hoc*, is of no more value than anyone else's opinion."

To which Scott retorted, "I think the opinion of the Prime Minister on a matter of government, even *post hoc*, is worth much more than most people's opinions."

Major replied, "I cannot, in retrospect, know what was in ministers' minds at the time, and I would not wish to mislead the inquiry by a judgment of which I could not be certain."

Major said he was unaware of the 1988 decision even when, as Foreign Secretary in July 1989, he participated in the Cabinet's Overseas and Defence Committee's discussion on the proposed sale of Hawk aircraft to Iraq. "I didn't pursue minor matters in the brief," he explained.

He distanced himself from heated ministerial debate about Iraq when he was Chancellor. In June 1990, Nicholas Ridley, then Trade and Industry Secretary, wrote to Thatcher warning that Britain stood to lose £1 billion in export credit guarantees if the threatened Matrix Churchill prosecution worsened relations with Iraq. Ridley, who called for an urgent meeting, copied his letter to members of the Cabinet's OD Committee, including the Chancellor and to the Cabinet Secretary, Sir Robin Butler.

"Did you see this document?" Baxendale asked Major.

"No, I did not," he replied.

Baxendale: "Why was it that you did not see the document?"

Major: "I believe the document was sent to the Economic Secretary [Richard Ryder, now Chief Whip] who was attending the meeting, and not to me as Chancellor, for I was not attending the meeting. Quite why at that stage I was not attending the meeting I do not know, but I did not see the document and I did not attend the meeting."

One meeting Major did attend was with Tariq Aziz, then Iraqi foreign minister, in New York in September 1989. He was given a detailed briefing by his officials about current issues facing two countries. Major told the Commons during the post-trial furore that the only reference to Matrix Churchill was as "an example of British media interest in Iraqi procurement activities in the UK. No further details were given and there was no other reference to United Kingdom defence exports to Iraq".

The inquiry witnessed a collective washing of hands, a chorus of "Not me, guv."

BARONESS THATCHER CALLED AS WITNESS TO THE INQUIRY/THE GUARDIAN/MARTIN ARGLES

5

Passing the Buck

"Press for a separate submission to go to the Prime Minister, as she was involved last time." Alan Barrett, MoD official.

Initially nervous, Thatcher quickly adopted a lofty tone. She was interested only with "the big things"– she singled out the proposal to supply Iraq with Hawk aircraft. In icy exchanges at the inquiry, she said she was concerned "with the policy, not the administration".

"I could never have done my job as Prime Minister on policy if I got involved in these things," she said, referring to the export guidelines. "Miss Baxendale," she sighed, "if I had seen every copy of every minute that I was sent in Government, I would have been in a snowstorm."

Baxendale reminded her of Sir Charles Powell's minute of September 1988 in which her private secretary reminded Whitehall that she "will wish to be kept very closely in touch at every stage and consulted on all relevant decisions".

Scott asked her whether the decision to revise the export guidelines was the sort of thing she would have expected to have been referred to her. Thatcher replied, "If they regarded this as a change of policy, yes, it should have come to me. It may have been mentioned to me by one of my secretaries. I have no recollection if it was."

Baxendale read out a letter from Clark to Waldegrave, dated January 10, 1989, in which the former trade minister revealed he "would favour the implementation of a more liberal policy, without any public announcement".

Thatcher replied that the proposals "were not submitted to me formally. Whether they were just mentioned to me, I have no recollection."

Baxendale: "Mr Waldegrave was seeing this as implementing a more liberal policy?"
Thatcher: "On a trial basis. And I do not like the use of the word 'liberal'."
Scott: "Lady Thatcher, what I do think you can help me with is giving me an indication as we go through these letters, of whether you think the point had been arrived at which you ought to have been informed."
Thatcher: "If there is a material change in policy, I would have preferred to have been informed. And if I am informed, I must be informed in a letter to me. Of course, it would have been easier if I had been informed of any change. I assume that the reason that they did not inform me was that they thought there was not a change of policy, but a change of circumstances, to which the policy applied."

Baxendale then took Thatcher to a briefing drawn up by Alan Barrett of the MoD for the December 1988 ministerial meeting which paved the way to the revised guidelines. In it, Barrett told Lord Trefgarne, "The Prime Minister agreed that, in order to protect the intelligence source, the licences already granted should not be revoked ... More disturbing intelligence coming to light. Press for a separate submission to go to the Prime Minister, as she was involved last time."

During Barrett's evidence, Baxendale asked him, "At that time, you clearly thought the Prime Minister had been involved in the initial consideration of the Matrix Churchill lathes?"

Barrett replied, "That is what I wrote at this time, yes. I would like, at this stage, to read what I have actually written in my actual submission to you: 'I cannot now find any papers to corroborate the statement in the aide-memoir I drafted then. I can only assume now that I was mistaken.' "
Baxendale: "You have referred to the Prime Minister twice in one paragraph. This is no casual dropping of the name in. I cannot imagine you would casually drop the Prime Minister's name in. It seems to me that would have been a rather peculiar thing to do."
Barrett: "I certainly did not make it up."

When Baxendale asked Thatcher if she had any idea why Barrett should have thought she was involved, she replied, "No."

Baxendale referred to an answer Thatcher gave to a parliamentary question from the Labour MP, Harry Cohen, on April 21, 1989. Cohen asked the Prime Minister "whether Her Majesty's Government proposes to change its current policy of prohibiting the export to Iraq of any weapon which could enhance its offensive capability or will agree to granting export licences for weaponry to Iraq to accommodate the United Kingdom exhibitors at the Baghdad fair?"

Thatcher had replied, "The Government have not changed their policy on defence sales to Iraq. Applications for export licences continue to be considered on a case-by-case basis, according to the guidelines as announced in the House by the Foreign and Commonwealth Secretary [Howe] on October 29, 1985," then she added, "and in the light of developments in the peace negotiations with Iran."

Asked by Baxendale whether she thought the answer was correct, Thatcher responded, "It is a mixed question, is it not?"
Scott: "It is a mixed answer."
Thatcher: "Yes, indeed. It is a mixed question and it may require a mixed answer."
Scott: "It is the shift from 'weapons' in the question, to 'defence sales' in the answer. That is the problem."
Thatcher: "It would, I am afraid, my Lord [Thatcher addressed the judge wrongly – this was not a court trial], come back to the same point we have been concerned about for quite a long time – was it a change of policy? To which my advisers would say, 'No, it was a change of circumstance.'"

Later, Baxendale asked Alan Clark why he said in his written statement to the inquiry: "The Prime Minister most certainly was informed of the new approach and indeed included it in her parliamentary answer to Harry Cohen MP."

Scott intervened, "When you say: 'She would certainly have been given it' – certainly have been given it by whom?"
Clark: "She must have had something, because otherwise she would not have tagged on to the answer 'and in the light of developments in the peace negotiations with Iran'. That indicates a loosening, you see, that was the agreed form of words. The trail was laid."

Clark has since said he had no direct knowledge of Thatcher's involvement. That, he said, was a matter for Sir Charles Powell, her private secretary. He also says it was Waldegrave's responsibility to keep

Number 10 informed since the Foreign Office was the "lead department" on policy towards Iraq. When Waldegrave indicated that he was sending minutes to the Prime Minister, Clark says he assumed that was happening.

Howe told the inquiry that at the beginning of 1989, at the time of worsening relations with Iran over the Rushdie *fatwa*, he "would certainly have discussed the whole topic with the Prime Minister". About Iraq, he said, "There is no doubt that the Prime Minister was as anxious as the rest of us that we were re-expanding our trade base there." There is no documentary evidence available showing that Thatcher personally knew about the 1988 decision, the running debate within Whitehall about relations with Iraq, or the Matrix Churchill prosecution. We know, however, that she took a keen interest in other related cases. In a letter, dated April 2, 1990, following convictions (since quashed) in the so-called "nuclear triggers" case, she asked Sir Brian Unwin, chairman of Customs and Excise, to pass on "my warm congratulations to all those engaged in the operation ... The whole nation has reason to be grateful to those concerned." She also took a close interest in the activities of the intelligence agencies. "Margaret, an avid reader of the works of Frederick Forsyth, was positively besotted by them," noted Nigel Lawson, the former chancellor, in his autobiography, The View From No 11. Robin Robison, a former official in the Joint Intelligence Committee, remembers how she took the highly unusual step for a Prime Minister of attending a meeting of the committee. She was eager to boost arms sales, one of the few sectors in which Britain could compete with the rest of the world. And on her specific instructions, Whitehall set up the Working Group on Iraqi Procurement to monitor Saddam Hussein's weapons programme.

"Thatcher would not have been told in writing about Whitehall's decisions relating to Iraq," according to a well-placed civil servant. "She would be careful not to put her signature on documents. But she would have been informed orally."

The one person who would know is Sir Charles Powell. Surprisingly, the inquiry did not summon Powell to give evidence in public and only requested written evidence from him in the summer of 1994, six months after Thatcher's testimony to the inquiry. Powell told Channel 4's

Dispatches programme, in answer to a series of written questions in April 1994, that, at that stage, he had not been asked to give evidence, and he had not volunteered any. In an interview in The Times newspaper on September 6, 1994, he said: "You have to take some things on your own shoulders, you've got to turn things away, to let a Prime Minister free from the detail." He added cryptically: "At the outset, the inquiry accepted that the Prime Minister knew everything about everything. In general, it was good to cultivate that view, but not in this case."

The inquiry highlighted the extraordinary power of officials in ministers' private offices. "There is a freemasonry among private secretaries, where they have more licence to express their personal views than some of the rest of us," Sir Robin Butler, himself a former principle private secretary at 10 Downing Street, told the inquiry with more seriousness than jest. Private secretaries control the flow of papers coming to ministers and decide what should be placed, and in what order, inside the red boxes ministers take home at night and at weekends. One senior civil servant told the author, "Private secretaries are more important than permanent secretaries. They keep ministers informed, but they also take decisions on what ministers see."

"Five hundred documents come into my private office a day," Michael Heseltine told Scott. "One hundred of them come through to me." Major told the inquiry it was quite normal for ministers not to see everything that came into their offices. "There is a huge flow. The reality is that if every piece of paper that came into that office was seen by the minister concerned, they would do nothing but read it, so there has to be a filtering process."

In June 1990 Nicholas Ridley circulated a memo critical of Customs' threats to prosecute Matrix Churchill executives. But Major told MPs in November 1992: "Papers in connection with Matrix Churchill were copied to my office in the Treasury in June (1990) ... [The Treasury] do not indicate whether I saw those documents, but I have no recollection of doing so."

Two years earlier, in November 1988, Alan Clark had written to William Waldegrave about Matrix Churchill exports, ending his letter: "I recognise, of course, that whatever is agreed between us will require the PM's approval in the light of her private secretary's letter of

2 September." Thatcher, as we have seen, insisted she was not involved in any agreement to clear exports to Iraq.

Deciding what papers ministers must see is a genuine problem in modern government. It also allows ministers to pass the buck. "I just cannot keep tabs on all this," said Thatcher, exasperated by Baxendale's determination to talk her through the documents. "It just has to be delegated." It was a recurring theme all the way down the line. "Junior ministers," said Howe, "are people of substantial independent importance who do not try to trouble secretaries of state or prime ministers unless they have to ... I think the process whereby this happened was cumulative and geological." Although he added, "I think they [– junior ministers –] were perhaps confused as to what they were doing."

Douglas Hurd, Howe's successor, told the inquiry, "There has to be extensive delegation ... By definition, ministers are not going to reach down [for information] because they do not know what there is to reach for." Butler said, "It was all happening below my eye-sight level." Ian McDonald of the MoD told the inquiry, "I'm not a believer in hierarchic management."

All this begs the question of just who is democratically responsible for the actions and decisions of Government. According to the well-established constitutional convention, ministers are responsible to Parliament for all the actions of their departments. But that does not mean they take the consequences and resign if things go wrong. The doctrine of "ministerial responsibility" was laid down by Sir David Maxwell-Fyfe, then Home Secretary, in 1954. He gave four generic instances:

"i. Where there is an explicit order [to a civil servant] by a minister, the minister must protect the civil servant who has carried out his order;

ii. Where the civil servant acts properly in accordance with the policy laid down by the minister, the minister must protect and defend him;

iii. Where an official makes a mistake or causes some delay, but not on an important issue of policy ... the minister acknowledges the mistake and he accepts responsibility,

although he is not personally involved. He states that he will
take corrective action ... He would not, in those
circumstances, expose the official to public criticism;
iv. Where action has been taken by a civil servant of which
the minister disapproves and has no prior knowledge, and
the conduct of the official is reprehensible, then there is no
obligation on the part of the minister to endorse what he
believes to be wrong, or to defend what are clearly shown to
be errors of his officers. The minister is not bound to
defend action of which he did not know, or of which he
disapproves."

Maxwell-Fyfe was addressing the Commons in July 1954, in the wake
of the Crichel Down affair where Sir Thomas Dugdale, the Agriculture
Minister, resigned after it was revealed that officials made serious
mistakes involving the sale of land requisitioned during the war.
Contrary to widespread assumption, Dugdale did not resign because he
took responsibility for the actions of civil servants. He resigned because
he had lost the confidence of his backbenchers. So, too, Sir Leon Brittan,
then Trade and Industry Secretary, resigned over the 1986 Westland
affair, not because of officials' wrongdoing – in this case, the leak of part
of a letter from the Solicitor-General – but because the Government,
and the Tory Party as a whole, needed a scapegoat.

In the arms-to-Iraq affair, Maxwell-Fyfe's first and second points are
relevant to the issue of whether officials were merely carrying out their
ministers' bidding. The third and fourth go to the issue of whether civil
servants were acting on their own behalf without ministers' knowledge,
and to the question of competence.

In a written statement to the inquiry, Sir Robin Butler appeared to
absolve both ministers and Whitehall permanent secretaries – of which
he is the most senior – from virtually any mistake, misdemeanour, or
malpractice in the government machine.

According to Butler's doctrine of government: "While ministerial
heads of department must always be accountable for the actions of their
departments and its staff, neither they nor senior officials can justly be
criticised for shortcomings of which they are not aware, and which could
not reasonably have been expected to discover, or which do not occur as

a foreseeable result of their own actions.

"Ministers and senior officials can only be criticised personally for deficiencies in the organisation if those deficiencies either occur as a foreseeable result of their instructions, or they could reasonably be expected to have known about them or discovered such deficiencies and taken action to amend them.

"While ministerial heads of department must always be accountable for the actions of their department and its staff, neither they nor senior officials can justly be criticised in a personal sense for shortcomings of which they are not aware."

Butler said, in general, he agreed with Maxwell-Fyfe's thesis, but he took exception to one word in a phrase used by the former home secretary in the course of his long speech to the Commons back in 1954. Instead of the principle that ministers were "constitutionally *responsible* to Parliament", Butler preferred "constitutionally *accountable* to Parliament". "I want accountability to be a blame-free word," Butler told the inquiry. Parliamentary criticism following a mistake or wrongdoing should "only lead to blame, and possibly resignation", he insisted, when "personal responsibility" was involved.

But while ministers were absolved from responsibility for the errors of their officials, ministers would determine which officials should give evidence to Commons committees. For civil servants, according to Butler, "represent the minister" when questioned by MPs.

Where does that leave John Goulden's evidence in 1992 to the Commons Trade and Industry Committee? If Goulden was wrong in his statement that the export guidelines had been changed – as ministers, notably Waldegrave, insisted he was – then surely that was the responsibility of ministers. Butler skirted over that question.

Scott and Baxendale then challenged him on a separate point – the right of MPs to decide for themselves who should give evidence to Commons committees. Butler argued that since civil servants appearing before parliamentary committees were "representatives" of ministers, it was for ministers, and not MPs, to decide which officials should appear.

Retired civil servants could not give evidence, even though they had direct knowledge about what the committee was inquiring into, according to Butler, because "they are no longer under the instructions of the minister and, therefore, can no longer properly represent the minister". Thus the Government prevented Bob Primrose and Roger Harding, two former MoD defence sales officials, from giving evidence to the Commons Trade and Industry Committee's inquiry into the Iraqi supergun affair. The two men were would have been asked about deals involving Astra, the British defence contractor which took over PRB, a Belgian company which supplied propellants for the supergun.

Butler did not say why the Government prevented Eric Beston and Tony Steadman, two key DTI officials, from giving evidence to the committee. Butler told Scott that parliamentary select committees usually reached "an amicable understanding" with the Government over which civil servants should give evidence. Scott told Butler it was "extraordinary" that a minister, accountable to Parliament, had the right to prevent a former civil servant from giving evidence to a Commons committee even though that ex-official had first-hand evidence of the subject of investigation, while the evidence of the existing civil servant chosen as a witness by the minister would merely be hearsay. That argument, Scott pointed out, would never stand up in a court of law.

Where does Major stand on the issue of ministerial responsibility? He told the inquiry that "A minister in charge of a department is accountable to the department for all aspects of the department's operation ... He must account to Parliament and for that matter, the public, because he, as head of the department, is the parliamentary and public interface and responsible for policy." Echoing Butler, he then added, "What does not follow from this is that the minister is personally responsible for everything that goes on within his or her department."

Waldegrave also exonerated ministers from blame. "Constitutional Government," he told the inquiry, "consists of ministers, and when they make decisions, they do so on the evidence available to them." The trouble with the arms-to-Iraq affair was that "those who took the decisions didn't have the right information".

Officials were not amused by this implied attack from Waldegrave, the minister responsible for the Civil Service at the time he gave evidence to the inquiry. He fuelled increasing concern among members of the First Division Association, which represents about 11,000 senior civil servants, about their relations with ministers. It had already accused some of their political masters of abusing their position. The Scott inquiry gave a further fillip to their demand for a statutory code of ethics. Such a code became more urgent in light of the Government's plans to introduce personal contracts for senior civil servants. Coupled with pay based on an individual's personal performance, the plans could make it easier for ministers to hire and fire officials on political or personal grounds, threatening the traditional concept of a politically-neutral Civil Service. Waldegrave later told the Commons Civil Service sub-Committee that he was not enamoured with the idea of a code of ethics. "Putting morals in laws nearly always ends in tears," he said.

The consensus view, said the FDA, was that the civil service was governed by three principles identified by Sir Robin Butler in evidence to the Commons Civil Service sub-Committee in March 1993. They were: ministerial accountability; objectivity and political neutrality; and fair and open competition in recruitment and promotion.

As civil servants have moved more into the public eye, partly by appearing in parliamentary select committees, questions had arisen "about what an individual civil servant should do if he or she believes that his or her minister is seeking to evade ministerial responsibility by, for example, misleading the House of Commons, or the public. Further ethical dilemmas are posed, for example, when individual civil servants believe that they are being required to undertake work which is properly for party political staff."

The key paragraph 9904 of the Civil Service's Pay and Conditions of Service Code states: "Civil servants must exercise care in handling the information that has come into their possession in the course of their official duties and should not forget that they are employed for the purposes of the department in which they are now serving. They owe duties of confidentiality and loyal service to the Crown. Since, constitutionally, the Crown acts on the advice of the ministers who are answerable for their departments in Parliament, these duties are for all practical purposes owed to the Government of the day."

The code is backed up by the 1987 Armstrong memorandum, named after the former cabinet secretary and head of the Civil Service, Sir Robert (now Lord) Armstrong. This states that "The civil service as such has no constitutional personality or responsibility separate from the duly constituted Government of the day." Civil servants have, therefore, no direct responsibility to Parliament.

The FDA told Scott that the phrase: "For all practical purposes" was "too sweeping" since it set aside civil servants' duties in three important respects: "A duty to other authorities, such as the duties to the courts, which would be binding upon civil servants who are lawyers, and upon civil servants who have specific statutory duties; the duties individual civil servants would have to their own professions, for example, the professional duties as statisticians, and; the duties that all civil servants have to maintain the confidence not only of serving government ministers but also of those who may become government ministers in their political neutrality."

The FDA acknowledged that "Civil servants must not deliberately withhold information from ministers," and that it was for ministers, not civil servants, to decide what official information should be disclosed. But it told Scott that "The absolute statement [in the Armstrong memorandum] that a civil servant has no duty to Parliament is, at least in our view, incomplete." The FDA noted, for example, that the Commons Procedure Committee had stated that Parliament has the power to enforce its right to secure information from civil servants.

It also pointed out that paragraph 27 of the official document, Questions of Procedure for Ministers, states: "Ministers are accountable to Parliament, in the sense that they have a duty to explain in Parliament the exercise of their powers and duties and to give an account to Parliament of what is done by them in their capacity as ministers or by their departments. This includes the duty to give Parliament, including its select committees and the public, as full information as possible about the policies, decisions, and actions of the Government, and not to deceive or mislead Parliament and the public."

Evidence heard by the inquiry gave the paragraph a particularly hollow ring.

JOHN MAJOR, FORMER CHIEF SECRETARY AT THE TREASURY, AND FORMER FOREIGN SECRETARY/THE GUARDIAN/GRAHAM TURNER

6

Parliament and Secrecy

"Half the picture can be true." Sir Robin Butler, Cabinet Secretary and head of the Civil Service.

"Justice is exposed to emotional misunderstandings in this country." Lord Howe.

At the height of a heated row provoked by the inquiry about whether or not it was ever right to mislead or lie to Parliament, John Major referred to the by now often-quoted paragraph 27 of Questions of Procedure for Ministers, in response to a letter from Labour MP, Giles Radice. "It is clearly of paramount importance," he told the MP on April 5, 1994, "that ministers give accurate and truthful information to the House. If they knowingly fail to do this, then they should relinquish their positions except in the quite exceptional circumstances of which a devaluation or time of war, or other danger to national security have been quoted as examples."

British exports to Iraq could scarcely be described as such an exception.

The Government had legitimate arguments to deploy in defence of secrecy, of not telling Parliament every detail of its sensitive relations with Iran, Iraq and other Arab countries. Ian Richter, Diane Parrish and Observer journalist, Farzad Bazoft, were held hostage by Saddam Hussein. Groups holding British hostages in the Lebanon were under the influence of Iran. The trouble, as Scott reminded Waldegrave, was that the genuinely delicate issue of the hostages was never used by the Government as a reason to keep Parliament in the dark about the secret tilt towards Iraq.

Like Thatcher before him, Major – as we have seen – denied any knowledge of any of the relevant decisions taken by ministers and officials. "Every parliamentary answer that I have given or letter that I have dispatched has been based on the position as I understood it to be," he told John Smith on November 12, 1992. Five days later, he went further, telling Smith, "The suggestion that ministers misled the House is a serious and scurrilous charge and has no basis whatsoever in fact."

Confronted by tenacious questioning that put MPs to shame, Civil Service witnesses to the inquiry admitted that ministers' replies to parliamentary questions were misleading, inaccurate, or simply wrong. Officials admitted that answers they drafted were misleading. They also blamed other officials for drafting misleading minutes. The FO's William Patey, for example, said the DTI's Tony Steadman's argument in a letter to the MoD's Alan Barrett that Matrix Churchill machine tools were "not necessarily" going to be used by the Iraqis to make weapons was "not accurate". Patey said Barrett's advice to Lord Trefgarne that Whitehall officials were satisfied that the exports were for "general industrial use" was "clearly wrong".

Ministers gave MPs a string of misleading answers:

On April 20, 1989, four months after the guidelines had been secretly relaxed, Alan Clark told MPs, "Applications for such licences are examined against the guidelines on the export of defence equipment set out by the Foreign Secretary, Sir Geoffrey Howe, in 1985."

On May 3, 1989, Waldegrave told the Labour MP, Nigel Griffiths, "The Government has not changed their policy on defence sales to Iraq or Iran. These are governed by strict guidelines ..."

On December 14, 1989, six months after Whitehall officials warned that British equipment was helping to build up Iraq's arms industry, Lord Trefgarne told his fellow peers, "We do not sell arms to Iraq ... The sale of such items to Iraq and Iran is subject to very close guidelines."

On July 1, 1991, Archie Hamilton, Armed Forces Minister, told MPs, "There were certainly no arms sales to Iraq from British firms. That is what I have always said and I confirm it absolutely."

In answer to a question by the Labour MP, Ann Clwyd, on March 14, 1989, Eric Forth, junior DTI minister, referred her to an answer given by Alan Clark to the Tory MP, Teddy Taylor two months previously. Clark had told Taylor, "The guidelines are being kept under constant review in the light of the ceasefire and developments in the peace negotiations."

Tony Steadman, head of the DTI's Export Licensing Unit who advised Clark that publicity would make it "more difficult" for machine tool companies seeking approval for exports to Iraq, admitted the answer was misleading. It made no mention of the Government's secret policy shift the previous December. Asked by Baxendale whether a full answer might have provoked criticism and a debate in Parliament, Steadman replied, "I agree we should have gone further."

On April 20, 1989, Clark told the Labour MP, Chris Mullin, that the Government was still applying the 1985 guidelines. "Licence applications," added Clark, "are considered on a case-by-case basis, in accordance with stringent export control procedures which include, in particular, an assessment of the human rights record of the country concerned."

"That's just wrong, isn't it?" asked the QC.

Eric Beston, Steadman's boss, agreed, adding, "The avoidance of controversy was not an uncommon concern in the presentation of policy – or, in this case, the non-presentation of policy."

Clark later admitted that Tim Sainsbury, the Trade Minister, misled Parliament on December 5, 1990, when he told MPs the Government had "scrupulously followed" official guidelines on exports to Iraq. Sainsbury made his inaccurate statement after press reports that Clark had given companies a "nod and a wink" encouraging them to sell weapons-making machinery to Iraq. Clark said Sainsbury's comment was the result of a departmental "muddle ... lifting stuff from the word processor".

Asked by Lord Justice Scott why he did not put the record straight, Mr Clark replied, "It is not for me to say [to Mr Sainsbury] the whole department is ignorant and you haven't been properly briefed."

Baxendale asked Beston about Thatcher's answer to the Labour MP, Harry Cohen on April 21, 1989. "Knowing what you did, does that leave a misleading impression?" asked Baxendale.

"I'm afraid it does," Beston replied, in another demonstration of how, with the exception of Butler and Gore-Booth, officials were more ready than ministers to admit that Parliament had been mislead.

On November 10, 1989, Thatcher gave an answer, almost identical to the one she gave Cohen, to the Labour MP, Dale Campbell-Savours. "Supplies of defence equipment to Iraq and Iran continue to be governed by the guidelines introduced in 1985," she said.

John Redwood, then Trade Minister, now Welsh Secretary, on November 13, 1989, told the Labour MP, Mo Mowlam, "I have no reason to believe that the company [Matrix Churchill] has contravened United Kingdom export controls." The DTI had ample evidence by then that the company was supplying parts to Iraq that could be used in missiles, as Mowlam had indicated in her question. Scott suggested to David Gore-Booth that Redwood's answer was an "evasion" of the question. The answer to the question, he said, "would have been an extremely embarrassing one". He described the answer as "admirable".

Gore-Booth made it abundantly clear he resented being asked to travel to London to give evidence to the inquiry in person. Scott and Baxendale were more than a match for this arrogant diplomat. After some initial uncontroversial exchanges, Baxendale went straight in. "Can I ask you," she said, "about asking questions in Parliament? If there is a question, it should be fully answered, should it not? The answer should be sufficiently full to give a true meaning?"

Gore-Booth: "Questions should be answered so as to give the maximum degree of satisfaction possible to the questioner."

Baxendale: "I am not sure you really mean that, because that is rather like people just giving you the answer you want to hear ... I do not think you quite mean that."

Gore-Booth: "No, it might be the answer you do not want to hear."

Baxendale: "That does not give you much satisfaction. Should the answer be accurate?"

Gore-Booth: "Of course."

Baxendale: "And they should not be half the picture?"

Gore-Booth: "They might be half the picture. You said, 'Should (they) be accurate?' And I said, 'Yes, they should.'"

Baxendale: "Do you think that half the picture is accurate?"

Gore-Booth: "Of course half a picture can be accurate."

Baxendale then asked Gore-Booth about an answer Lord Glenarthur, a junior FO minister, gave to the House of Lords on April 20, 1989, four months after the decision to relax export controls to Iraq. "British arms supplies to both Iran and Iraq," said Glenarthur, "continue to be governed by very strict guidelines preventing the supply of lethal equipment to either side. I can assure the House that these guidelines are scrupulously applied."

Asked by the judge whether he thought that was a satisfactory answer given the decision to adopt a more liberal approach towards exports to Iraq, Gore-Booth replied, "I think the statement as made by Lord Glenarthur is absolutely correct. Given that it had been decided that there would be no announcement of the modification of the guidelines, that seems to me to be an entirely appropriate response."

Gore-Booth's attention was then drawn to another, similar, answer Lord Glenarthur gave to Lord Kilbracken in April 1989. Glenarthur referred to the original guideline (iii) making no mention of the "tilt" towards Iraq.

Baxendale: "That is completely ridiculous, is it not, in the light of the fact that it has been amended for Iraq, to completely different words?"

Gore-Booth: "I do not think so at all. We come back to the point of whether you think the British public and Parliament are so dumb as to realise that there has not been a ceasefire."

Baxendale took Gore-Booth to a Ministry of Defence document – similar to those distributed to officials in other Whitehall departments – warning civil servants that "Ministers generally prefer to give parliamentary questions that are factual and straightforward"; that answers "must be meticulously accurate and worded in clear and unambiguous terms"; and that "an error of fact or an answer that misleads the House can be dreadfully embarrassing." Asked whether Glenarthur's answer complied with the guidelines, Gore-Booth replied, "Yes ... It had been agreed that there should be no public announcement of the reformulation of the guidelines ... because there are all sorts of reasons why the Iraqis were not very popular, even though they were slightly more popular than the Iranians: ... Kurds, chemical warfare and so on, on the one hand, and also that we were trying, rather unsuccessfully I must admit, to establish and maintain a relationship with Iran. Of course, one of the factors that would have complicated that would be the Iranians knowing that we were giving the Iraqis slightly better treatment than they were getting. There was a myriad of foreign policy reasons tucked away."

The inquiry had earlier questioned Sir David Miers, also a former head of the FO's Middle East Department, now British ambassador to the Netherlands. When Baxendale suggested the 1988 guideline decision was "a major change", Miers – who accused the QC of bowling him "googlies", a cricketing term with which she said she was unfamiliar – replied, "Yes. Please forgive me, when you asked if I thought this was a change, I was wondering whether you expected me to say I did not think it was a change."

"I just wanted you to say what you thought. It seems to me to amount to change, but you never know what witnesses are going to say," responded Baxendale who suggested they should go to the question of what Parliament should have been told.

"This is something that you believed that ministers would feel under an obligation to tell Parliament about?" she asked.

Miers: "Yes."

Baxendale: "It is not just that they want to tell them, but you think that there is an obligation to tell Parliament?"

Miers: "Well, I mean, that is really for them to decide. When you say 'an obligation', a moral obligation, a legal obligation, we are touching on the very heart of the question which Sir Richard has been pursuing, are we not, on exactly what obligations there are and what political protests there may be, and so on? I would not wish to prejudge this great constitutional question. Certainly I think they were under an obligation to tell Parliament about the changes in the guidelines."

Baxendale: "Not least morally?"

Miers: "Moral, political, parliamentary, all sorts of obligations."

How would Sir Robin Butler, an extreme proponent of official secrecy, handle the inquiry? So concerned was he that he might be tripped up, before he gave evidence he privately rehearsed some of his prepared questions with senior Treasury officials. He entered the ring on February 9, 1994. By now the judge and his QC had got their teeth into the whole question of secrecy.

Baxendale reminded Butler that he stated in his written statement to the inquiry: "The Government should always give as full information to

Parliament as is possible and should take care, save in the most exceptional circumstances, not to give a false or misleading answer. Answers should also be sufficiently full to avoid giving a misleading account of an issue."

Baxendale asked whether this covered a "half answer".

Butler replied, "What I am saying is, if you are asked a question about a particular subject, you can never give, in an answer, all there is to know about that subject. You have to be selective about the facts." There were certain circumstances, said Butler, when it was justified to give half an answer, although "you should try not to mislead".

He offered two examples. The first was government denials that it had "negotiated" with the IRA. The denials were raised in the Commons after newspaper disclosures in November 1993 that the Government had sanctioned informal contacts with the IRA and Sinn Fein leaders, including Martin McGuinness. The denials, said Butler, did not give "a complete picture, as subsequent events showed, but most people, I think, including the majority of Parliament thought that, in the circumstances, it was a reasonable answer". Though Butler acknowledged that ministers' responses to questions from MPs – namely that the Government had not negotiated with the IRA – were "incomplete", he denied they were "misleading". "It was a half answer, if you like," he told a sceptical Scott, "but it was an accurate answer, and went to the point of what people were concerned about."

Baxendale suggested it must have given the wrong impression. Butler replied, "No, I do not think so. It did not deny that there had been contacts. It simply did not cover the point. It was an incomplete answer." It was an answer "which was true but not complete, not designed to mislead".

The second example was Lord Callaghan's reaction in 1967, when he was Chancellor, to questions about whether the Government intended to devalue the pound. Butler assumed – wrongly, as an angry Callaghan soon reminded him – that the former chancellor had denied the Labour Government had any intention of devaluing, shortly before it actually did so. "That was an answer that was false," Butler told the inquiry. "It was not misleading. It was false, and it was false for a reason that Parliament thought subsequently was defensible." Pressed by the judge

SIR ROBIN BUTLER, CABINET SECRETARY AND HEAD OF THE CIVIL SERVICE SINCE 1988/THE GUARDIAN/MARTIN ARGLES

who was clearly irritated, if not confused, by Butler's word-play, Butler added that Callaghan's supposed answer about devaluation "went further than misleading. It was an untrue answer."

But these were very exceptional cases. In general, Butler explained, "You do not mislead. You give some information that you safely can. You do not give all the information that is available to you. By doing that, it does not follow that you mislead people. You just do not give the full information." He went on, "I would have thought that an answer that there had been no negotiations with the IRA would have been an answer which was half the truth. I was really thinking of the David Gore-Booth instance: ... 'Half the picture. Half the picture can be true'."
Scott: "A tenth of the picture can be true, if it does not matter that the whole picture is being perceived in a sense that is different from the truth. The percentage of the picture that you give is immaterial."
Butler: "These are difficult lines to draw. It is not justified to mislead, but very often one is finding oneself in a position where you have to give an answer that is not the whole truth, but falls short of misleading."

Butler side-stepped questions about whether the Government should have told the Commons about the 1988 change in the guidelines on the grounds that he was not personally involved.

Scott asked him, "In your experience of government – and you have had a very great deal – do you think there is anything in the proposition that the convenience of secrecy ... about what the Government is doing, because it allows government to proceed more smoothly without the focus of attack that might otherwise be levelled, does in practice inhibit the giving of information about what [the] Government is doing?"

"You can call that a matter of convenience, if you like," Butler told the judge. "I would call it a matter of being in the interests of good government."

A month after Butler gave his evidence, his friend Waldegrave provoked a storm by telling the Commons Civil Service sub-Committee that it was sometimes right for ministers not to tell the truth to Parliament. "In exceptional circumstances, it is necessary to say something that is untrue in the House of Commons." He added there were "plenty of cases" – particularly relating to diplomatic matters – when a minister "will not mislead the House ... but he may not display everything he knows about the subject". Waldegrave went on, "Much of government activity is much more like playing poker than playing chess. You don't put all your cards up at one time."

They were provocative remarks given the drip-by-drip evidence at the Scott inquiry about the Government's contempt for Parliament. It also coincided with contradictory evidence being given to the Commons Foreign Affairs Committee about whether or not arms sales had been linked to British aid to the Malaysian Pergau Dam Project. What made matters worse was that Waldegrave had picked up Butler's example of Callaghan's handling of the 1967 devaluation.

Callaghan sharply denied the suggestion he had lied to the Commons. The records show that on November 16, 1967, he told the Commons: "I have nothing to add to or subtract from anything I have said on previous occasions on the subject of devaluation." Back in the summer of 1967, Callaghan had said devaluation was "not the way out ... The Government rejects the notion".

Butler returned to the fray to defend Waldegrave. Callaghan's intervention was "defensible but false", he told the Commons committee. "It is always wrong to lie or mislead anyone and it is particularly wrong to do so to Parliament. But any first-year student of moral philosophy will be able to tell you that there are very rare occasions when a greater wrong is done by not lying than by lying."

Back at the inquiry, Waldegrave was brought down to earth. He acknowledged a letter he wrote to Tom Sackville, Tory MP for Bolton West and now junior Health Minister, in 1989 in which he maintained that the Government adopted a policy of impartiality towards Iran and Iraq, gave "a false impression". "Openness is not the only criterion," said Waldegrave.

Baxendale drew him into what had now become a test question: Lord Glenarthur's claim in April 1989 that the Government "should continue to scrutinise rigorously all applications for export licences for the supply of defence equipment to Iraq and Iran".
Scott: "Why is not the right answer to say there is the flexible interpretation, the flexible policy, call it what you like, in relation to Iraq?"
Waldegrave: "Because it was judged that there were overriding reasons

for giving misleading information about tilts to one side or another, [not] to put British citizens there at risk, and all the rest of it."

Scott: "Is it not a very healthy feature of a mature democracy that serious issues of this sort can be debated."

Waldegrave: "But it is also, Sir Richard, a definition of what a mature democracy means, I think, that it knows from time to time, in relation to foreign affairs, it is going to be necessary not for everything to be said in detail."

Mark Higson, an official on the FO's Iraq desk who resigned because he could no longer put up with official deceit and hypocrisy, summed it up this way: "We were doing a juggling act. There was a lot to gain and and there was a lot to lose. We had prisoners [by which he meant hostages], we had an enormous amount of concern from the public, Parliament and non-governmental organisations over Iraq's human rights record. To come out openly and say, 'We are relaxing our policy towards Iraq' was, I believe, seen as not tenable."

Asked by Scott whether he meant the policy was untenable for domestic political reasons, Higson replied, "I think the policy in general was tenable ... because the policy that we could actually achieve greater trade relations and greater influence was politically sound. I am saying it would not have been tenable domestically. We also could not afford to, if you like, drop behind everyone else in the race to pick up on Iraq after the end of the [Iran-Iraq] conflict."

Higson was reminded of an answer the now-famous Lord Glenarthur gave, this time to Lord Kilbracken on May 8, 1989: "British arms supplies to both Iraq and Iran continue to be governed by very strict guidelines." Higson had no hesitation in agreeing that the answer was untrue and misleading. On January 31, 1991, John Major told the Liberal Democrat MP, Sir David Steel that "For some considerable time, we have not supplied arms to Iraq." Commenting on the answer in a newspaper interview before the inquiry, Higson said: "He either knew or his officials were negligent in not telling him."

Alan Barrett, the MoD official who described the guidelines as "a convenient tool" was asked by Baxendale whether the point was that the Government wanted to change its policy "with the least trouble. That is why you needed no public announcement because as soon as you have a public announcement you get trouble?"

Barrett: "The trouble is – "

Baxendale: "Because of the public perception of Iraq and the Kurds?"

Barrett: "Yes, indeed."

Baxendale: "In that way, they wanted to change the policy, but they knew that if they announced the change, there would be trouble?"

Barrett: "Yes."

Baxendale: "Is that how you understood it at the time?"

Barrett: "Yes."

Baxendale: "I am not just creating ..."

Barrett: "Not at all. The public generally was not concerned."

Baxendale: "But there was a group who were very concerned?"

Barrett: "Indeed."

Baxendale: "They appeared in the press, public and in Parliament, and the House of Lords?"

Barrett: "I cannot remember about the House of Lords, but I think so too ..."

Baxendale: "Going to your statement, you say: 'If we amended the guidelines now to appease industry, we would find it difficult to explain the change in such a way that would satisfy industry without upsetting public and parliamentary opinion and Saudi sensibility.' The public at the time were anti-exports going to Iran and Iraq were they not?"

Barrett: "Certainly anti-Iraq."

Baxendale: "Very anti-Iraq?"

Barrett: "It was the Kurds."

The inquiry revealed that to get round a Foreign Office veto on Ministry of Defence arms salesmen visiting a Baghdad military fair in April 1989, the ministry released for a few days David Hastie, a British Aerospace director on secondment to the MoD, so he could attend as a "BAe representative". The decision was taken by senior officials, including Sir Colin Chandler, then the MoD's chief arms salesman, after the Iraqis refused a visa to the BAe executive originally chosen.

"Mr Hastie was an official before he got on the plane, and an official when he got back, and he attended [the fair] as a BAe representative," Scott remarked.

In February 1991, the Labour MP, Tony Banks, had asked whether an

MoD official attended the fair. Alan Clark answered, "No." Asked by the judge why "a complete answer could not be given", Ian McDonald, head of the MoD's Defence Sales Secretariat, replied, "It was a complete answer." The inquiry heard that Clark's answer led to an internal MoD inquiry with Sir Michael Quinlan, the then permanent secretary, concluding that "The department sailed close to the wind."

McDonald explained that MPs were repeatedly misled because the ministry relied on "stock replies in word processors" to give "treadmill responses". But it was not as simple as that. "Truth is a very difficult concept," he told the inquiry. For Eric Beston, former head of the DTI's export control department – since transferred to the East Midlands where he is the DTI's regional director – answering parliamentary questions is more of an "art form than a means of communication".

Ministers suppress information from MPs and the public to avoid political embarrassment. Civil servants – the permanent Government – withhold information from ministers to control their "political masters". Official secrecy also means an easy life. Greater openness equals more work, more explanation. The message is in the eleventh commandment: "Thou shall not be found out."

Officials advise their ministers never to apologise, nor to admit mistakes. Thus cover-ups begin, more often to hide cock-ups rather than conspiracies. Here, there was concerted Whitehall-wide subterfuge to avoid controversy and public debate.

Christopher Sandars, a senior official in the MoD's Defence Services Organisation, advised against any publicity on exports to Iraq "as it would simply re-open arguments we were trying to close off", He added, "I don't think we should wish to encourage debate ourselves as officials."

The former trade and industry secretary, Paul Channon, told the inquiry that MPs could always demand a debate on government policy towards Iraq. "But a debate without knowledge?" replied Scott.

That happened "very often", responded the worldly Channon with a look of astonishment at the judge's apparent naivety.

Scott suggested to witnesses that arguments over the "very important matter" of export guidelines took place "under the table by officials and was not ventilated publicly". Baxendale took up the theme suggesting to Ian Blackley, an FO witness, that "the entire machinery of government" was run "under the table".

Blackley retorted, "That does not necessarily mean what has gone under the table is negative."

"Did a decision [to change the guidelines] depend on the public not being told?" asked Scott.

Blackley replied, "If there had been an outcry, I am not sure it would necessarily have reflected the view of the country, only of the number of people prepared to comment."

Scott, at one point, suggested to Howe that the former foreign secretary was adopting "a sort of 'Government-knows-best' approach".

Howe replied, "It is partly that. But it is partly, if we were to lay specifically our thought processes before you, they are laid before a world-wide range of uncomprehending or malicious commentators. This is the point. You cannot choose a well-balanced presentation to an elite parliamentary audience."

Scott: "You can, can you not, expose your hand to people of this country?"

Howe: "There are reasons for caution. Justice is exposed to emotional misunderstandings in this country."

Such patronising arrogance reflects a widespread view in Whitehall. It is deployed as an excuse for secrecy – the only people who really want to know what the Government is up to are mischievous individuals or self-serving pressure groups.

Secrecy surrounds the simplest of questions about Britain's arms exports. Asked by the Labour MP, Harry Cohen, in January 1991 "what ... the precise purpose for which the machine tools to be exported by Matrix Churchill were to be used", Peter Lilley, then Trade and Industry Secretary replied, "It has been the practice of successive governments not to discuss information concerning individual export licences."

In May 1992, Jonathan Aitken, then Minister for Defence Procurement and once a champion of open government told the Commons, "It has been the consistent policy of successive governments not to discuss particulars of defence sales with other countries as these are matters of commercial confidentiality ... Since 1984, the United Kingdom has refused to supply any equipment which could prolong or exacerbate the Iran-Iraq conflict."

A year later, Aitken refused to disclose information about Britain's £20 billion Al Yamamah arms deal with Saudi Arabia, with the refrain: "It has been the practice of successive governments not to comment on detailed matters concerning individual defence export sales."

Meanwhile, Richard Needham, Minister for Trade, told the Commons, "I see no reason to change the policy followed by successive administrations that details of individual export licence applications should not be made public."

Scott described the claim that MPs could not be given figures about arms sales as "almost unjustifiable by any coherent argument".

Government secrecy embraces more than arms sales. It went to the roots of justice – and to Britain's system of parliamentary democracy. Sir Patrick Nairne, a former Whitehall permanent secretary, has said: "The secrecy culture of Whitehall is essentially a product of British parliamentary democracy; economy with the truth is the essence of a professional reply to a parliamentary question."

Secrecy also envelops the role and activities of the intelligence agencies, crucial in the arms-to-Iraq affair.

DAVID MELLOR, FORMER HOME OFFICE AND FORMER FOREIGN OFFICE MINISTER/THE GUARDIAN/GRAHAM TURNER

7

Intelligence

"They are cornflakes in the wind." Lord Howe.

The role of the intelligence agencies – and MI6 in particular – was a vital ingredient of the arms-to-Iraq affair. It is also central to the whole question of ministerial responsibility, of Whitehall incompetence, of lying in court, of the suppression of information. And Paul Henderson, chief defendant in the Matrix Churchill trial was an MI6 informer.

Ministers explained their decision to approve exports to Iraq they knew would be used to make weapons on the grounds that MI6 needed to protect its source – whom they assumed was an Iraqi, not Henderson – and to maintain its flow of intelligence about Saddam Hussein's arms build-up. In secret sessions at the inquiry, MI6, however, disputed this, suggesting that ministers used the question of source protection merely as an excuse.

The demands of MI6 were cited by ministers and civil servants as the reason why they approved arms-related exports to Iraq. Perhaps this was why so many witnesses were so keen to debase the value of intelligence reports.

As far as David Mellor, former home office and foreign office minister, was concerned, they did not contain "shattering information about who was doing what to whom ... They were significantly less rivetting than the novels would have you believe. They weren't as interesting as the metal boxes marked, 'Eat after reading'. They didn't tell you all you wanted to know about life."

Gore-Booth told the inquiry, "Intelligence is a very imprecise art as a matter of fact."

Howe recalled, "In my early days I was naive enough to get excited about intelligence reports. Many [intelligence reports] look, at first sight, to be important and interesting, and significant and then when we check them, they are not even straws in the wind. They are cornflakes in the wind."

Howe also claimed that one of the most difficult tasks in Whitehall was to ensure the prompt availability of intelligence. "Everywhere it should have been available while at the same time ensuring that it was not available anywhere else." It was like trying to "design and operate a high-speed, multi-directional, leak-proof sieve", explained Howe.

Douglas Hurd said, "There is nothing particularly truthful about a report simply because it is a secret one. People sometimes get excited because a report is secret and they think that, therefore, it has some particular validity. It is not always so in my experience."

As with other Whitehall documents, so too, with intelligence reports. Ministers blamed the sheer volume of paperwork for their ignorance. "The total number of intelligence reports," Major told the inquiry, "is indeed huge. The amount of intelligence reports reaching the Foreign and Commonwealth Office, for example, would be around 40,000 a year, and that would ... probably ... be GCHQ and SIS [Secret Intelligence Service, more commonly called MI6]. Split down: about two-thirds GCHQ and one-third SIS."

Major continued, "They would be of varying grades. Some of that intelligence would be extremely valuable, others not so. Quite a strong filtering process is needed. It is clearly absurd that ministers should read 40,000 pieces of intelligence, but it would be filtered through the appropriate machinery and, where intelligence was thought to be relevant, validated and reliable – reliable being a key point – the officials would endeavour to put that before ministers." What was put before ministers was always a "value judgment".

MI6 and Defence Intelligence Staff drew up a whole series of reports showing how British exports, notably machine tools, were being used to make Iraqi bombs and missiles. Since 1985, they had been specifically tasked by the Joint Intelligence Committee to investigate Iraq's arms procurement programme. Evidence from intelligence agents to the inquiry was heard in secret. But enough was heard in public to make taxpayers wonder about the use of a panoply of intelligence agencies, whose effectiveness is damaged by the very mystique and lack of accountability which the agencies insist are essential to their efficiency.

Witness after witness described how crucial intelligence reports were ignored, forgotten about, mislaid, withheld from ministers, or misinterpreted. It was difficult to know whether civil servants responsible for distributing intelligence reports to decision-makers in Whitehall were incompetent buffoons or devious manipulators. Whitehall, it seemed, learned nothing from the last inquiry into intelligence failings – the Franks report on the events leading up to the Argentine invasion of the Falklands in 1982. The report contained damning criticism of intelligence assessors in the Cabinet Office. The Franks committee of Privy Counsellors – which, unlike the Scott inquiry, met entirely in secret – noted, for example, that "The changes in the Argentine position were, we believe, more evident on the diplomatic front and in the associated press campaign than in the intelligence reports."

Just as intelligence assessors in the Cabinet Office did not foresee the the Argentine invasion of the Falklands, so too MI6 failed to predict Saddam Hussein's invasion of Kuwait. (MI6 in London had dismissed a warning about the invasion from one of its agents in the Gulf.)

Many of the intelligence reports on Iraq's arms programme were, to use Major's phrase, "extremely valuable". One MI6 report, marked "UK SECRET", and dated November 11, 1987, was distributed to the DTI, MoD, and the FO. Though extremely relevant to their case, it was not passed on to Matrix Churchill defence lawyers until well into the trial.

Entitled "Iraq: The Procurement of Machinery for Armaments Production", it said: "According to a British businessman involved in some of the deals, the Iraqi government has been signing contracts with British, West German, Italian and Swiss firms for the purchase of general purpose heavy machinery for the production of armaments in Iraq. Details of those contracts about which the businessman knows are as follows – TI (Tube Investments, the former owners of Matrix Churchill), £19 million worth of multi-spindle and Computer Numerical Control (CNC) lathes."

A passage of the report handed to the defence was blacked out until paragraph (iii) which read: "Iraq intends to use machinery purchased to manufacture its own munitions. According to Anees Wadi of Meed International, Iraq has been paying inflated prices for finished products from the Soviet Union and now wishes to manufacture its own cartridge shell cases and mortars and projectile nose cones.

"The armaments production is to take place in two main factories in Iraq: the Hutteen General Establishment for Mechanical Industries in Iskandaria, and the Nassr General Establishment for Mechanical Industries in Taji, near Basra. Both factories are large by western standards and the annual production targets for the Nassr factory (the smaller of the two) are as follows:

  i.   10,000 122mm missiles per annum
  ii. 150,000 130mm shells p.a.
  iii. 100,000 mortar shells (80mm and 120mm) p.a.
  iv. 3000,000 fin stabilised 155mm shells p.a. (similar to those produced by PRB in Belgium).

"Most of the technical drawings used as blueprints for production at the Nassr factory are Russian. The one exception noted was a set of American drawings used for a large bomb. British businessmen visiting

LORD TREFGARNE, FORMER MINISTER OF STATE FOR DEFENCE, FORMER MINISTER OF TRADE/SEAN SMITH

the factory were told that it was a 1,000lb bomb. The businessmen were also told that all the Soviets had been expelled from the factory."

The report was based on information provided by Mark Gutteridge, Matrix Churchill's former export sales manager and Henderson's former colleague. Gutteridge – now unemployed – provided MI5 with details of Iraq's orders with Matrix Churchill. (MI5 passed on the intelligence to MI6. Gutteridge's contact was an MI5 agent known as "Michael Ford" who gave evidence at the trial because, in his early days in export sales, Gutteridge provided information on Soviet and east European trade delegations visiting Britain, MI5's bailiwick.)

DTI officials told the inquiry they read the report, then forgot about it. They weren't alone. William Patey, an FO witness, said the report remained "in our cupboard" until the middle of the following January. Asked why it was not followed up immediately, Sir David Miers, senior to Patey, replied, "I mean 'immediately' is a relative term. It depends on what else you have in your tray, does it not?"

Despite clear and detailed intelligence information, later that month – January 1988 – ministers cleared a batch of Matrix Churchill machine tools for export to Iraq. They were to clear another batch in February 1989, and a third in November 1989. Officials told the inquiry that the ministers involved – William Waldegrave, Alan Clark, and Lord Trefgarne – made decisions on the basis, firstly that MI6 needed to maintain its intelligence source and, secondly, that intelligence was too vague.

Yet in January 1988, an anonymous Matrix Churchill employee sent a letter to Howe at the Foreign Office warning him that the company – which had been taken over by the Iraqis the previous year – was "working on a large order for Iraqi munitions". This, as government witnesses conceded at the inquiry, provided "collateral" to the information provided by Gutteridge. According to Patey, the letter never reached ministers. Meanwhile, however, a stream of intelligence reports corroborated the earlier warnings.

In December 1988, a Defence Intelligence Staff report referred to Hutteen and Nassr – Iraq's two main arms factories to which Matrix Churchill and other machine tool company's exports were destined. It warned: "We could be guilty of far greater folly if we gave ground now."

It was ignored. The same month, a classified report of the Restricted Enforcement Unit – a secret Whitehall committee of officials from the DTI, the MoD, the FO, MI6 and Customs – warned that "The same procurement network [Habobi] had attempted to obtain gas centrifuge components from the UK."

On June 23, 1989, a secret report of the Working Group on Iraqi Procurement – set up on Thatcher's personal instructions – warned that Matrix Churchill "now had a firm order from Iraq for these lathes ... but the end-user was known to be the Iraqi missile programme". The inquiry heard that the DTI cleared the lathes for export – and ministers approved – without going through Whitehall's inter-departmental monitoring procedures. Alan Barrett, a member of the working group, later advised ministers there was only "circumstantial evidence" that British machine tools were being used by Iraq to make weapons. He told the inquiry, "I suspect I had forgotten that particular meeting." Further intelligence reports identified the missile programme as Project 1728. William Waldegrave admitted that Project 1728 was covered by the international Missile Technology Control Regime to which Britain is a party.

The warning was discussed by the working group on three occasions during the summer of 1989. Eric Beston told the inquiry that he and his deputy, Steadman, had forgotten about it during the summer holidays.

In August 1989, Waldegrave's private office warned FO officials: "Assuming the [Matrix Churchill] equipment has been used specifically for arms production, this is in contravention of our policy on defence sales to Iran and Iraq."

In September, three further MI6 reports warned that Matrix Churchill machines were going to Saddam Hussein's weapons plants. A month later, GCHQ – Government Communications Headquarters which gathers intelligence by intercepting radio, telex and telephone messages – warned that a British company was selling equipment to Iraqi arms factories. This warning was first discussed at a meeting of the Restricted Enforcement Unit, chaired by Beston.

Yet in November 1989, Beston advised ministers in an official briefing that "We have no reason to suspect that the company [Matrix Churchill] is supplying parts for missiles to Iraq or to believe that the company has in any other way contravened UK export controls."

GCHQ identified three specific contracts, including a deal with Carlos Cardoen, the Chilean arms manufacturer, which three years later featured on the indictment at the Matrix Churchill trial. The REU meeting took place before the crucial November 1 ministerial meeting.

The GCHQ report was distributed throughout Whitehall, including Customs. No one raised the question of which company was involved at the meeting of the REU in October 1989. The question was asked at the next meeting of the unit in November, but the company was not finally identified as Matrix Churchill until December. The GCHQ report mentioned further arms-related Matrix Churchill exports in the pipe-line. But still no action was taken. (Paradoxically, the REU was set up to improve the monitoring of intelligence.)

When Scott and Baxendale presented Waldegrave with the most important, most specific, intelligence reports, he said he was unaware of any of them. "Common sense seems to suggest that I should have known," he said, referring to the GCHQ report. It is clear, however, he had received some warnings from intelligence agencies suggesting the machine tools were being used by Iraq to make weapons. Experienced Whitehall officials insist that intelligence reports are usually highlighted as a priority when documents are prepared for the relevant ministers to read.

Waldegrave referred to intelligence reports frequently in minutes to his ministerial colleagues. He specifically asked to be kept in touch with Iraq's arms procurement network operating in Britain. In November 1989, he told Clark and Trefgarne that "Matrix Churchill's exports probably went into the Iraqi armaments industry."

Self-serving it may have been, but Waldegrave exposed a scandal of stupefying Whitehall complacency – and perhaps worse. He explained that he gave Matrix the benefit of the doubt. He added, "I take the view ... maybe wrongly and certainly wrongly with hindsight, but it looked reasonable at the time, that the priority in Iraq had changed and that [Iraqi] industrial plants were going to be [put] to civil use."

Gore-Booth may not have done himself any favours by his arrogance, but he was one of the few senior civil servants who consistently opposed the sale of machine tools to Iraq on the grounds that they were likely to be used by Saddam Hussein to make shells and missiles. He based his judgment on common sense, without the benefit of intelligence reports that would have strengthened his hand.

When Waldegrave was asked about the use of gathering information if it was not used, he replied that that had been "a constant problem with intelligence over the years". In a prepared written statement to the inquiry, Waldegrave claimed that "Officials and ministers worked carefully and consistently to interpret the usually conflicting evidence that was available at the time."

Waldegrave then referred to machine tools. "Such dual-use exports [were] allowed if it was believed they were to be used to produce weapons." Whitehall documents in the hands of the inquiry demonstrated that was inaccurate. Ever since early 1988, civil servants had admitted they knew that machine tools were being used by Iraq to make weapons. Waldegrave himself had strongly suspected that they were being used to make weapons. He finally conceded his statement was incorrect.

Baxendale reminded him that by November 1, 1989 – the date of the ministerial meeting at which Waldegrave allowed himself to be overruled by Clark and Trefgarne – the Government knew British equipment had been destined for an Iraqi missile project.

Waldegrave replied, "The point I am making ... is that those who took these decisions did not actually have ..."

Baxendale: "The right information."

Waldegrave: "That is correct."

Scott then intervened to ask whether "the Government was indivisible in that sense"?

Waldegrave agreed the information "had gone into the state machinery". The problem, he said, was that it "did not come out in the right place of course". So Waldegrave took the easy option and blamed the system.

Alan Clark also blamed the system. He told the inquiry that intelligence showing that British machines were being used by Iraq to make arms should have "broken out of the ring fence in which it was fermenting". He had "no personal knowledge" as a minister. He was "a spectator". He referred to the "obsessional possessiveness" of the intelligence agencies. He, too, however, contradicted himself. He did see some intelligence reports – he spoke, at one stage, of having to take part in a "swearing-in ceremony" when they were shown to him. He also used the "intelligence card" as a reason for not being frank at a meeting of machine tool company executives in January 1988. "I could not give [the companies] any justification for thinking I knew what the machines were going to be used for," he said.

Most ministers involved claimed they had no idea Paul Henderson was an MI6 informer. According to Clark, "No one knew before 20 minutes before [the trial] happened that one of our own intelligence operatives was being tried." He called it an "absurd paradox. Intelligence was telling you what they were being used for. But the machines had to be provided [to Iraq] in order to protect the source telling you how they were being used. It was a total circularity."

Documents released to the inquiry revealed that Hurd told Heseltine, his Cabinet colleague, about his "unease" that MI6 had not told ministers about the agency's association with Henderson.

There were times when the agencies could not agree among themselves. Defence Intelligence Staff consistently took a harder line towards exports to Iraq. Yet the DIS position was weakened because it failed to ensure that even Ministry of Defence arms salesmen saw its reports. Air Marshal Sir John Walker, head of DIS, acknowledged these shortcomings in a private meeting with Lord Justice Scott and members of his inquiry team.

Part of the problem is the "need-to-know" principle, a principle endemic in Whitehall and nowhere more so than among those responsible for distributing intelligence reports provided by MI6, MI5 and GCHQ which spend hundreds of millions of pounds every year gathering the stuff. Reginald Hibbert, a former senior FO official responsible for liaising with MI6, once warned of the risk "in ministers and leaders and top officials becoming absorbed into a culture where secrecy comes to be confused with truth and where, after a time, contact is lost with earthly awkwardness".

But for intelligence agents on the ground, the "need-to-know" principle can go up as well as down. As Baxendale told Ian McDonald, the MoD official who prided himself on delegating, "If you were not told about something, you don't know if you need to know it."

The possessiveness of intelligence agencies, the deference shown to them by Whitehall departments, and the "need-to-know" principle severely limits the number of officials who can see intelligence reports. They are subjected to a long positive-vetting security clearance procedure. Simon Sherrington was advising ministers about sensitive issues relating to trade with Iraq before he was PV'd and thus unable to see intelligence reports. Steadman was only cleared to see MI6 reports months after he was first appointed head of the DTI's Export Licensing Unit. DTI officials had to visit a specially-guarded Sensitive Document Unit to read intelligence reports. Customs cited excessive secrecy as one of the reasons why they did not see all relevant documents before the Matrix Churchill prosecution.

According to Gore-Booth, "Only if intelligence were incontrovertible would it be possible to argue against the reasons for allowing the trade [with Iraq] to go ahead."

If intelligence needs to be "incontrovertible", yet was at the same time "a very imprecise art", and often ignored, why then bother with intelligence agencies at all?

The use and abuse of intelligence throughout the arms-for-Iraq affair also raises the now familiar question of just who is responsible? The way intelligence reports were handled was "a matter of concern", Thatcher admitted to Scott. "Either the machinery was not being used effectively, or the machinery itself was defective." In a remark which appeared to be aimed at Waldegrave, she said, "As a matter of common sense, you would have expected the person taking the meeting to see that the relevant information was there, and that meant seeing if there was any, or asking someone to put an inquiry through to see if there was any."

The Scott inquiry drew up a paper extending the official guidance on ministerial responsibilities and behaviour – Questions of Procedure for Ministers – to apply specifically to intelligence. It said:

"i. Ministers are ... entitled to rely on their permanent
secretaries to establish an organisation and structure which
ensures that, for the purposes of taking decisions, all relevant
information (including intelligence) is available to officials
and ministers involved in the decision-making process.

"ii. Accountability, however, requires that a failure in the organisation and structure of which results in a failure by the Government to carry out its policies is a matter for which the relevant minister must answer."

In a paragraph specifically naming Waldegrave's evidence, it continued:

"Answerability requires not only accountability in Parliament after the event, it may require the minister to take an active interest in the organisation and structure of his department. "iii. Specifically, where a minister has the responsibility for taking decisions in a sensitive area and knows of the sensitivity of the decisions which he is taking, he has the duty personally to assure himself that he is adequately briefed. That means, in appropriate cases, asking relevant questions about the briefing, and testing the conclusions and recommendations. It is inherent in the process that he satisfies himself that the structure and organisation are sufficient for the purpose."

Hurd broadly agreed, but emphasised that ministers have to rely on their permanent secretaries. Major agreed that "A minister has a responsibility to see that he is adequately briefed." He added, "In practice, a minister could not personally check the accuracy of every piece of information that is given to him." Major also said, "What is certain is that, if a minister has any reason to suspect he may be inadequately briefed, [or has] any reason to suspect that, then he should clearly ask for more information."

The inquiry's paper, and witnesses' replies to questions about it, leave Waldegrave in a particularly exposed position. They also have implications for Sir Robin Butler who, as Cabinet Secretary, was the most senior official responsible for overseeing the efficiency of the intelligence agencies and the way their reports were distributed around Whitehall. At the end of the day, however, it is the Prime Minister who is accountable to Parliament for the activities of the agencies.

DAVID GORE-BOOTH, FORMER HEAD OF THE FO'S MIDDLE EAST DEPARTMENT/P.A./SEAN DEMPSEY

8

The Whispering Campaign

"An inquisition in double-barrelled form." Lord Howe.

"Damage ... has been unfairly done to our system of government, to the reputation of the Civil Service and to individuals." Sir Robin Butler.

It was not long before a Whitehall increasingly concerned about the direction in which the inquiry was heading resorted to a traditional tactic – off-the-record, unattributable, even personal, criticisms of Scott and his inquisitor, Presiley Baxendale.

It started as early as the summer of 1993, after Scott and Baxendale had shown up the arrogance of senior Foreign Office officials who, with one or two exceptions – adopted a hostile, resentful manner which served only to be counter-productive. Sir David Miers accused Baxendale of asking "trick" questions. David Gore-Booth referred, with a hint of mockery, to discussions about his travel plans "with a doctor in Riyadh before coming [who] referred me to something called a retrospectrascope, which you stick into people and it enables you to look backwards". After he suggested that Baxendale's questions were "inappropriate", Scott intervened, "I think you have to rely on me to make a fair use of your answers."

It was still rankling a year later. Gore-Booth said on BBC2's True Brits series on the Foreign Office that the way the inquiry was structured, "it's almost as though you had killed [your] next-door neighbour". Questioning, he said, seemed to be directed at "trying to prove, in some way, you've committed an offence". British policy towards Iraq, he insisted, was "as close to being honourable as international circumstances permitted ... yet we're in the dock. It's a very curious feeling."

Senior civil servants muttered privately that Scott did not understand the way Whitehall worked, that with everyone overworked, delegation was essential, that many decisions were taken informally – orally – and that the documents did not tell the full story. Scott made a virtue of his lack of direct experience as a Whitehall "insider", and used *faux naiveté* as an effective weapon. "My familiarity with the way Government works has been formed entirely by what I have seen in this inquiry," Scott told Tristan Garel-Jones. "I do not have anything else." But he was genuinely exasperated by civil servants' dissembling, lack of candour and failure to give straight answers to straight questions. He was frustrated by another of Whitehall's traditional weapons – delay. In July 1993, he told Major that delays in obtaining relevant documents "have had the consequence of hindering the efficiency of the questioning of witnesses ... The process of formulating the questions to be dealt with by witnesses in their written evidence has been made much more burdensome and time-consuming by the piecemeal manner in which documents have been forthcoming." Major promised to chivvy up Whitehall departments.

Six months later, on January 8, 1994, Scott wrote to Michael Heseltine – who as Trade and Industry Secretary would be the initial recipient of the final report – saying that Whitehall departments had created "unnecessary burdens" by withholding documents. "I regret to say ... that there have been a number of occasions when documents have been submitted long after they should have been." He warned Heseltine that his investigations had "raised important issues about the relationship between ministers and Parliament and between civil servants and their ministers" – a clear indication of what was to come in his final report.

Simmering resentment in ministerial and Whitehall circles erupted into the open six days later when it was Lord Howe's turn to give evidence. In a prepared written statement, the former foreign secretary accused Scott of being "detective, inquisitor, advocate and judge" all at the same time – a reference to Lord Denning's description of his role as official investigator into the Profumo affair in 1963. With no prior warning to Scott, Howe accused the inquiry of ignoring "cardinal principles" set out by Lord Salmon following the Denning report

31 years earlier. These were that witnesses should have advanced warning of allegations made against them, the opportunity of being examined by their own advocate, and the chance to cross-examine on evidence against them.

Those who had already given evidence, and those watching the proceedings from outside, Howe went on, were "bound to be less enthusiastic to accept the conclusions" of the inquiry. The attempt at a pre-emptive strike produced a sharp retort from Scott who asked Howe whether he was speaking on behalf of anyone in particular. "Are your clients, so to speak, say, a number of anonymous individuals in some department or other?"

"No," Howe replied, though still refusing to identify those individuals. He added simply, "All those to whom I have spoken, both concerned with the case and outside the case, have expressed surprise that the procedure has taken this form. The point I am making is that, in so far as surprise is expressed ... that [it] represents a handicap for you, sir." He said he was motivated by a concern to protect the reputation of ministers and people he described as his "former flock" – a likely reference to Foreign Office officials – in a presumably unintended echo of Lord Healey's famous remark that being attacked by Howe was akin to being savaged by a "dead sheep". There was no doubt that Howe was reflecting widespread resentment in Whitehall and among some ministers about the forthright nature of Scott's and Baxendale's questioning and their determination to get to the truth. There were murmurings in Whitehall that Major had reacted too pre-emptorily in setting up the inquiry in the first place – that Thatcher would have brazened out the furore following the collapse of the Matrix Churchill trial. But ministers officially distanced themselves from Howe's outburst. Heseltine told Robin Cook, shadow trade and industry secretary, that Howe had given evidence "as a private citizen ... The comments he made are his own responsibility."

Scott took the unprecedented step of releasing an immediate retort to Howe through Christopher Muttukumaru, the inquiry's secretary. "No complaint" he said, had been made to the inquiry about its procedures either by the FO or by the Government. The inquiry's procedures had been established "with a view to ensuring its efficient conduct while paying full regard to the need to safeguard the interests of individuals. The procedures were agreed after consultation both with government departments and interested individuals." Given the complexity of the issues which he was investigating, it would have been "ludicrous" to allow legal representation to everyone who might have had an interest in particular issues.

The judge pointed out that detailed written questionnaires giving a clear idea of what they would be asked about were sent to witnesses before they were asked questions in public hearings. All witnesses had the opportunity to have legal advice paid for out of public funds – indeed, Howe had advice from the Treasury Solicitor's Department.

Lord Trefgarne, who also criticised the inquiry's procedures and said he eventually decided, "A refusal to appear would have exposed me to the criticism that I had something to hide", came accompanied by a legal adviser – Sir Patrick Neill, former warden of All Souls, Oxford.

Howe later said the impression gained by witnesses questioned by both Scott and Baxendale was "of an inquisition in double-barrelled form". He told readers of The Times that one unidentified witness had written to him saying: "You spoke for all of us who have had to undergo humiliation, even degradation, for doing our duty in good faith and – in fact if not in the fiction which passes for it these days – with honour and a reasonable degree of success."

But Scott made plain from the start that before making any criticism of a witness in his final report, that witness would be given a draft of the relevant passage and have an opportunity to make any comment he or she wished. Muttukumaru drove the point home in a meeting with Whitehall "Scott Units" – groups of officials set up to help witnesses provide documents to the inquiry, and co-ordinate evidence. Muttukumaru also said that the Civil Service could make representations about what information or documents sent to the inquiry should be kept secret, but he reminded Whitehall that Major had given Scott "unfettered discretion" about what to publish.

The irony behind Howe's attack was that it was John Major who established the inquiry's status and terms of reference, overruling objections by the Opposition. John Smith had called for a statutory tribunal under the 1921 Tribunals of Inquiry (Evidence) Act with witnesses giving evidence under oath and with cross-examination by their lawyers. Major rejected the idea on the grounds that that would take far too long. In its own guidance to prospective witnesses, the Government said: "Legal representatives may attend the inquiry ... but witnesses will be expected to speak [for] themselves and not through their lawyers." Asked in the Commons what he thought about Howe's outburst, Major said, "It was the Government who set up the inquiry and gave Lord Justice Scott the freedom to pursue it as he thinks fit."

In the ensuing row, Scott received support from Denning. In a letter to The Times, the former law lord said: "The expedient which Lord Justice Scott has adopted of not allowing lawyers has been a useful and practical device to avoid undue prolongation of the inquiry and even greater expense." Lord Donaldson, a former Master of the Rolls, also backed Scott. He told the BBC, "I can very well understand that if you have a collection of witnesses who are highly intelligent, highly articulate, and you're inquiring into a matter which is very fully documented, you might well conclude that there was no need for them to be legally represented." If witnesses' lawyers had the opportunity to cross-examine, "it wouldn't be an inquiry, it would be a circus". Others pointed to the similarities between the Scott inquiry and the DTI inspectors' investigations under the Companies Act, criticised on the grounds that the "accused" did not have a fair trial in an independent court. Scott, however, gave witnesses early warning of questions, and witnesses' legal costs were funded by the taxpayer.

Sir Robin Butler was careful not to criticise Scott or the inquiry's procedures. Instead, he directed his fire at the media, accusing it of damaging Britain's "system of government" and the reputation of Whitehall. Whitehall's task of preparing evidence had been made "more fraught and onerous by grossly distorted and prejudicial allegations", he said in a prepared statement. "The victims are often middle-ranking officials who could not have expected to be thrust into the limelight in the way in which they have." Although he forewarned Major about the general thrust of his statement, he said his attack on the media was delivered in his role as head of the Home Civil Service, after consulting Sir David Gillmore, head of the Diplomatic Service.

He asked Lord Justice Scott to "put the record straight" and said the

*Crest for the tie designed by journalists
covering the Scott Inquiry, drawn by Mathew
Lawrence, sketch artist for Channel 4 News.
A serpent is wrapped round a Roman three
– the clause of the Howe guidelines secretly relaxed
to allow more arms-related equipment
to be exported to Iraq.
The motto reflects Sir Robin Butler's description
of media coverage of the inquiry.*

inquiry should "undo ... the damage which has been unfairly done to our system of government, to the reputation of the Civil Service and to individuals". Butler spoke of the "the meticulous way in which records were kept and preserved" – a claim which did not prevent the judge from rebuking him for the failure of the Cabinet Office to release documents relating to meetings involving the Cabinet Secretary, the Prime Minister, and Alan Clark over allegations that Clark gave "a nod and a wink" to British firms selling equipment to Iraq's arms industry.

Baxendale asked Butler, "Do you think there are lots of other documents like this we haven't seen in the Cabinet Office files that have handwritten comments [by Sonia Phippard, Butler's private secretary] on them?"

In a calculated message directed at both Whitehall and the public, the judge frostily added that the inquiry had still not received a substantive response to a written request two months earlier for an assurance that all relevant Cabinet Office documents would be made available.

Journalists covering the inquiry reacted to Butler's attacks by designing a tie with the words "distorted, wild, prejudiced" proudly blazened below a fork-tongued serpent. They presented a tie to Butler. The Cabinet Secretary accepted it in what he called, "A spirit of (I hope) mutual understanding and I shall wear it with much pleasure." He added, "Whatever else happens, it will be a memento of a remarkable episode in all our lives."

Butler and the media were to hear more evidence which shed even worse light on the Government and the antics of Whitehall.

CUSTOMS DISCOVER PARTS OF THE SUPERGUN/NORTH NEWS/CARL RUTHERFORD

REPUBLIC OF IRAQ.
MINISTRY FOR INDUSTRIES
AND MINERALS.
PETROCHEMICAL PROJECT.
BAGHDAD.   IRAQ.
P.O. NO. 3-839-988.
GROSS WT. 44,750 KGS.
NO. 45.
O/NO. 5997184.

9

The Supergun

"[Customs and Excise] were given very little indication of what they had to look for ... They actually thought they were collecting a huge shipment of drugs, and they took sniffer dogs." David James, chairman of Eagle Trust, on the discovery of supergun parts.

An unbroken thread in the tangled case of Matrix Churchill and its extraordinary repercussions can be traced back to the seizure by Customs in April 1990 of a consignment of large pipes at Teesport and the decision, seven months later, to drop charges against two men in connection with the proposed export.

The pipes, made by Sheffield Forgemasters and Walter Somers, a West Midlands firm, were destined for Iraq, which claimed they were for a petrochemical plant. They were believed by the Department of Trade and Industry which told the companies that the pipes did not need an export licence.

Although the seizure and its aftermath quickly became known as the supergun affair, the pipes were widely assumed to be for Saddam Hussein's Project Babylon, a plan – dreamt up by the Canadian engineer, Gerald Bull – to produce a number of large guns, theoretically capable of delivering short-range nuclear or chemical warheads. Alternatively – as Christopher Cowley, a metallurgist working for Bull's Space Research Corporation and one of those charged, insisted – they were part of a plan to launch satellites. Following the Iraqi invasion of Kuwait, United Nations observers found a large supergun in the mountains of northern Iraq. However, a single, giant supergun would have been nonsense from a military point of view, difficult to prepare for fire and a vulnerable, static target. A senior DTI official later told the Commons Trade and Industry Committee that "The Ministry of Defence thought Operation Babylon was connected with buying cluster bombs or artillery – not a supergun."

A week before the seizure of the pipes at Teesport, Gerald Bull was assassinated in Brussels. The widespread assumption was that it was the work of Mossad, the Israeli secret service, though Whitehall privately put it about that Bull may have been killed by Iranians. Cowley has claimed that Bull had kept British intelligence fully informed about the Babylon project since June 1988. In October 1989, Paul Henderson of Matrix Churchill handed MI6 plans for Iraq's ABA missile, believed by British intelligence experts to have been part of the Babylon project. At about the same time, Gerald James, chairman of Astra, the defence contractor, warned the MoD of his suspicions. Astra had recently taken over PRB, the Belgian explosives company which had been supplying Iraq with special propellant for the project. Bull was killed shortly after having lunch with Christopher Gumbley, Astra's chief executive.

The controversy turned, not on who might have killed Bull – who had many enemies – but on the Government's prior knowledge of the supergun project, and its subsequent decision to abandon a prosecution in connection with it. Civil servants, intelligence agencies and ministers prevented details emerging about the Government's knowledge of the affair – both on the floor of the Commons and during the investigation by the Commons Trade and Industry Committee. The committee's report, published just before the 1992 general election, referred to the "obstruction" it had faced from Whitehall. It said it found it "particularly strange" that senior Customs officials consulted the then Attorney-General, Sir Patrick Mayhew, and John MacGregor, then Leader of the Commons, before giving evidence. Sir Patrick, the committee noted, "endorsed the intention of the [Customs] Commissioners not to disclose evidence that had been revealed to them in the course of their investigations". Alan Clark, then Minister for Defence Procurement, told the committee he was "unable to illuminate on the role of the security services".

Back in June 1988, Dr Rex Bayliss, managing director of Walter Somers, contacted Sir Hal Miller, then Conservative MP for

Bromsgrove, and told him of his concerns about a prospective order from Space Research Corporation. Bayliss said that, after studying the initial Iraqi order, he thought it looked like "a giant pea-shooter" that might be used for launching missiles. He then noticed that the Iraqi specification for tubes was constantly increasing, approaching the pressures associated with gun steels. Miller later told the Scott inquiry how Bayliss was prepared to drop the order or mark the consignment with "pink spots" so that the intelligence agencies could identify its destination.

Miller, whose revelations provoked a smear campaign directed by 10 Downing Street – he later said he had never come across "so much lying in high places" – declined to give evidence to the committee, preferring to hold his fire for the Scott inquiry, where he electrified the proceedings by claiming that Mayhew had urged him to suppress crucial evidence.

He told the inquiry that after Bayliss' call, "the first person I reached for was the Minister of Trade's [then Alan Clark] private office". Clark's office apparently directed him to the DTI's Export Licensing Unit. The same day, Tony Steadman, director of the unit – who Miller described as having "played for the long grass" – contacted the MoD.

Miller said he also contacted the MoD and "another agency", a reference either to the Defence Intelligence Staff or MI6. Bayliss told the committee that Miller had given him the name of Bill Weir, an MoD metallurgy expert. Concerned that Whitehall was not properly investigating the Iraqi order, Miller alerted the MoD in 1989 – where he was told that "everything was under control" – and again in early 1990.

At the time of the seizure, Nicholas Ridley, then Trade and Industry Secretary, told the Commons that "The Government recently became aware in general terms [of the Iraqi project] ... Until a few days ago, my department had no knowledge that the goods were designed to form part of a gun."

His claims were described by Alan Clark in evidence to the Commons committee two years later as an "exaggeration".

A key player in the search for truth about Whitehall's knowledge of the supergun was Nicolas Bevan, then a senior official at the MoD. On January 22, 1992, he told the committee, "We have no evidence of Sir

SIR HAL MILLER, FORMER CONSERVATIVE MP FOR BROMSGROVE/MICHAEL WEBB

Hal Miller having talked to the Ministry of Defence on this subject."

A month later, on February 27, 1992, Clark contradicted Bevan. He said he had "records" of Sir Hal's contacts with Whitehall in 1988 and 1990. Miller later told the Scott inquiry that Bevan's evidence to the committee was "rubbish, because the private office confirmed to me that all the conversations were correctly logged and fully logged". He suggested that Whitehall knew the pipes were for military use by Iraq even before his approaches. He described how he warned a "Mr Anderson", an intelligence officer – "a jolly-hockey-sticks sort of character" – about the Iraqi order in June 1988. "The officer replied, 'Jolly good of you, old boy. This confirms everything we know.'"

Yet Bevan had told the Commons committee that the Government's awareness that British companies were involved in the Iraqi project only "began to come together in the second half of March 1990". He said ministers were not alerted until the Customs seizure in April 1990.

Miller's account was challenged by an extraordinary gung-ho version of events presented to the inquiry on June 30, 1993 by David James, chairman of Eagle Trust, which had taken over Walter Somers. Britain's involvement in the supergun project, he said, was exposed by a year-long hunt by MI6 and Mossad. He claimed that MI6 believed the gun was designed to deliver a tonne of anthrax – a virulent biological warfare agent – up to 1,400 miles, bringing Israeli cities well within its range. His evidence – which appeared at times more like a Biggles adventure set in the world of John le Carré – was the full story behind the affair, although apart from other facts, he ignored such details as the inaccuracy of the supergun. Had it been fired, the gun would have poisoned the Arab population within a five-mile target, including the Gaza strip.

James argued he had withheld information from the Commons Trade and Industry committee because, he said, intelligence agencies were not a "parliamentary affair". He described how he was alerted during a visit to the Walter Somers factory at Halesowen in January 1990, when he noticed three steel pipes, one of which looked like a "thumping great muzzle, just like a cartoon representation of a siege gun". He was accompanied by Peter Mitchell, who had taken over as managing director of Walter Somers. Mitchell explained the pipes were for an Iraqi petrochemical plant. James said he decided to make "discreet inquiries".

Without telling Mitchell, he shared his concerns with Charles Whyte, one of the company's senior engineers. On March 20, 1992, he telephoned MI6 about his suspicions. He refused to comment on how he knew MI6's telephone number.

A week later – three days after Bull was assassinated – James said he met an agent identified as "Mr Z". He gave Mr Z a rough sketch of the 330mm steel pipes. Although the MI6 agent told James that the find was the "first tangible evidence" that parts for large Iraqi guns were being made in Britain, his initial reaction was disappointing. The pipes were too small for the "monster gun" MI6 had been looking for a year earlier at the request of Mossad. On March 30, 1990, James obtained letters of credit from the "international banking circuit" which showed that another British company, Sheffield Forgemasters, had arranged to supply Iraq with bigger pipes. James said he immediately telephoned Mr Z who responded with "whoops of joy".

In search for further evidence, and using the cover story that bankers wanted to check the company's files, Whyte took 900 documents from Walter Somers' offices. They were photographed secretly through the night with special MI6 equipment set up in a room at a Halesowen hotel, booked by James. On April 11, 1990, Mr Z phoned James, informing him that the Sheffield Forgemasters pipes had been found at Teesport "ready to go". Customs rushed to the scene. In order to disguise Whyte's help, James said he asked Douglas Tweddle, head of Customs' investigation branch, to subject Whyte to an "aggressive interview to maintain the cover".

James adorned his picaresque account by telling the inquiry, "I do not think it has been said anywhere before, but Customs and Excise later explained to me, at quite a high level, [that] one of the problems they had here was that the whole of the advice from MI6 came so quickly, as a reaction to the discovery that shipment was imminent, and the confidentiality required that they were given very little indication of what they had to look for – and they actually thought they collecting a huge shipment of drugs, and ... took sniffer dogs."

James' extravagant evidence was a sideshow. A week earlier, Miller had claimed before the inquiry that when Sir Patrick Mayhew was Attorney-General, he was urged by him to suppress evidence about how the Government misled MPs about its knowledge of the supergun project. Miller had threatened to give evidence in defence of his business contact, Peter Mitchell, who had been charged with Cowley in connection with the affair.

Miller said he approached Mayhew in the Commons lobby with detailed evidence about events leading up to the Customs charges against Mitchell and Cowley. Miller outlined the exchange to the inquiry:

Miller: "There was a stage when I consulted the Attorney-General and the Solicitor-General [Sir Nicholas Lyell, the present Attorney-General] about the evidence available to me. I first of all asked them as lawyers whether ... contemporary notes [and the fax from the DTI constituted] evidence, in a strict sense, and was assured that they were.

"I said [to Mayhew] I then intended to go into court and produce them if Somers were charged. An attempt was made to persuade me not to do that, and I said, 'You must be joking. You charge them – I will go into court,' and then there was a sort of: 'We do not charge them. Customs are independent,' and I remember saying, 'Come on, Paddy, you are the Attorney-General, I cannot believe people really get sent into court without you at least having some say in the matter.' He said, 'No they are completely independent.' So I said, 'Fine, in which case I will go to court.' "

Baxendale: "Who made an effort to stop you going to court? You said someone made an effort to stop you going to court."

Miller: "He sought to dissuade me from producing the evidence in court."

Scott: " 'He' being?"

Miller: "Paddy Mayhew. He said, 'You would not do that, would you?' To which I replied, 'Just watch me.' "

Baxendale: "Did he say anything else?"

Miller: "No. It was a conversation in the lobby ..."

Scott: "He did not say anything else?"

Miller: "I was seriously concerned for these people. To my knowledge, they had done nothing wrong at all, and they had given every co-operation and every assistance and people were just washing their hands and letting them go to jail. This is Britain ..."

Miller's evidence was immediately rejected by Mayhew. He flew from

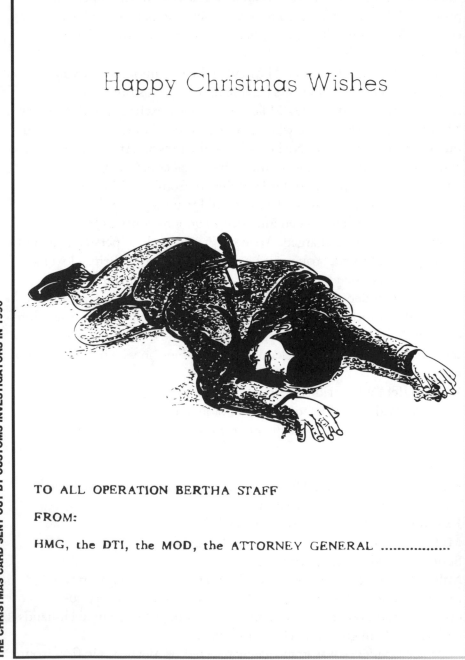

Happy Christmas Wishes

TO ALL OPERATION BERTHA STAFF

FROM:

HMG, the DTI, the MOD, the ATTORNEY GENERAL ....

THE CHRISTMAS CARD SENT OUT BY CUSTOMS INVESTIGATORS IN 1990

Northern Ireland for a specially-convened session of the inquiry three days later, on May 27, 1993. In a prepared statement, he said he had known Sir Hal Miller for many years and he was sure the former MP's evidence "represents what is now his honest recollection". He then added, "I disagree with it, however, in one crucial respect. I assert my absolute confidence that I never attempted, as he alleges, to persuade him not to go into court and produce documents if Somers were charged."

Mayhew said he recalled "a chance encounter" with Miller in "a crowded and noisy" Commons lobby. Miller had described "some relevant documentary evidence in his possession ... I think it quite possible that I did tell him they could in principle be admissible as evidence." He added, "I certainly cannot recall the words of my response – but their character, I am confident, was 'so be it' or 'that is up to you'. I am sure I did not say, 'You would not do that, would you?' Or say anything calculated to convey pressure on him not to do so.

"And the reason is this. To try to persuade someone not to produce evidence in the circumstances I have described would have been wholly wrongful. It would have been inconceivable to me, both as a private person and as a member of the Bar, let alone as its Leader, the Attorney-General. I have never done such a thing. If I had done so, whether in this perfunctory conversation in a crowded lobby or at all, the memory of it would, I am sure, remain vividly with me. Yet I recall no such action."

Customs investigators on the case were shocked when charges against Mitchell and Cowley were suddenly dropped in November 1990. They believed the case should have been put to a jury. Their view was expressed in a Christmas card they sent out that Christmas showing a body with a knife in its back (see illustration). Mayhew gave his account of the decision. He said that he became directly involved in the case in July 1990 when Julian Bevan, Customs' senior prosecuting counsel, told the then Attorney-General that he had concluded a jury "would be reluctant to convict these employees given the background". In a reference to the Code for Crown Prosecutors, Bevan said, "If asked the ultimate question, we [Bevan and his junior counsel] are of the view that we have a less than 50 per cent chance of securing a conviction." That was the view directed particularly at Mitchell's case – with Cowley there was said to be "a reasonable prospect of success", but it was later considered it would be difficult to continue against one of the men, letting the other one go.

In August 1990, senior Customs officials asked Mayhew if he would appoint a new leading counsel to replace Bevan. Sandy Russell, a Customs Commissioner, warned that failure to go ahead with a trial would expose "government ambivalence" over arms sales to Iraq and deal "a hammerblow" to Customs' ability to enforce sanctions against Iraq. Mayhew responded that this was not a proper "public interest" consideration to justify a prosecution. Although the Attorney-General has the power to drop prosecutions – by issuing a *nolle prosequi* – Mayhew insisted that the final decision whether to go ahead with the prosecution was one for Customs, an independent prosecuting authority.

The inquiry heard later that Russell acknowledged Customs was entering "highly-delicate territory", but told Sir Brian Unwin, then chairman of Customs and Excise, that he was "deeply unhappy about throwing in the towel". Russell blamed Whitehall departments – and, above all, the DTI – for the failure to secure prosecutions in the supergun case. The DTI's performance in the supergun case had been "less than brilliant", he said. "Quite detailed drawings had been sent by Sheffield Forgemasters to the DTI, and had that been fully explored and properly dealt with, there is the chance alarm bells would have rung."

On November 14, 1990, the day before the charges were dropped, Unwin sent a letter to the then Chancellor, John Major – alerting him to the intention not to continue with the case. The same day, Sir Robin Butler sent a similar letter to Sir Charles Powell, Thatcher's private secretary.

Butler's involvement was outlined in unpublished written evidence sent to the inquiry by Sir Hal Miller. Miller describes an extraordinary meeting with Sir Robin on April 24, 1990, a few days after Customs' seizure of the steel pipes at Teesport. Miller alleges that Sir Robin initially accused him of making up the evidence, warning him that he could be in serious trouble if he persisted in his accusations. But after Miller produced his handwritten notes containing the evidence, Miller says Sir Robin's attitude suddenly changed. The official Cabinet Office minute of the meeting gives an anodyne version of the exchange. The

minute also records – wrongly – that the MoD, the DTI, and the
intelligence agencies had no recollection of Miller's previous approaches
to them. Sir Robin wrote to the inquiry denying Miller's account of
the meeting. Meanwhile the Government's concern about the whole
affair was reflected in its decision to set up a special "Gun Committee"
in the Cabinet Office.

A month after he was told to drop the supergun prosecution, Unwin
wrote a memo about the next case on the horizon – the Matrix Churchill
prosecution. After attending a crisis meeting with Butler to discuss
newspaper allegations that Alan Clark had given Matrix Churchill
"a nod and a wink" to carry on selling machine tools to Iraqi weapons
factories, Unwin wrote: "To put it crudely, I don't want a repeat of the
gun affair ... Apart from the damaging effect on morale, we don't have
the resources to waste on complex cases that are unlikely to lead to a
successful prosecution." He said the lesson of the supergun affair made
Customs even more determined to investigate thoroughly the Matrix
Churchill case.

His comments are now resonant with irony. But what Unwin did not
say was that, after the collapse of the supergun prosecution, Customs
was more determined than ever to go ahead with the Matrix Churchill
case, come what may.

NICHOLAS RIDLEY, FORMER TRADE AND INDUSTRY SECRETARY/THE GUARDIAN/GRAHAM TURNER

10

More Panic ...

"There was scope for all sorts of interesting things to come out of the woodwork." Michael Coolican, senior DTI official.

"Things are lurking! ... They knew it was for military use! ... In reality the DTI probably did suspect." Customs lawyers on the DTI.

On June 21,1990, an anxious Nicholas Ridley, the Trade and Industry Secretary, wrote an urgent minute to the Prime Minister, with copies to Sir Robin Butler and members of the Cabinet's Overseas and Defence Committee. "I understand," he said, "that Customs are today making an ostensibly routine visit to [Matrix Churchill] and will report on what, if anything, they uncover. But any action following that visit is likely to worsen relations with Iraq." He warned that the Export Credit Guarantee Department's exposure in Iraq amounted to £1 billion. Consequences of a systematic Iraqi default would be "extremely serious" with implications for the Government's controls on public expenditure.

The previous day, Martin Stanley, Ridley's private secretary, wrote to Simon Woodside, Sir Brian Unwin's private secretary at Customs and Excise. "We noted that your officers propose to make a routine visit to the company ... but you had given DTI ministers the opportunity to object. You assured me that the visit would be used for fact-finding only, and no action would be taken as a result without consulting ministers." He copied the letter to Sir Charles Powell, Thatcher's private secretary, and to the private secretary of then Chancellor, John Major.

The DTI's panic was graphically explained by Michael Coolican, who had taken over from Eric Beston in charge of export control policy.

Coolican, who knew about the MI6 report, said, "The dirty washing liable to emerge from the action proposed by Customs will add to the problems posed by the [super] gun," he warned his ministers on June 14. "The timing is extraordinarily embarrassing given the recent correspondence between ourselves, the Foreign and Commonwealth Office and the Ministry of Defence." He added, "Needless to say, we were not aware of Customs' knowledge and activity when we briefed the ministers for trade" – a reference to Lord Trefgarne who approved a batch of Matrix Churchill exports even though the Government was told the equipment had been sold to Iraqi weapons factories. "Are ministers willing to have the 1987 and subsequent decisions exposed, and made the subject of courtroom argument?" asked Coolican. "Are ministers willing to face a worsening in our relations with Iraq?"

Asked at the inquiry by Presiley Baxendale why he wrote the urgent memo, Coolican referred to MI6 reports which confirmed that the machine tools were for military purposes. "There was scope for all sorts of interesting things to come out of the woodwork." He later warned James Meadway, his boss at the DTI, that documents which could be disclosed at a trial would make the department "look like a bunch of bungling amateurs".

In early November 1990, Sir Peter Gregson, the DTI's permanent secretary – the department's top official – had become involved. He came to see Butler at the Cabinet Office. Butler claimed at the inquiry that Gregson was concerned about the intelligence connection, with the clear – and misleading – implication that the DTI's hands were tied because it could not tell Customs that MI6 had an interest in Matrix Churchill sales to Iraq.

A secret MI6 minute, dated July 7, 1990, showed that Customs was already well aware of the intelligence connection. An identified MI6 agent – possibly John Balsom, Henderson's contact – noted: "As I had been tipped off, first by [name blanked out] and then by [name blanked out] before the visit I knew in advance and managed to speak to Peter Wiltshire in Customs, who is aware that we have a source in Matrix Churchill Ltd. Both then and since, Peter Wiltshire has been very helpful in keeping me informed on the general thrust of the investigation and detailed points about it. He has in no way resented my inquiries: he describes the case as sensitive and political not because of our interest but because of the relevant matters involved in export licence applications, with the companies sending large amounts of documentation, including component drawings, to the DTI. Therefore, any prosecution would risk a large amount of potentially-damaging government documentation being produced in court."

What concerned Gregson – and, it seemed, Butler too – was not the intelligence aspect, but ambiguous remarks made by Alan Clark, then Trade Minister, to members of the Machine Tools Technologies Association in January 1988. This is made plain from a note of a telephone call Butler made to Sir Brian Unwin on November 7, the day after his meeting with Gregson.

In a note of the conversation, Unwin said Butler had referred to "the reported remarks by Mr Alan Clark", and added that he "hopes he has safeguarded our statutory position" – a clear suggestion that Unwin was already worried that pressure would be put on Customs to drop the case, or as Butler put it to the inquiry, "[Customs were] warning me to keep off the grass".

Clark's meeting with the MTTA was raised later that month when Whitehall discovered that the Sunday Times newspaper was about to publish a damaging article about the former minister. Butler warned Andrew Turnbull, then Major's private secretary, that the Matrix Churchill defence was likely to be that Clark had "implicitly encouraged them to undertake this trade". So a full two years before the trial, Butler and the Prime Minister's office were already forewarned of the case for the defence which ultimately led to the trial's collapse.

The Sunday Times duly printed the allegations against Clark and calls by Paddy Ashdown, the Liberal Democrat leader, for the minister's resignation. The article provoked anguish in Whitehall. Butler hastily called a meeting. "This was another panic morning," Butler later told the inquiry. The meeting was attended by Gregson, Gerald Hosker – the DTI's legal adviser, now Treasury Solicitor – David Gore-Booth from the FO, Sir Brian Unwin from Customs, Sir Michael Quinlan, permanent secretary at the MoD, and other Cabinet Office and DTI officials.

Later that morning, Clark was summoned to 10 Downing Street for a meeting with Major, attended by Butler. A minute of the meeting drawn up by Butler recorded that Clark had told the MTTA companies to "downgrade specifications so that they could not be used for military purposes". Clark denied this and amended the minute with new wording, stating that he agreed to specifications "so that they would not be seen as suitable for military purposes" – a subtle but crucial distinction, a significant weakening of Clark's advice and one more consistent with his evidence at the trial. Until Clark came to give evidence in December 1993, the inquiry had not been given the amended version of the minutes. Asked by Scott why the Cabinet Office had not supplied him with it, Butler replied, "As a result of an oversight, I guess. You can be assured that there was no conspiracy to keep it from you." Neither prosecution nor defence lawyers were aware at the trial of Clark's corrected minutes of the meeting.

Butler conceded that notes of the MTTA meeting of which he was aware back in December 1990 showed that Clark's comments could have been open to "misinterpretation" by the companies – so they could have believed they were being encouraged to sell arms-related equipment to Iraq. He was then asked by Scott why the prosecution had not seen Cabinet Office records of these meetings until October 1992, nearly two years later, and just days before the trial began. Butler suggested that only a lawyer would know whether or not the Cabinet Office records were relevant – a suggestion Scott strongly contested – and that it was the job of prosecution and defence lawyers to ask for papers.

Butler then revealed to an angry Scott that his private secretary, Sonia Phippard, had drawn up rough notes of the Cabinet Office meeting early on the morning of December 3, 1990. They, too, had not been disclosed to the inquiry. Phippard wrote: "Implication AC colluded in [the export sales]". She noted that Len Appleyard, a senior Cabinet Office official – now ambassador to China – who also attended the meeting, remarked: " 'If conceal factory to which tools going, could be conspiracy, because defendants could say Alan Clark encouraging false statement.' "

Appleyard then said that the DTI record of the MTTA meeting was "ambiguous" – it could be read either to support what the defendants were arguing, or what Clark was saying he meant. Butler said he could not remember whether he raised the ambiguity point with Major. (He later said he did not do so on the grounds that the Prime Minister had already heard Clark's version of events.)

According to Phippard's notes, Gregson remarked at the meeting: " 'Official record encouraged nod and wink people. Would need to brazen beyond that' " – meaning that the Government would have to deny it was official policy to give the companies "a nod and a wink".

In November 1991, at the time of the committal hearings against the Matrix Churchill 3, William Reeves, a Cabinet Office official, warned, "One point which has always worried me is that the DTI brief for Clark's meeting with the industrialists indicated knowledge of the military purpose of some of the machine tools. This document struck me as potentially damaging to the prosecution case and at the same time difficult not to disclose in the interests of justice." The Government did its best to try and prevent it from getting into the hands of the defence.

Customs lawyers at this stage expressed confidence about the prosecution on the grounds that whatever the Government knew, this did not negate the company's obligation to be honest. There was already worry, however, about Clark's potential performance as a witness. Sir Michael Quinlan, permanent secretary at the MoD, wrote of his then minister: "We had a number of concerns, both as to the likely performance of Mr Clark as a witness, given his views on record that he was in favour of exports to Iraq, and his occasionally idiosyncratic behaviour, [and] more generally concerning the principle of putting ministers in a witness box."

A few days later, on November 15, 1991, Butler sent a note to Andrew Turnbull, John Major's principle private secretary. He warned it was likely to be part of the defence case that the Government were aware that the exports were specially designed to have a military application. Butler then added: "The Government deny that they were so aware of what Mr Clark and Lord Trefgarne had in their minds in their dealings with the company."

Butler's note worried Martin Stanley, private secretary to Peter Lilley, who by then had succeeded Ridley at the DTI. He dispatched a minute to Sir Peter Gregson, his permanent secretary, referring to a conversation he had had with Sonia Phippard. Phippard, Stanley said, had agreed with him that Butler's phrase: "The Government denied they were so aware" was "simply wrong". Stanley added that she "clearly felt a jury were unlikely to convict and she could not understand why Customs were pressing on with the case". She noted: "It had not taken Customs long to drop the supergun prosecutions", and she clearly wondered whether this case, too, would ever get a full hearing.

Another DTI official was equally unhappy. Michael Coolican alerted his colleagues that the Prime Minister had been given a "misleading steer" about the Government's connivance in the trade with Iraq. As early as February 1991, Coolican had told Lord Trefgarne, his Trade Minister, that Matrix Churchill lawyers' main defence would be that the Government knew all along the machine tools would be used by Iraq to make arms.

Butler told the inquiry that he did not correct his minute to the Prime Minister's office in the light of Phippard's observations, on the grounds that the comments of Coolican and Stanley were "misconceived". Asked by Baxendale whether his decision not to amend his minute was "a high-handed thing to do", Butler suggested that Phippard was not aware of what had been going on in other parts of Whitehall. He put Phippard's views down to "gossip" among the "freemasonry" of private secretaries. Asked by Scott if he held any common views about the prosecution with Phippard, Butler responded, "No. I cannot remember sharing my view with her. As you realise, I am not now going to share it with anybody else."

At the DTI, anguished officials were beginning to manoeuvre as it became clear Customs was pressing ahead with the prosecution. Tony Steadman warned that it would be "extremely embarrassing" if evidence was to come out showing how the Government cleared the export licences at the height of the Iran-Iraq war. Eric Beston conceded later to the inquiry that he knew the main defence argument was likely to be that the Government knew the machines were being used by Iraq to make weapons, but had done nothing about it. He also agreed there was no evidence the company had misled the Government in its export application forms – the main plank of the prosecution's case.

But he told his colleagues before the committal proceedings in November 1991 that he would "do [his] very best to avoid embarrassment" to ministers and civil servants. He acknowledged it was a "rather pompous and self-indulgent" admission, but he had been "in a state of considerable uncertainty" about what to do. The same month, Michael Coolican warned his minister, Peter Lilley, of the "unhelpful publicity" which might emerge at the committal.

But Customs lawyers ignored deep misgivings within Whitehall, and side-stepped politically-embarrassing questions, in their determination to prosecute. They noted an attitude of "general reluctance" about the prosecution within the DTI. Another note warned: "Things are lurking! i.e. They knew it was for military use!"

Annabelle Bolt, a Customs solicitor on the case, was to tell the inquiry she believed the DTI's reluctance to go ahead with the prosecution was fear they would be shown in a "less than favourable light", particularly in the way it had handled export licence applications. When Scott suggested that the DTI was also concerned about the damaging evidence that would emerge in court about how the Government knew the machine tools were being used to make arms, but did not care, Bolt replied, "They didn't at any stage say, 'Please stop'."

Some DTI officials tried. Coolican wanted to deal with the Matrix Churchill case by calling in the defendants and "slapping them across the wrists" rather than by a prosecution. Others were more reticent. Meadway warned his colleagues that if they pushed to stop the prosecution, they might end up in a Customs "interrogation suite".

Sir Brian Unwin acknowledged that in a series of meetings and telephone conversations, senior civil servants warned him of "storm signals" that lay ahead, in particular allegations that Alan Clark had given Matrix Churchill "a nod and a wink" to arms exports. But he said the warnings in the end amounted to little more than a "general background noise of unease", and did not divert him from his view that a prosecution was the right course.

Asked by Lord Justice Scott if "officials, in the nicest possible way, were trying to make you think twice about the prosecution?" Unwin replied that they were telling him only that it was "a jolly difficult case with potential for embarrassment all round". And in any case, Customs was an independent prosecution authority.

ALAN MOSES QC, CUSTOMS' CHIEF PROSECUTION COUNSEL/REUTERS/PAUL HANNAH

11

Documents Withheld

"I can't understand why on earth I didn't know about this." Alan Moses QC, chief prosecution counsel.

It was "a high-profile case at an early stage", Peter Wiltshire, the Customs agent in charge of it, told the inquiry. It had "a political dimension ... Notes were winging their way upwards." DTI officials, in particular, tried to mount a Whitehall campaign to get Customs to scale down their investigation into Matrix Churchill. They shared the view, expressed forcibly to the inquiry by Alan Clark. He described the prosecution as "ludicrous" and without any justification. Customs, he said, enjoyed a degree of autonomy that was "a perpetual mystery".

Alan Barrett of the MoD told the inquiry he was aware "there were people around who believed the prosecution shouldn't be brought and were making overtures to try to ensure that it didn't take place". Asked to be more specific, he named the three DTI officials most closely involved in monitoring exports – Coolican, Beston, and Steadman.

Michael Petter, former head of the DTI's Middle East branch, told the inquiry he was worried that high-profile investigations would damage Britain's trade link with Iraq and risk £2 billion in export credits. He said that the FO was equally concerned, pointing to a telegram from the British ambassador in Baghdad warning of the Iraqis' "extreme degree of concern" at what was perceived as a deliberate campaign against them.

Petter accused Customs of going about some of their previous raids "in a rather gung-ho way. There had been a fair amount of press reports about them and it appeared to get under the skin of the Iraqis." His suggestion to ministers that Customs scale down their activities earned a severe rebuke from Len Appleyard, a senior Cabinet Office official. Appleyard described Petter's call for "less assiduous" investigations as an "entirely improper interference in the independence of Customs".

But not all Customs officials were sanguine. Pat Blackshaw, a senior Customs officer cautioned his colleagues, suggesting that "political guidance" was needed on how to proceed with the case. Asked by Presiley Baxendale why Blackshaw had referred to "political guidance", Annabelle Bolt replied, "I've no idea." She assumed it was a reference to the role of the intelligence agencies.

While the DTI eventually backed away, MI6 was quick to dump Henderson. Internal MI6 documents show that Balsom dropped contact as soon as Henderson was arrested in October 1991. "Obviously," Balsom noted: "I will have no further contact with [Henderson] and if he telephones me, I will play it very cool." At the trial, personal conscience or institutional self-interest led Balsom to describe Henderson as a "very brave man". This unscripted intervention electrified the proceedings.

Among ministers, Douglas Hogg, FO Minister of State, grasped the point – after the trial's collapse. His private secretary warned Hurd's private office: "Mr Hogg thinks that for us [the FO and the intelligence agencies] the real question is whether we acquiesced wrongly in a prosecution when we or they by official or ministerial action had acquiesced in what Henderson or others were doing." Hogg, his office noted, had reached no conclusion but "remains concerned that the intelligence agencies did not alert the FO ministers to their connection with Henderson when they knew that a prosecution was going ahead".

Michael Heseltine – well advised by the civil servants in his private office and untainted by any involvement in the arms-to-Iraq affair – was astute enough to identify the dangers that lay ahead. He was warned that the press would have "a field day" if they discovered ministers had tried to suppress documents at the trial. His officials told him that Henderson had been providing information to MI6. They told him about the informant letter from a Matrix Churchill employee, and the fact that no action had been taken following the letter. As Heseltine was later to tell the inquiry, "I had come across paragraph 10 [in a submission from an official], where it says: 'The involvement of the security services ... The case against the defendants is not that the goods were used for manufacturing military equipment, but that they had lied as to whether the machines were specially designed.' So my question was, if the real crime was the export of this equipment, why were they not being prosecuted for that as opposed to just the fact that they filled in a form inaccurately? We then went on to the two question marks which are here: 'The case for the prosecution is a good one, but unfortunately it may appear to the uninformed reader that the Government did not and does not care that Matrix Churchill was selling equipment for manufacturing weapons of war, and only that lies were told.' That is exactly what people would say.

"We then go on: 'It is also true that, when the security services man called upon Matrix Churchill, the defendant had told the reception that the visitor was from the Department of Trade and Industry, and so the cover had to be maintained. Parliamentary questions were tabled at the time this information became public, but were given a suitably uncommunicative blocking answer.' "

Heseltine explained to an attentive audience, "Here we have a line and a question mark, because what this was telling me was that the security services at that time were in touch with Matrix Churchill. If they were in touch with Matrix Churchill and we were prosecuting them for lying about forms and not for the manufacture – at this time, I began to be preoccupied that we knew more than the superficialities of this official submission would indicate.

"Then we go to paragraph 12. This is where it really became rather more serious: 'A further consideration is that in 1988, a Matrix Churchill employee wrote to Sir Geoffrey Howe telling him that Matrix Churchill were making machine tools to produce mortar shells.' That got three lines under it, because we knew, apparently. It then goes on: 'No action appears to have been taken on this letter by the Ministry of Defence, to whom it was sent, or by the DTI's Export Licensing [Unit] or the security services, who also received a copy.' By that time you have two or three lines, because it told me that *everybody* knew."

After abandoning the attempt to stop the prosecution at the end of 1991, Whitehall resorted to a second self-serving tactic – withholding documents from Customs that would reveal government implication in

ANDREW LEITHEAD, AN ASSISTANT TREASURY SOLICITOR/THE INDEPENDENT/GERAINT LEWIS

exports to Iraq in breach of the publicly-stated guidelines, or as Lord Justice Scott put it, "In the Nelsonian sense, [they] turned a blind eye."

Whitehall documents crucial to the Matrix Churchill case were withheld from prosecution lawyers, in some cases until shortly before the trial opened at the Old Bailey. They included intelligence reports, MoD and DTI papers which showed the Government knew that the company's machine tools were being used by Iraq to make weapons. Peter Wiltshire described how "a major debate was going on and all records of that debate were classified". Sandy Russell, deputy chairman of Customs and Excise, described the DTI's handling of the Matrix Churchill case as "incompetent". On at least three occasions, Customs officers asked senior DTI officials if they were reluctant to bring charges, but "answer came there none". He said there was not the slightest doubt that Customs did its best to ensure there were "no skeletons rattling in the cupboard".

The inquiry heard that MI6 tried to prevent references to documents being made on ministers' Public Interest Immunity certificates, since it would alert the defence to their existence. (Alan Moses argued later that the disclosure of the documents were not needed "because the witnesses [were] going to make clear their state of mind".)

Ten times Scott asked Douglas Tweddle, then head of Customs' investigation department, why his officers did not pick up the GCHQ report, before Tweddle – who admitted he had had no personal experience in conducting an investigation – finally conceded that his investigators should have paid more attention to the intelligence agencies. Two Customs officials had attended an earlier meeting of the secret Working Group on Iraqi Procurement, where it was disclosed that Matrix Churchill had won a contract to supply machine tools to Iraq. This information was never passed to the Customs officials who later investigated the Matrix Churchill case, apparently because all intelligence reports were destroyed after six months.

Tweddle admitted Customs officers should have made inquiries with other departments, including the Foreign Office and the Ministry of Defence. He explained that the Matrix Churchill case was sensitive because of the involvement of ministers – a reference to Alan Clark and Lord Trefgarne.

Scott also chided customs officers about the way they arrested Peter Mitchell, former managing director of Walter Somers, the Midlands steel firm, in connection with the supergun affair in 1990. The judge suggested that the search warrant did not comply with the requirements of the 1984 Police and Criminal Evidence Act to spell out the reasons for an arrest. Tweddle told the judge he would look into the matter. "The sooner you do, the better," responded Scott.

While Whitehall departments were holding back papers from the prosecution, and Customs were taking insufficient steps to get relevant information from the departments, government lawyers tried to withhold key documents from the defence in apparent contravention of the Attorney-General's guidelines. Andrew Leithead, an assistant Treasury Solicitor, admitted to the inquiry that he had tried to retrieve secret papers released to the prosecution so they would not have to be disclosed to the defendants.

"How can you justify a government department setting out to make it more difficult for a defendant to get government documents which under the Attorney-General's guidelines, properly applied, he would be expected to get?" asked Scott.

Leithead explained that the documents were originally shown to Customs investigators by the DTI. DTI lawyers had decided the documents should not actually be handed over to Customs as, under the Attorney-General's guidelines, they would be liable to be disclosed to the defence.

But as a result of what Leithead called a "misunderstanding", Customs obtained a set of the papers from MI6. It was then that Leithead said he wrote to Customs seeking to recover the documents. He said DTI lawyers "seemed very keen to get the return of the documents and that seemed to me the right line to take".

Alan Moses, Customs' senior prosecution counsel and a QC, had a lot to answer for. He had told the judge in pre-trial hearings, in the absence of the press, that after reading Whitehall documents relating to the case, he concluded, "They do not assist in any way the defence." The documents were to prove crucial to the defence after Brian Smedley, the trial judge, ordered their release.

Moses gave evidence towards the end of the public hearings in March

1994. It was damning. He told the inquiry he would have abandoned the prosecution if he had known about crucial evidence contained in documents concealed by Whitehall officials before the action came to court. Whitehall withheld information which anyone "with a basic sense of justice" should have disclosed.

The documents included evidence that DTI knew Matrix Churchill machine tools were being used by Iraq to make weapons, as well as the minute of the December 1990 meeting attended by John Major and Sir Robin Butler about the Sunday Times allegations against Alan Clark. Butler had told the inquiry that, in his view, the minute was not important.

Moses said the "most disturbing" omission was the GCHQ intelligence report linking Matrix Churchill to Iraq's military programme. The report – dated October 1989, four years before the trial opened – referred specifically to contracts cited in the prosecution indictment. "It seems to me to be the clearest possible indication of (government) knowledge," Moses said. "I can't understand why on earth I didn't know about this ... I don't think I would have gone on with the prosecution if I had." Unable to control his anger at the way the trial had been handled, he said privately later that he would never want to touch a Customs case again.

The true position "about all this equipment", said Moses, "was that we knew as near as dammit it was going for military production. I can't understand why the departments weren't saying, 'We did know'."

Moses was also unaware of a memo written by Steadman of the DTI and a prosecution witness at the trial. In the memo, Steadman told his colleagues that Alan Clark may have given the impression he was encouraging companies to disguise the true purpose of the sales. "That is the end of the case if that is the view of the official sitting there," said Moses. "That directly contradicts what he said in oral evidence to the trial ... You don't sit back and wait and hope it turns out for the best at the trial. There were people there who had worked for years with Mr Clark, who knew exactly the cut of his jib."

The DTI had shown "great reluctance" to help the prosecution team, Moses told the inquiry. "They didn't like the prosecution because it was going to expose all the defects in their system and also they had allowed equipment to be escorted despite their suspicions."

He described how he was only given access to crucial Cabinet Office papers three days before the start of the trial. Accompanied by Peter Wiltshire, he was shown into the Cabinet Secretary's room where a table was covered with files. "There was a far table on the right with a box of individual documents, some of which were Cabinet Office minutes. Nobody else was there. We were just left to get on with it. I was furious. What I should have done was to walk out and say I wanted to make it abundantly plain that these were not the circumstances – on the last working day before a trial – for me to look at anything sensibly."

Moses did not limit his attacks to the DTI and the Cabinet Office. He said he was surprised that Customs investigators did not interview Ministry of Defence and Foreign Office officials involved in shaping policy towards Iraq. It was "absurd", he said, that he did not see MoD documents until shortly before the trial opened in October 1992.

Annabelle Bolt had earlier told the inquiry that the failure to check key MoD documents until shortly before the trial opened was "an oversight". She also said in her evidence she was unaware of a DTI document sent to Coolican by Steadman, admitting that officials "knowingly went along with the deception" over the Matrix Churchill exports.

Moses went on to say he was unaware of what he called Customs' "hidden agenda" – the decision to tailor charges to try to avoid politically-embarrassing evidence emerging in court. Customs framed a charge that Henderson had deceived the Government by wrongly claiming that Matrix Churchill machine tools could be used for both civil and military purposes, whereas, in fact, they were "specially designed" only to make weapons. Customs came up with this "brainwave" – as Scott cynically described it – so it could argue that the documents showed that the Government only *suspected* the machines were being used by Iraq to make weapons, and the documents were, therefore, irrelevant. Customs also hoped the tactics would avoid having to ask ministers and Whitehall officials awkward questions about divisions within Government on the whole question of exports to Iraq.

The description, "specially designed" had never before been used by Customs or the DTI to describe machine tools. Export Control Orders referred only to machine tools as "dual-use", i.e. they could be for civil or military purposes. Machine tools were not included on Customs' own official "munitions list". By this new device, Customs introduced an element of certainty which, it hoped, would win the day.

"Put simply," Cedric Andrew, Customs' senior investigator on the case told the inquiry, "evidence of 'special design' would effectively have removed any reasonable doubt which those sympathetic to more exports could use to support their arguments for granting licences." He acknowledged it would make it more difficult for the defence. It would not have been enough, Andrew said, for the defendants to show that the Government knew *some* of the machines were used to make weapons.

As Bolt was to argue, Whitehall documents which reflected only government suspicion that the exports might be used for military purposes were not good enough. To be relevant to the case, the documents would have to *show* that Henderson had specifically told the DTI of the absolute certainty the equipment would be used to make arms, and had no other use.

DTI officials had privately warned Customs that unless it argued the "specially-designed" case, the entire basis of the prosecution case would be "shot out of the water". Customs responded by trying unsuccessfully to lean on the DTI to change its official licensing procedures just weeks before the trial opened at the Old Bailey.

Scott was not amused. "We have seen no document showing that 'special design' was a factor in anybody's mind," interjected the judge. He told Andrew Biker, another Customs solicitor involved in the case, "You were embarking on a prosecution which was speculative. It depends on a legal proposition that has not been tested in the courts."

At the end of two days of questioning, Scott told Moses that he was still troubled by the QC's claim at the trial that the documents Whitehall was trying to suppress would be no help to the defence. At the very least, Scott suggested, they were important "building-blocks" for use by defence lawyers in cross-examination. Looking back, Scott asked if that had been the right submission to make. Moses replied, "It obviously was not right because the judge ruled against me."

There are no heroes in this story.

TONY STEADMAN, FORMER HEAD OF THE DTI'S EXPORT LICENSING UNIT/PHOTO NEWS SERVICE

12

... And Worse

"I quite simply misled myself on what I thought the situation was." Eric Beston of the DTI.

When a trial became inevitable, the Government and prosecution adopted more outrageous tactics. They interfered in witness statements; and having lost their fight to stop the trial, DTI witnesses succumbed to pressure from government lawyers and Customs officers to give misleading evidence.

Tony Steadman, head of the DTI's Export Licensing Unit, was told he should delete references to intelligence information which showed the Government knew Matrix Churchill machine tools were being used by Iraq to make weapons. Andrew Leithead, an assistant Treasury Solicitor, and Peter Wiltshire, a senior Customs investigator, advised Steadman that intelligence reports were not relevant evidence. This was even though the reports were precisely the reason Steadman knew the equipment was being used to make weapons. Government knowledge that the exports were destined for Iraqi weapons was a key defence argument at the trial.

Wiltshire admitted that the changes he made to Steadman's pre-trial statement left a false impression. He finally relented after Lord Justice Scott had asked him three times whether the changes meant the statement was "truthful". The changes suggested the Government's suspicions that the exports were destined for weapons were overridden by "reassurances" from Matrix Churchill that the machine tools were for civil use.

Steadman acknowledged that was inaccurate. Indeed, Whitehall documents already seen by Customs showed that Steadman had previously conceded that the company "assumed we knowingly went along with the deception" – a reference to the "nod and wink" from Alan Clark. The prosecution was worried as much about Steadman as a witness as it was about Clark. An internal Customs document sent to Douglas Tweddle, Customs' chief investigation officer, warned that Steadman was "likely to be a weak witness on this aspect of the case".

Baxendale raised with Leithead, the assistant Treasury Solicitor on the case, the original wording of Steadman's witness statement. Steadman had said: "I recall there was concern by ourselves and departments involved in advising on licence applications as to whether these machine tools might actually be used by the Iraqis for military production." Then he added: "There was no evidence as far as I am aware to support these suspicions."

Leithead crossed that out. Asked by Baxendale why he had done so, Leithead replied, "It did not seem a sensible thing for a witness to say. Of course, there must have been some evidence if there were some suspicions. You know, it is precisely the sort of thing a witness gets caught out on when being cross-examined in a witness box."

In his statement, Steadman had gone on to say: "The background briefing that I gave to the minister [Alan Clark before the MTTA meeting] was on the basis that, despite our concerns these machine tools could have dual-use civil/military." Leithead had also crossed this out.

Steadman continued: "I was aware of suspicions, but in the face of assurances from Matrix Churchill, we relied on statements in the licence applications." That, too, was deleted by Leithead.

"What," asked an astonished Scott, "are the officials doing, including the lawyers of whom you were one, in drafting what Mr Steadman is going to say in his witness statement? What business have officials got to be drafting something like that?"

Leithead replied, "Well, it is merely suggesting to Mr Steadman what the correct position would be."

Scott: "His evidence in a criminal case, or perhaps a civil case too for that matter, is not evidence on behalf of anybody. It is evidence as to the truth as known by the witness, is it not?"

Leithead: "Yes."

Baxendale then asked the assistant Treasury Solicitor whether he remembered that there were two strands to the defence case – that the DTI turned a blind eye to the military uses of the machine tools and, secondly, that since Henderson had been involved with MI6, the Government were in any event fully aware of what was going on. Leithead replied that he had been apprised of the defence's arguments.

Leithead, at one point almost crumpled, explaining he had great difficulty in answering the questions. But Baxendale persisted, reminding him that he, not Moses, was the one who agreed the statement. "You settled it. You approved it. Who wrote those words? Who thought up: 'It is improbable that such documents can have any significant relevance', or was it just put on the Xerox copy?"

"Certainly not," said Leithead. Pressed by Scott, Leithead finally conceded that Steadman's briefing for Clark was, indeed, relevant, "but that is with the benefit of hindsight".

Baxendale had earlier taken an increasingly nervous Steadman through the scandal. She pointed out that a sentence suggesting he had "no hard evidence" that machine tools were being used to make Iraqi weapons had been crossed out from his witness statement. Asked if he was concerned about the deletion, Steadman replied, "I assumed there was good reason why that had to be deleted."

Baxendale: "At the time, did you read it and think, 'This is not representing the truth'?"

Steadman: "It is not that it was untrue, but that it did not go as far as obviously the previous witness statement had."

Scott: "It is more than that, is it not? You knew those licences were going to make munitions?"

Steadman: "Yes."

Scott: "To say, 'We accepted their assurances', is more than not accurate. It just is not true."

Steadman: "Yes."

Scott: "Why [then] did you let it stand like this?"

Steadman: "I had legal advice, and I assumed that the legal advice was correct."

Scott: "It is you who [has] to sign things to swear that it is true."

Baxendale noted that Steadman's references to briefing ministers had also been deleted from his witness statement, and then asked, "You knew, did you not, that the defendants were likely to run a defence that the Government knew [the machine tools were going to Iraqi arms factories]?"

"Yes," replied Steadman, who agreed that the companies could have drawn the wrong conclusions from the MTTA meeting with Clark.

Asked whether he was worried that "things were being taken in and out of [his witness statement] at will"?

Steadman replied, "I assumed that people were acting in good faith."

The saga of Steadman's witness statement ended when Alan Moses advised that Steadman's reference to his "suspicions" about the use to which the machine tools would be put should be re-inserted into the statement. Moses gave his advice on the grounds that the trial judge was more likely to order disclosure of the documents to the defence if prosecution witnesses went so far as to claim they had no suspicions. The documents would show this was clearly not plausible.

But the witness statement remained inaccurate – as Steadman admitted – for it maintained he had no "hard evidence" linking Matrix Churchill with Iraqi arms factories. He told the inquiry he had forgotten about the intelligence reports which had produced the evidence.

The extraordinary stream of admissions continued. Eric Beston, Steadman's boss, admitted he had misled the jury in the Matrix Churchill trial on issues crucial to the defence. He admitted he was wrong to have told the court that the DTI did not know Matrix Churchill machine tools would be used to make weapons. He disclosed that senior DTI civil servants had, in fact, warned him before the trial about the prospect of "extremely embarrassing" information being disclosed in court, and that his cross-examination could prove "tricky" if the case went ahead. Beston also wrongly claimed that the company had assured Whitehall that the machines would be used for civil purposes. He had failed to tell the court about the 1987 MI6 report describing how machine tools were being used in Iraqi arms factories and he wrongly claimed that no new intelligence emerged during 1989 confirming the original report.

Beston had read the MI6 report in early 1988, and again in 1991 when he was asked by Customs, the prosecuting authority, to sign a pre-trial witness statement. He said that in court he had "simply overlooked" a meeting of a secret Whitehall committee which heard in June 1989 that Matrix Churchill machines were known to be used in an Iraqi missile programme.

Beston explained to the inquiry, "I think there was an element of mutual reinforcement of belief or misunderstanding, started because we had a situation in which Customs said that no prosecution would go ahead if there is any clear evidence about end-user and so on ... The situation became very confused ... I quite simply misled myself on what I thought the situation was."

A second witness statement by Beston was changed to omit any reference to the Government's secret change in the export guidelines in 1988. Scott raised this with Gerald Hosker, then DTI legal adviser, and since appointed chief Treasury Solicitor responsible for giving legal advice to all Whitehall departments. He asked why Beston's statement was changed.

"I don't know," Hosker replied. He then admitted he had "some hesitation" about the prosecution after seeing evidence which suggested that Alan Clark might have given an ambiguous message to machine tool companies about what they could export to Iraq. (Asked later why a Whitehall memo sent to him about pre-trial tactics was stamped, "Secret", Hosker replied, "Sometimes classification of a document is a mystery to the recipient.")

The judge retorted, "So you have all these stamps at your elbow and select the one which seems most appropriate?"

Hosker replied that officials had since been urged to adopt a "more intelligent use of classification".

The Government continues to maintain that the trial collapsed, not because of mounting evidence in Whitehall document, revealing it had breached its own export guidelines, but because of the "inconsistencies" in Alan Clark's evidence at his pre-trial witness statements, compared to what he then said from the Old Bailey witness box.

The controversy centred on Clark's meeting with the MTTA on January 20, 1988. The meeting was called because the companies were concerned about the delay in approving export licences. Clark knew of the intelligence connection – MI6's argument that it wanted the exports to go ahead to maintain its flow of information about Iraq. And some

Matrix Churchill employees knew that the Government knew the machine tools would be used by Iraq to make weapons.

The official note of the MTTA meeting on January 20, 1988 read: "Choosing his words carefully, and noting that the Iraqis would be using the current orders for general engineering purposes, Mr Clark stressed it was important for the UK companies to agree to a specification with the customer, in advance, which highlighted the peaceful – i.e. non-military – use to which the machine tools would be put."

Baxendale asked Clark whether the use of the phrase, "general engineering" implied the Government did not mind if the machine tools were to end up making weapons. Clark replied, "I had to indulge in a fiction, and invite them to participate in a fiction."

Clark said in his pre-trial statement drafted by Customs that the advice he gave to the companies "was based on the assumption that the exports were intended for civil applications". Two years later, he told the inquiry that it depended "on how strongly you are bound by the term 'assumption'." When Scott said Clark's prosecution statement suggested the companies had deceived ministers and officials, Clark conceded it may have included "an element of sleight of hand".

Asked by Baxendale if his witness statement for the trial set out what actually happened at the MTTA meeting, Clark replied, "It set out what happened at the meeting. It omits my knowledge."

At the trial, Clark admitted it was unlikely that the machines would be put to peaceful uses. He also conceded at the trial that while he did not explicitly advise the companies to say "nothing military" in their export licence applications, they got the message "by implication".

At the inquiry, Clark argued that Customs investigators did not probe him about his views of the impending prosecution, even though he expressed his scepticism about it. Nor did they did tell him that the defence was going to argue – in the event, successfully – that the Government knew all the time the machines were being used by Iraq to make weapons.

"Now looking back, I should have been more attentive," said Clark. He said he thought at the time a trial was "ridiculous", and Customs simply wanted a statement to close their file on the company. He said he thought it was "highly improbable" that the trial would go ahead. He was blind to the damage that had been done, and could not understand the deterrent effect it bore. And he did not know what the three Matrix Churchill directors were being charged for when he signed his witness statement for the prosecution.

Clark might have indulged in dissembling, but, for more than a year before the trial, he had made his views about exporting to Iraq clear within Whitehall. As early as December 1990, Sir Robin Butler agreed Clark had given an "ambiguous" message to the machine tool companies at his meeting with them in January of that year. Clark's admissions under cross-examination by Geoffrey Robertson QC, Henderson's counsel, were the catalyst which provoked the end of the trial.

The Government blamed Clark alone for the trial's collapse, although the case had already been undermined by strong evidence of government involvement in arms-related exports to Iraq – evidence which four ministers had told the trial judge should not be seen by the defence.

To drive home the Government's claims that Clark was uniquely responsible, its lawyers reported him to the Crown Prosecution Service. The CPS, however, took no action after a police investigation into whether Clark's alleged inconsistency during the Matrix Churchill trial had constituted a breach of the law.

IN THE MATTER OF:

COMMISSIONERS OF CUSTOMS & EXCISE

- v -

HENDERSON, ABRAHAM AND ALLEN

CERTIFICATE OF
MR TRISTAN GAREL-JONES MP

1.   I am the Minister of State at the Foreign and
     Commonwealth Office ("FCO"). I make this
     Certificate on behalf of the Crown.

2.   I am advised that Counsel instructed by H.M. Customs
     and Excise who are prosecuting this case has
     examined FCO papers and advised that under the
     Attorney General's Guidelines certain of such papers
     are disclosable to the defence. The purpose of this
     Certificate is to explain to the Court why for
     reasons of public interest, such documents should
     not be so disclosed.

8.   The disclosure of any sources or alleged sources of
     intelligence information, and any aspects of the
     means by which it was gathered (including dates and
     times and associated transactions) would cause
     unquantifiable damage to the functions of the
     security and intelligence services in relation to
     their role both in the United Kingdom and abroad.

     for such document. I understand that Ministers from
     the MOD and DTI will be making certificates in
     respect of documents originating from their
     respective departments where public interest
     immunity ought to be claimed.

156

13

In the Public Interest

"I think the word 'unquantifiable' can mean unquantifiably large or unquantifiably small." Tristan Garel-Jones.

As the extent to which ministers had tried to conceal their role in misleading Parliament, and the way in which civil servants and lawyers had interfered in the Matrix Churchill prosecution, became disturbingly clear, attention began to focus on Public Interest Immunity certificates.

Hitherto a little-known weapon in Whitehall's armoury of secrecy, PII certificates are signed by ministers – occasionally by senior civil servants or police officers – to prevent information about the inner workings of government from being disclosed in court. Although a final decision whether the information or documents should be released to the defence is up to the trial judge, in practice it is extremely rare for a judge to overrule PII claims put forward by ministers.

Originally called "Crown Privilege", in 1973 the concept was given the more user-friendly description of "Public Interest Immunity" – rather like changing the name of Windscale to Sellafield.

Sir Nicholas Lyell insisted, after the collapse of the Matrix Churchill trial, that ministers had a duty to sign PII certificates covering certain categories, or classes of information. That duty, he insisted, cannot be waived. It was a claim that was to be challenged by lawyers, by Scott himself, and by revelations that former and serving ministers – more conscientious than those ministers who signed certificates in the Matrix Churchill case – had refused to sign PIICs in the past.

Four ministers had signed certificates in the case: Kenneth Clarke, the Chancellor who was then Home Secretary; Malcolm Rifkind, the

Defence Secretary; Tristan Garel-Jones, then Minister of State at the Foreign Office (standing in for Douglas Hurd, the Foreign Secretary, who was abroad at the time); and Michael Heseltine, the Trade and Industry Secretary. Heseltine, who initially refused to sign, was eventually persuaded by Lyell to do what his government colleagues had done without asking awkward questions.

Other ministers had signed PII certificates earlier on in the proceedings. Kenneth Baker, the former home secretary, was one. He acknowledged at the inquiry that he had signed a PII certificate at the committal stage without knowing the circumstances of the case. Although his certificate was designed to suppress information relating to the intelligence agencies, he was unaware that Henderson, the chief defendant, had been an MI6 informer. Asked by Scott if he should not have been "properly briefed about what the case was about so you could direct your mind about what would matter?"

Baker replied he was merely following precedent.

"It is the absence of any questioning that I am finding a little difficult to understand," the judge commented. "There was a pretty shrewd notion in government circles what the defence would be."

Baker replied, "It was certainly not known to me." Baker said he had been assured by Sir Clive Whitmore, his permanent secretary at the Home Office, that there were no intelligence reports relating to the case. His certificate was drawn up in broad and almost identical terms of other PII certificates handed to ministers by government lawyers and civil servants – so broad in its scope, Scott suggested, that it would have prevented the defence from asking questions "the answers to which might be wholly innocuous". Baker also signed a PIIC during the trial, in early 1992, of three executives of Ordtec, a military engineering firm, charged with selling arms to Iraq via Jordan. That certificate, framed according to Scott, "in much wider terms than necessary", would have prevented evidence from Stephen Wilkinson, a police Special Branch officer who was passed intelligence about Iraq's build-up by Paul Grecian, one of the Ordtec defendants.

Peter Lilley, then Trade Industry Secretary, also signed a PIIC for the committal hearings. He did so despite having serious doubts about the validity of the prosecution. In remarkably frank evidence to the inquiry, he said he believed the prosecution would "almost certainly fail" and thought it "strange" that it went ahead. He said he made no attempt to hide his views. At one point, he considered approaching Customs to "call off" the prosecution. He was prevented from doing so by government lawyers who told him such action would be "grossly improper". He told the inquiry, "It left me with a certain sense of frustration." The lawyers included Gerald Hosker and Alan Moses who told him he had not choice but to sign a PIIC which, if upheld, would have suppressed information crucial to the defence.

Lilley said he believed the prosecution would fail after he was told by his officials in the DTI that Henderson had provided MI6 with information about Iraq's military procurement programme. He was also concerned about allegations that Alan Clark had given a "nod and a wink" to Matrix Churchill to go ahead with their exports though it was known the company's machine tools were being used by Iraq to make weapons. Although the allegations were known to the rest of the Cabinet, including John Major, Lilley was the only serving minister to admit doubts about the prosecution and the only minister who was told at the time about Henderson's role.

"I just couldn't see the jury convicting in those circumstances," he told Lord Justice Scott. "It seemed to be strange at that stage that the case should be continuing." His view was not based on any detailed knowledge of the case, he said, "it was simply a knowledge of human nature". Lilley's views, as we have seen, were shared by Sonia Phippard, private secretary to Sir Robin Butler, the Cabinet Secretary.

Lilley had been presented with documents which Hosker advised him "fell clearly within an established class for which public interest immunity has to be – not merely can be – claimed". They included an official briefing for Clark before his alleged "nod and wink" meeting with machine tool companies, and a Whitehall minute referring specifically to a Matrix Churchill export licence cited by the prosecution.

Although these and other documents, when released by the trial judge, proved vital to the defence, Lilley was told to certify that it was "improbable [they] can have any significant relevance to the proceedings". On the advice of Moses, he was told by Hosker to sign a second certificate, without a list of documents attached. Moses' aim, said

Hosker, was "to reduce the risk the judge will call for copies of the documents". Lilley also signed a PIIC designed to suppress crucial evidence before the Ordtec trial. He insisted, however, he had done nothing improper. The PII system was designed to protect civil servants' advice to ministers. It was important, for that advice to be candid, that it should be kept confidential.

Rifkind – a QC – said in his certificate that he had read all the relevant MoD documents and had "formed the opinion" that their disclosure "or any requirement of witnesses to give oral evidence as to [their] contents ... or the meetings recorded in such documents, would be injurious to the public interest and that it is necessary for the proper functioning of the public service that the documents should be withheld from production".

Rifkind willingly signed a PIIC after Jonathan Aitken, then Minister for Defence Procurement, demurred, partly because he had been a director of BMARC, a defence company which had former dealings with Matrix Churchill. Like Baker before him, he was chided by Scott for trying to prevent innocuous information from being disclosed. In acerbic exchanges at the inquiry, the judge suggested that Rifkind had wasted the court's time by signing a certificate designed to suppress

MALCOLM RIFKIND, DEFENCE SECRETARY SINCE 1992/THE GUARDIAN/GRAHAM TURNER

Whitehall documents the Government clearly had no need to withhold. Scott said it was difficult to claim "any sort of sensible justification" to protect the sort of documents covered by Rifkind's certificate.

"One of the problems of lumping all documents together in a class," said Scott, referring to humdrum official correspondence as well as highly-confidential papers, "is that it deprives the certificate of any weight." The weight Rifkind asked the trial judge to give to some of the papers the minister said should be withheld would have been "trivial".

Rifkind argued that ministers had a duty automatically to sign PII certificates to protect certain classes of information – including all advice from civil servants – regardless of their contents. He conceded that PIICs were presented to ministers by officials "in a standard form", even though they were drawn up to imply they were the result of a minister's personal value judgment. The practice had been followed by successive governments over the past 40 years.

Scott retorted that trial judges were faced with an "impossible process" if ministers did not consider the issues seriously. "A judge's time is simply being wasted unnecessarily." Rifkind's own officials seemed to prove the point. When it became clear the Matrix Churchill trial judge was going to overrule the certificates, Rifkind was advised by Ian McDonald, "We can live with this sort of release." Referring to Rifkind's claim before the trial that the disclosure of documents would impair official advice to ministers, Scott asked whether the Defence Secretary had since "discerned any change in the quality of advice". Rifkind confessed that he had not. He said he saw no reason why "routine reports" drawn up by Whitehall officials should not be covered by PII claims in future.

The most over-arching PIIC in the Matrix Churchill case was signed by Tristan Garel-Jones. Curiously, for such a cosmopolitan and worldly man – a former minister for Europe, with a Spanish wife, a former Whip, by no means on the right of the Tory party – he unashamedly and forthrightly defended his action. He said in prepared written evidence distributed to the media at the inquiry: "I would say that I have never had the slightest doubt about the propriety of signing the [PIIC]." He has since made it plain that, in his view, the Scott inquiry, was wholly unnecessary. He went so far as to suggest that the trial judge's decision to disclose documents to the defence had undermined "the public's confidence in ministers and civil servants".

His certificate said in part: "I am advised that counsel instructed by HM Customs and Excise who are prosecuting this case has examined FCO papers and advised that under the Attorney-General's guidelines certain of such papers are disclosable to the defence. The purpose of this certificate is to explain to the court why for reasons of public interest, such documents should not be disclosed. The documents identified by counsel fall into three categories:

"Category A consists of two documents: a document from a confidential informant who is a member of the public and whose personal security and livelihood may be jeopardised if his or her identity is disclosed and a second document which is also in Category B (described below) which discussed the first document and identified the informant.

"Category B consists of minutes, notes and letters passing between ministers and ministers, between ministers and officials, and officials and other officials, either within the FCO or inter-departmentally with the Ministry of Defence, and Department of Trade and Industry. It also includes notes or records of meetings between such persons. All these documents relate to the formation of the policy of HM Government in particular with regard to relations with and the export of military and quasi-military equipment to foreign countries.

"Category C consists of documents as described in Category B and which either include material relating to secret intelligence emanating from the Security and Intelligence Services primarily relating to Iraq and other Middle Eastern countries, or which discuss such intelligence information.

"I have read all the documents ... and have satisfied myself that they are of the nature described.

"With regard to the documents in Category A, it is undoubtedly in the public interest that the identity of a person carrying out his duty to inform the authorities of suspected wrongdoing, and thereby jeopardising himself and his livelihood, should as far as possible be kept confidential.

"With regard to the documents in Categories B and C, I have formed the opinion that, for the reasons hereinafter set out, the production of such documents or any requirement of witnesses to give oral evidence as to the meetings, discussions and deliberations would be be injurious to the public interest and that it is necessary for the proper functioning of the public service that the documents should be withheld from production.

"All these documents fall into a class of documents which relate to the formulation of government policy and the internal dealings of government departments. Such policy was decided at a high level, for the most part by ministers of the FCO, MoD and DTI, although the documents include documents preparatory to advice given for the benefit of ministers in office during the relevant period. Decisions made by ministers are frequently preceded by detailed discussions within and between government departments and by consideration of the various possibilities open to ministers. It is out of such discussion and consideration that the advice to be tendered to ministers is often formulated (frequently, initially in the form of drafts of documents intended for the consideration and approval of ministers). This is true of the present case. It would, in my view, be against the public interest that documents or oral evidence revealing the process of providing for ministers' honest and candid advice on matters of high-level policy should be subject to disclosure or compulsion ...

"With regard to documents in Category C there are additional reasons why disclosure ... would be contrary to the public interest. The very nature of the work of the Security and Intelligence Services of the Crown requires secrecy if it is to be effective. It has for this reason been the ... policy of successive governments of the United Kingdom not to disclose information about the operations of the Security and Intelligence Services and neither to confirm nor deny matters relating to their work. Evidence about the identity of members of the Security and Intelligence Services could put their lives at risk and would substantially impair their capability to perform the tasks assigned to them ... In particular, any disclosure of these matters [or any sources or alleged sources of intelligence information] would substantially impair the work of the Security and Intelligence services in protecting the United Kingdom and its allies from threats from hostile or potentially hostile foreign powers ...

"Where the ... [information-gatherers] are human, the information is provided in the knowledge that what is imparted will be treated as having been imparted in confidence and any breach of confidentiality by the Crown in revealing the identities would cause unquantifiable damage ..."

Picking up Garel-Jones' use of the word "unquantifiable", Scott told him, "The question that troubles me is whether the nature of that damage to the public interest, which is no more than a fear that the Government might be exposed to what has been described as 'captious and ill-informed criticism' is enough to justify non-disclosure."

Garel-Jones: "I think the word 'unquantifiable' can mean unquantifiably large or unquantifiably small."

Scott: "So when the text of your certificate reads: 'The disclosure of any sources or alleged sources of intelligence information would cause unquantifiable damage to the functions of security and intelligence in relation to the United Kingdom and abroad', the trial judge should have read that as covering both unquantifiably great and also minuscule?"

Garel-Jones: "Yes."

Of all the ministers who signed PIICs, Kenneth Clarke – like Rifkind, a QC – is most exposed. On BBC1's Question Time in January 1994, he was asked by John Prescott, now Labour's Deputy Leader, if he would resign if the inquiry showed him to be "at fault" in signing Public Interest Immunity certificates before the Matrix Churchill trial. He instantly replied, "Of course I will."

It is a hostage to fortune. The inquiry showed his approach was both cavalier and inconsistent. Clarke signed a certificate on June 16, 1992, the very day, Henderson says in his book, The Unlikely Spy, that the defence wrote a letter demanding the documents. It was three days before the letter was handed over to the prosecution – one of many indications, according to Henderson, that telephones of the defence team were being tapped.

Clarke claimed in his certificate that any disclosure of information about "the organisation, procedures and capabilities" of the security and intelligence agencies "could substantially impair their operational efficiency" – a phrase identical to that used by ministers in other cases involving MI5 and MI6.

He said he had been advised that an officer of the security and intelligence services would appear at the trial to give evidence for the prosecution – Officer A, "John Balsom", Henderson's MI6 contact. Balsom's written statement had been made freely available to the defence without any PII certificate in apparent breach of Clarke's claims that this class of information should be protected by PII. In a second certificate, signed just days before the trial opened, Clarke contradicted the sweeping claims of his first certificate by sanctioning the disclosure of MI5 and MI6 documents with passages "redacted" – Whitehall's word for blacking-out.

His first certificate echoed the words in Garel-Jones' statement about the need for secrecy surrounding the work of the security and intelligence services and that disclosure was likely "to cause serious and unquantifiable damage". Clarke added for the benefit of the judge that the disclosure of information relating to the agencies "would assist those whose purpose is to injure the security of the United Kingdom, and whose actions in the past have shown that they are willing to kill innocent civilians". Disclosure could "put their [MI5 and MI6 officers'] lives at risk".

Clarke began his testimony to the inquiry in relaxed mood. Asked whether he had underlined a particular passage in a document "in a thick, black pen", he replied, "I have a habit, which I think I acquired at the Bar, of underlining when I read documents. There are occasional exceptions to that. I do not underline when I am in bed, because you get ink on the pillow. And I do not underline when I am in a car because the underlinings tend to go all over the document."

As the questioning continued, he cast doubt on government claims made to Parliament that ministers had no choice but to sign the certificates. He admitted that ministers had discretion about which documents they advise the court should be suppressed and which could be disclosed. Asked by Scott whether the duty – described by Lyell as one that could not be waived – was, after all, subject to discretion, Clarke replied, "Yes, I agree with that."

Clarke's own certificates, the judge suggested, "refuted the proposition that in recognised classes, a minister has no discretion".

The judge could not understand the need to protect whole classes of documents if ministers only needed to protect particular contents of specific documents. Having agreed that ministers enjoyed discretion, Clarke – who soon lost his initial bonhomie – then appeared to contradict himself by saying there was no discretion, only to add, "The definition of 'class' is not very fixed."

Clarke, as we have seen, agreed in his certificate that Balsom could give evidence provided his true identity was protected. Balsom had signed a written witness statement which had already been given to the defence without Clarke's knowledge, even though the statement contained precisely the kind of information Clarke insisted in his certificates could not be given to the defence, at least without the approval of the trial judge.

Confusion which belied Lyell's certainty about PIICs – echoed later in the Commons by John Major – was further illustrated when the inquiry disclosed that a MI5 officer, code-named "Michael Ford", had given evidence without Clarke's knowledge and without any Public Interest Immunity certificate covering what he could reveal. Clarke said he was not aware that the MI5 officer had given evidence at the trial until he was preparing his testimony for the Scott inquiry well over a year later.

More important was the impact of Clarke's second certificate in which he told the judge that documents he had seen would put the lives of "innocent civilians" at risk. The documents were nothing more than MI5 and MI6 records of meetings with Henderson and Gutteridge, containing references to the very export contracts over which Henderson was accused of deceiving the Government. The only life at risk was Henderson's.

Clarke's certificate, with its references to grave damage to national security and innocent lives were designed to frighten the trial judge. The inference was that Judge Brian Smedley would have blood on his hands if the documents were given to the defence. Indeed, Smedley – who was also a senior judge at the British army bases in Cyprus – rejected defence demands for disclosure. He succumbed only after Alan Moses, having heard appeals by Geoffrey Robertson QC, Henderson's counsel, left the court to make a telephone call to Whitehall. Fifteen minutes later, Moses returned to the court and said, "The prosecution can well see how the balance tips clearly in favour of the defence, seeing the records ... " It was an astonishing *volte-face* – placing Clarke's dire warnings of putting innocent lives at risk in true perspective.

The documents finally disclosed included standard MI5 and MI6 "contact notes" which Clarke said could not be seen because their format was secret (they could have been re-typed; it was not the information in them, but their form that was relevant to the defence). Their disclosure may have led to government embarrassment, but they did no damage to national security.

Yet at the inquiry, Clarke – whose Public Interest Immunity certificates could easily have prevented the defence from getting vital information for its case – told the inquiry, "Neither of my certificates had the slightest bearing on the conduct of the trial."

"Nothing that was relevant to Mr Henderson's case was cut out by my certificate," said Clarke. "No one has ever claimed that Mr Henderson was prejudiced by this certificate."

To which Henderson made the obvious retort that "Had the judge upheld [Clarke's] certificate, we would not have had the documents and that would have prejudiced the outcome of the trial."

Clarke's cavalier use of PII certificates was revealed shortly after he gave evidence, when the High Court revealed that, while Home Secretary, he prevented the disclosure of information that would have freed a man who spent more than a year in jail awaiting trial. The court ruled that there had been "procedural impropriety" in the way Paul Bennett, a New Zealand pilot, had been brought to Britain from South Africa. Clarke's PII certificate, issued in July 1992, covered a Crown Prosecution Service lawyer's memorandum which showed that Bennett was the victim of collusion between South African and British police forces. It revealed that the South African police noted that Bennett would "conveniently stop at Heathrow" where Special Branch "have agreed to nick him". Bennett, who was officially being taken to New Zealand, claimed he was illegally kidnapped following accusations he had obtained a loan by deception.

MICHAEL HESELTINE, PRESIDENT OF THE BOARD OF TRADE/DON McPHEE

14

Hezza v the Attorney

"Up with this, I will not put." Michael Heseltine.

"Claiming public interest immunity is an obligation not a privilege." John Major.

"I defend absolutely the system of public interest immunity, but it is a special privilege." Michael Heseltine

Michael Heseltine was not so compliant. His officials had alerted him to the dangers that lay ahead. Before he was asked to sign a PII certificate, he read a briefing note drawn up by his officials which explained how Matrix Churchill employees had warned Whitehall that the company's exports were being used by Iraq to make arms but the Government had taken no action. Michael Coolican told him about the anonymous letter from a Matrix Churchill employee. "Assuming the writer retains his public-spirited interest, it may well be that, as the details of the case get into the public domain, he may well feel moved to write again, but possibly to the press." Coolican explained that parliamentary questions about the exports had been met with "suitably blocking and incommunicative answers".

A passage from his briefing notes, Heseltine told the inquiry, "attracted five lines [written by Heseltine in the margin], and the reason it attracted five lines is because it became apparent to me that I would have to go and try to indulge in the process of – what is the word – 'incommunicative' answers, and I was not prepared to do that. So that was where we were when I first read this submission. I said, 'Up with this, I will not put.'"

Heseltine was presented with a PIIC almost identical to that signed without fuss by the other ministers. Phillip Bovey, a DTI legal adviser, recorded Heseltine's reactions: "The papers Mr Heseltine had seen suggested that Whitehall departments had been well aware of the intended military use, yet the defendants seemed to be being prosecuted for concealing it ... It would look as though Mr Heseltine had been engaged in a cover-up." Heseltine wanted to give the judge "the clearest possible signal" that the documents were relevant to the case. "It could not be right," said Heseltine, "to suggest that the documents were not relevant to the defence."

Heseltine was handed the draft PII certificate on September 3, 1992. He was told by government lawyers to have it ready signed by the next morning. Heseltine did not oblige, and instead he registered his concern with the Attorney- General's office. There, Juliet Wheldon, one of Lyell's legal advisers, telephoned the Attorney-General, who asked her to draft him a note about the problem and put it in his ministerial red box which he would read over the weekend.

"The problem," wrote Wheldon, "is that [Heseltine] thinks it is in the public interest for the documents in this case to be disclosed, despite the fact that they fall within a class. I gather he is unhappy about the Customs prosecution and does not want to be party to the suppression of documents which are helpful to the defendants."

After talking to Heseltine on the telephone, Lyell wrote him a letter on September 7. He said he "entirely understood" why Heseltine felt unable to sign the PIIC, and recognised that Heseltine believed he could not "conscientiously assert" that it would be contrary to the public interest to disclose the documents. But Lyell referred to a ruling by Lord Justice Bingham, now Master of the Rolls, in a 1992 police complaint case, Makanjuola v Commissioner of Police. Bingham said that public interest immunity "cannot in any ordinary sense be waived since, although one can waive rights, one cannot waive duties". Lyell sent Heseltine a redrafted certificate. "The drafting ... is unusual," Lyell assured Heseltine, "and the judge and defendants will be alert to its limited scope which can, if necessary, be emphasised by counsel for the Crown orally."

After referring to Garel-Jones' certificate, Heseltine's new PIIC stated: "I have been advised as to past decisions and, accordingly, it is my duty to assert the public interest grounds why such documents ought to be immune from production ... In making this certificate I emphasise that my concern is only with the question whether the documents to which I have referred fall within classes of documents which are *prime facie* immune from production. Whether, in fact, all or part of any individual document or documents should be disclosed is a matter for the court. I am aware that the court will consider this claim to immunity at the same time as considering whether in this case and in relation to each document there is a countervailing public interest that the requirements of doing justice in this case require their disclosure. I recognise ... that the ultimate judge of where the balance of public interest lies is not the person asserting the immunity but the court."

The following day, September 8, 1992, Lyell's letter to Heseltine was faxed to Andrew Leithead at the Treasury Solicitor's Department.

On September 10, Lyell called a meeting to "take stock" of the case. As well as Heseltine's doubts about the PIIC, Juliet Wheldon had warned the Attorney-General about uncertainty surrounding Alan Clark's position, and the attitude of the DTI. With remarkable premonition, she said, "The prosecution may yet come to a sticky end." Lyell later told the inquiry he agreed that the prosecution "always looked from the outside to be very difficult".

Present at this meeting were Sir Derek Spencer, the Solicitor-General, Juliet Wheldon, Alan Moses and Michael Saunders, a Customs solicitor. They discussed a recent interview with Clark in the Sunday Telegraph in which the former trade and defence minister was quoted as saying he had "tipped off our machine tool manufacturers as to how they should frame their export applications to get round the guidelines for trade with Iraq". (Clark at the trial denied he had "tipped off" the companies, but agreed, as we have seen, that "by implication" the message was they should keep quiet about the potential military uses.)

Lyell described the meeting, which lasted over 90 minutes, as "solid and serious". Yet, astonishingly, Heseltine's concerns were never raised. Lyell explained to the inquiry that he personally was not worried because the trial judge would see the different wording of Heseltine's PIIC. He regarded it as "inconceivable" that "any injustice" would be done by "non-disclosure of the documents".

Heseltine wrote back to Lyell on September 11. "I am glad a way has been found of reconciling the fact that I am under a legal duty, which I cannot waive, to claim immunity from disclosure of certain documents on the grounds of public interest with the fact that, in my view, at least some of them ought to be disclosed in the public interest."

Heseltine was appeased because of Lyell's personal assurance that his concerns would be made clear to the trial judge by the senior prosecution counsel, Alan Moses. But they never were. Heseltine's views were not passed on to the judge because Moses was never told about them. Moses was to claim that he never understood that Heseltine's views were any different from those of the other ministers who signed Public Interest Immunity certificates. "In the event," said Moses, "I argued, and the judge accepted that all ministers were adopting the same stance, and were not intending to make any comments as to how the balancing exercise should be carried out. I was never instructed to the contrary.' "

Further, at the trial Moses contradicted Heseltine's views – known to Lyell – by saying that Whitehall documents covered by the certificate were not relevant to the defence. In evidence highly damaging to Lyell, Heseltine told the inquiry that he had done all he "properly could to indicate to the judge what I thought the position to be ... I find it difficult to explain the way in which events worked out."

Heseltine's anger was fuelled by being given different advice by government lawyers on a separate case that arose shortly after the collapse of the Matrix Churchill trial in November 1992. He was told by Lyell that ministers did not have to claim PII in every case where disclosure of government documents was sought.

Heseltine said he found Lyell's advice "incredible" and felt "indignant" in the light of what had happened in the Matrix Churchill case. "In the Matrix Churchill case, he was told he had a duty to sign a PII certificate," his private secretary told Wheldon. "Now, however, he was told that the prosecuting counsel had a discretion denied to ministers ... Mr Heseltine said that in the Matrix Churchill case, no rational person who had looked at the files could have said that the documents should not have been disclosed. It would have been terrible if a defendant had gone to jail as a result of non-disclosure."

Lyell, the only person with constitutional authority to stop the prosecution, promised on the eve of his evidence to the inquiry that he intended to "stand out like a lighthouse". But, although he illuminated some of the darker recesses of the government machine, he failed to clear doubts about his role.

He admitted he did not know that crucial Whitehall documents were withheld from Moses – "You educated me," he told Lord Justice Scott. He confessed he "wasn't following the trial day by day". He told a visibly-irritated judge that even then he had not actually read the documents which, two years before the trial, he advised ministers should be covered by Public Interest Immunity certificates. For Scott it was "a little surprising" that Lyell himself had not looked at the documents to see whether they should be covered by PII certificates.

Lyell replied that the Attorney-General's role was limited to making sure that ministers' PII certificates were drafted in a consistent way. "How can you do that," asked Lord Justice Scott, "without knowing what documents ministers are trying to protect?"

Lyell dug a deeper hole for himself as he explained how, after initially being closely involved with the trial, he then left the conduct of the case to others. He acknowledged a series of errors, in particular the failure to ensure that relevant evidence – notably Heseltine's reluctance to sign a PII certificate – was transmitted to Moses.

Lyell acknowledged that his office did not send a separate copy of Heseltine's redrafted certificate to Moses. Nor did his office send Moses a copy of his correspondence with Heseltine. Instead, he passed the buck to others. He said he expected the Treasury Solicitor's Department, the DTI, and Heseltine's office, to have sorted it out. The "spadework" was being done by Wheldon and Moses – he could not be expected to be aware of the day-to-day "nitty-gritty" of the work of the Government's legal service. And, anyway, the PII certificates posed only a "tiny risk" of a miscarriage of justice.

Baxendale suggested that Lyell he could have "rung up" to ensure Heseltine's concerns were passed on. "Lots of things could have happened."

"Miss Baxendale," he replied, "masses of things *could* have happened."

Scott asked the Attorney-General whether he did not think he should have taken "some step to see a copy of the briefing sent to Mr Moses, or some other step to see the concerns of Mr Heseltine were adequately reflected?"

Lyell: "No."

Scott: "Did you give any instructions to the Treasury Solicitor's Department as to how they were to approach the briefing to counsel?"

Lyell: "No."

Scott: "Do you think you should have done more?"

Lyell: "No."

Scott: "Is there any more to be said than 'No'?"

Lyell replied that the Treasury Solicitor had a large department. For him to have gone further would have been "unusual". The judge commented that "The whole case was unusual; looking back, don't you think it was called for?"

"No," replied the Attorney, "seriously sir, I don't."

In the midst of the running controversy over the PII certificates, Lyell told the Commons on April 25, 1994 that the special nature of Heseltine's certificate "leapt from the page" – an assertion belied by Moses and the trial judge. Lyell claimed that "Nobody ... who had any understanding of the subject of public interest immunity could fail to realise that it was a special certificate."

Moses, praised by Lyell himself as a senior, experienced lawyer did not appreciate it. He told Lyell's legal advisers during the post-mortem after the trial's collapse, "I did not understand, and neither did the judge, that the other ministers were taking a different stance to that taken explicitly by Mr Heseltine."

Scott suggested that despite Heseltine's concerns, his certificate still "left ambiguous that which should have been unambiguous" – namely, that he had no objections to disclosure of the documents. Lyell agreed, acknowledging that Heseltine's objections could have been pointed out more clearly in the redrafted certificate. "For example," Scott suggested, "Heseltine could have said, 'I wish to raise no argument against disclosure.'"

Lyell conceded that would have been a clearer way to alert the judge. Lyell also told the inquiry that, until the trial, he was not aware of

Henderson's connection with MI6. "I don't think I really knew knew anything about Mr Henderson at all," he said. This was despite being warned by Sir Brian Unwin, chairman of Customs, before the trial, of the involvement of the intelligence agencies. Asked about Juliet Wheldon, his close adviser, being told that Henderson was in contact with MI6, Lyell told the inquiry that she "certainly did not hear it in her mind".

That aspect of the case, explained Lyell, "did not register". Baxendale asked him whether that was "the kind of thing you, as Attorney-General, when you are looking at these major cases would bear in mind when looking at the public interest in proceeding with a prosecution?"

"Yes," replied Lyell, who also agreed it would be "very relevant" to the key question of whether or not a jury would prosecute.

Lyell acknowledged mistakes were made. "A number of things didn't happen as they should," he admitted. Moses should have had "proper instructions". And despite his protestations that he did not get involved in the "nitty-gritty", Lyell, however, did get involved in detailed discussions about Heseltine's PII certificate.

He also told the inquiry, "I am a minister of the Crown. The Treasury Solicitor's Department is one of the four departments that fall under my responsibility and, therefore, I have ministerial responsibility. I accept that."

SIR NICHOLAS LYELL, ATTORNEY-GENERAL WITH CHRISTOPHER MUTTUKUMARU, THE INQUIRY'S SECRETARY/GRAHAM TURNER

15

Administrative Convenience

"It is damaging to the public interest to have any decision-making process exposed." Andrew Leithead, assistant Treasury Solicitor.

"If people say the law is an ass, I'm inclined to think it probably is." Douglas Hogg, Foreign Office Minister of State.

Sir Nicholas Lyell has insisted throughout that he acted "scrupulously and with complete integrity" during the Matrix Churchill affair. His thesis is a simple one. He told MPs the day after the trial collapsed, "Ministers have a duty to claim Public Interest Immunity certificates either in respect of specific documents or recognised classes of documents ... This duty cannot be waived ... Ministers, in claiming public interest immunity, were doing what they were obliged to do by law."

Although he did not say so, Lyell was quoting from a convenient passage of a recent ruling by a senior judge in a case called Makanjuola v The Chief of Police. By the end of two days of questioning at the Scott inquiry, his simple thesis was severely battered.

He began by insisting that it was not the role of the Attorney-General, the Government's senior law officer, even to see whether PII claims were justified. It was the duty of ministers merely to ensure that the documents in question were in "a class" traditionally protected by PII. That was as far as the role of ministers went. It was for prosecution counsel, rather than ministers, to decide whether or not the documents were relevant to the case.

Scott bluntly told Lyell that his view had "no legitimacy in authority". He told the Attorney-General, "This is the point where I start scratching

177

my head. The minister is the custodian of the public interest. If, in relation to his documents, he doesn't really mind whether they are going to be disclosed and he doesn't think there is going to be any damage to the public interest ... then why should he claim PII. What is the point?"

What, Scott asked, if ministers said the information was "piffling"? Were ministers still bound by duty? The Attorney-General appeared to be taking the view that whatever the courts decided, ministers "willy-nilly have to go along with it".

What "if documents which are low level are getting swept in because of an abundance of caution or excessive secrecy?" Ministers, added Scott, often took it on themselves to release documents without reference to the courts. They released information to Commons committees and in political memoirs without getting advice from counsel. Lyell acknowledged that was the case, but insisted that litigation was different.

But not even in litigation had the Government adopted a consistent approach. Baxendale raised the 1985 trial of Clive Ponting, the MoD official charged – and acquitted – under the Official Secrets Act for disclosing information about the sinking of the Argentine cruiser, the General Belgrano, during the Falklands war. Heseltine, then Defence Secretary, volunteered to the court – including the jury – highly-classified intelligence documents without mention of public interest immunity. Both Lyell and Heseltine argued before Scott that the Ponting case was special because the jury was vetted, and when the documents were discussed the trial was *in camera*. Another explanation is that Heseltine wanted to use the documents to further the prosecution case and impress upon the jury the need for secrecy.

Lyell was also challenged over the way statements by MI5 and MI6 officers were passed to the court in the Matrix Churchill trial without any ministerial PII certificates while ministers sought to deny the defence access to intelligence documents. "The prosecution doesn't seem bound by the PII rigours in the same way the defence does," remarked Lord Justice Scott.

"Not necessarily so," replied Lyell who insisted that the MI6 officer's evidence was vital for the prosecution to rebut the defence case. "If he failed to rebut it, the case would collapse." The other side of the coin was that without the documents which Whitehall did its utmost to suppress, through the use of PII, the defence case could have collapsed.

Lyell's proposition that ministers had no choice but to sign PIICs put in front of them was challenged by Lord Jenkins, the former Labour home secretary. He said he used to approach each PII claim with a healthy scepticism – "Some I signed, some I didn't." He told the London Evening Standard, "The duty of the Home Secretary, particularly because of his role in holding the balance between the authority of the state and the individual's rights, is to be sceptical of papers put to him to sign, and my experience is that he should be particularly sceptical of anything put to him to sign by the Secret Service."

Lyell's claims were further undermined by the refusal – before government lawyers approached Heseltine – of Baroness Denton, parliamentary secretary at the DTI, and Richard Needham to sign PII certificates. Needham's reluctance was based on his experience as a minister in Northern Ireland where, as one official has put it, PIICs are handed out "like confetti". We have seen that Jonathan Aitken did not sign a certificate when he was asked by his officials to do so.

Scott and Baxendale probed witnesses about the sheer breadth of the PII certificates, as well as about inconsistencies in the way they were used. They covered classes of documents and information – such as official advice to ministers – regardless of the actual contents. They embraced information merely because it was classified in Whitehall as "confidential", not because disclosure would cause real damage to the public interest.

Lyell said, at one point, that the disclosure of information would be "unhelpful" for those taking decisions, for example, on social security policy "which either because it is giving money to poor people or because it is taking money from poor people, is very sensitive". Scott turned round the Attorney-General's argument that secrecy was needed to prevent ill-informed criticism. "As to being ill-informed, the more information there is, the less likelihood there is of it being ill-informed."

Scott told Leithead, "What started as a very necessary protection given to particular *ad hoc* documents has become by rote protection of a very wide class of documents." The PII system "has been turned on its head ... If the Public Interest Immunity certificates had been confined to claiming protection for documents, disclosure of which would have caused damage ... it is at least arguable that the public perception of the Government would have been the better and not the worse."

Leithead admitted that government lawyers adopted a "generous" approach when asking ministers to sign PII certificates. He admitted they were often used "for administrative convenience", adding, "it is damaging to the public interest to have any decision-making process exposed."

Asked by Scott what he meant by "generous", Leithead replied, "Generous to the government departments."

Scott: "Who regards it as damaging to the public interest that any of this decision-making process should be exposed? Who?"

Leithead: "I think it is the general view of people who deal with this subject."

Scott: "The Government?"

Leithead: "Yes."

Baxendale: "Not necessarily the ministers concerned?"

Leithead: "No ..."

Scott: "Is this approach bred of a desire for convenient administration?"

Leithead: "I think so, yes. We go back to the point that the whole process of discussing the policy and advice is worthy of protection ... It is this whole process of confidentiality."

Scott: "Confidentiality has never been the basis of Public Interest Immunity certificates alone. What has been required is damage to the public interest."

Leithead: "What damages the public interest is the disclosure of a whole process as regards to ministers."

Scott: "Regardless of the contents?"

Leithead: "Yes."

Baxendale insisted that though ministers claimed in their certificates that disclosure of information would be damaging, in reality this was far from the case. A trial judge, she said, "has no yardstick to know that, in fact, these discussions between the officials really would not injure a flea, and it is just because it is convenient?"

"That is right," said Leithead.

Scott then asked Leithead whether he had "draft Public Interest

Immunity certificates in [his] department on the word processor?"

"No," replied Leithead, "we use the Xerox machine quite a bit."

Ministers could not use their own judgment about what was, and what was not, in the public interest. A minister either agrees, explained Leithead, or "is brought to agree with the policy".

"He is told he jolly well has to," suggested Baxendale.

"Well, he is advised, as ministers are," replied Leithead.

Asked whether a minister is entitled to have a view that disclosure would not damage the public interest, Leithead argued, "Well, I am not sure about that." A minister had no discretion, he added, echoing Lyell. "It was damaging to have any decision-making process exposed."

After a subdued Leithead left the inquiry room, it was the turn of his new boss, Gerald Hosker. "The point is this," Scott told the Treasury Solicitor, "the importance in a criminal case of relevant documents ... being made available to the defence, for the defence to make what they will of them in order to achieve justice, is so strong as to make it *unthinkable* that anybody could ever try to use PII to cover documents of which no more could be said than that they were confidential."

Scott challenged the Attorney-General's claims head-on. He told Hosker that by trying to withhold so many documents, ministers had been advised to act in a way that appeared to be inconsistent with recent legal judgments. "What we are examining at the moment," said the judge, "is whether the PII claim in the particular criminal case that we know about, the Matrix Churchill case, covering a vast range of relatively mundane communications between officials and ministers, between officials' internal memos, was the proper subject of PII claims."

"Yes," replied Hosker, quickly adding, "documents that appear to an outsider ... may very well appear to be mundane, but they could have a significance when they are read with the totality of the documents."

Hosker told the inquiry that the best argument the Government could put forward in defence of suppressing internal Whitehall documents was so as not to "fan ill-informed, captious, and political criticism" – a reference to Lord Reid's remarks in a ruling delivered in 1968.

Confidentiality, insisted Hosker, was "necessary for the proper administration of the public service", and ministers had to defer to government lawyers. Asked by the judge whether the old aphorism, "Officials advise, ministers decide" did not apply to PII claims, Hosker replied that they did not.

But he acknowledged it was difficult to provide "authority" to support his argument and conceded that the law on PII had not been applied "strictly enough". He said as a result of the Matrix Churchill case, he intended to draw up a new manual for government lawyers on how they should apply PII in future.

● ● ●

Never again will a Government use the notion of public interest immunity as freely as it has in the past. Douglas Hogg, Minister of State at the FO, who is tipped to be a future Attorney-General, said on BBC1's Question Time, a month before Lyell gave evidence in March 1994, that he hoped one of the consequences of the Scott inquiry "will be a recommendation to look again at the way certificates are issued ... The law is very odd. If people say the law is an ass, I'm inclined to think it probably is." He said the doctrine that ministers had a duty to sign PII certificates – a doctrine espoused by Lyell – was a dangerous one.

Douglas Hurd, the Foreign Secretary, told his officials that he found the role of ministers in signing the certificates "baffling". According to Carol Harlow, professor of Public Law at the London School of Economics, "No public lawyer would accept the black and white interpretation of the Attorney-General. The issue is shot through with discretion." She was one of many academics – and practising lawyers – who challenged Lyell's interpretation of the law.

"The customary formula for claiming PII is that 'It is necessary for the *proper* functioning of the public service' that documents should be withheld," Anthony Bradley, former professor of Constitutional Law at Edinburgh University, told The Independent newspaper. "What should a minister do if he or she is convinced that the public service has been functioning *improperly*? And that it is necessary for the proper functioning of the public service for the full facts to be known? Ministers must [decide] themselves; they cannot take cover behind the Attorney-General.

The origins of PII lie in the constitutional convention that the Crown

– initially the monarch, latterly "the Government of the day" – has the final say over what information should be disclosed, and what should be kept secret.

In 1947, the Crown Proceedings Act stated for the first time that the Crown could be sued. But it said the Crown need not disclose documents "when to do so would be injurious to the public interest".

Nine years later, Lord Kilmuir, then Lord Chancellor, urged that in future claims of Crown Privilege – predecessor of PII – should exclude "those categories of documents which appear to be particularly relevant to litigation and for which the highest degree of confidentiality is not required in the public interest". After referring to road accident reports, he said, "We also propose that if medical documents, or indeed other documents, are relevant to the defence in criminal proceedings, Crown privilege should not be claimed." But he then added, "The reason why the law sanctions the claiming of Crown Privilege on the class ground is the need to secure freedom and candour of communication with and within the public service, so that government decisions can be taken on the best advice and with the fullest information" – a statement which, in light of the arms-to-Iraq affair, seems wholly unfounded.

Then in 1968 came Conway v Rimmer, a case where a police constable sued his former superintendent for malicious prosecution. The House of Lords established that it was for the courts, and not the executive, to conduct the balancing act – to decide whether or not the interests of justice in disclosure outweighed any possible harm to the nation or the public service. Lord Reid dismissed Lord Kilmuir's argument about "candour", but defended the protection against disclosure of certain classes of documents, notably "Cabinet minutes and the like". He said, "To my mind, the most important reason is that such disclosure would create or fan ill-informed or captious public or political criticism. The business of government is difficult enough as it is, and no Government could contemplate with equanimity the inner workings of the government machine being exposed to the gaze of those ready to criticise without adequate knowledge of the background and perhaps with an axe to ground." It was a judgment that has been seized on with alacrity by successive governments ever since.

In the Matrix Churchill case, the Government took particular comfort from the words of Lord Justice Bingham in Makanjuloa v The Commissioner of Police, reported in 1992. The Government prayed in aid a passage in the judgment where Bingham said: "Public interest immunity cannot in any ordinary sense be waived since, although one can waive rights, one cannot waive duties" and that "where a litigant holds documents in a class *prime facie* immune, he should (save perhaps in a very exceptional case) assert that the documents are immune and decline to disclose them, since the ultimate judge of where the balance of public interest lies is not for him but the court ..."

But Bingham preceded this passage by making it clear that there was no obligation upon ministers to make such a claim. He said: "It does not mean that in any case where a party holds a document in a class *prime facie* immune he is bound to persist in an assertion of immunity even where it is held that, on any weighing of the public interest in withholding the document against the public interest in disclosure for the purpose of furthering the administration of justice, there is a clear balance in favour of the latter."

Anthony Scrivener QC, a former chairman of the Bar, is in no doubt that ministers have a discretion whether or not to claim public interest immunity. In a lecture, "Secrecy At All Costs?" to the City University in April 1993, he said: "A minister doesn't have to claim immunity and it is a nonsense to suggest otherwise. He is in command of his department. He can weigh up the issues ..."

In a 1990 case involving attempts by Lorrain Osman, a Malaysian banker, to fight extradition and PII certificates signed by ministers, Lord Justice Mann told the Court of Appeal, "Where the interests of justice arise in a criminal case touching or concerning liberty, the weight to be attached to the interests of justice is plainly very great indeed."

Scott brought Osman's words to the attention of government lawyers. The implication was that by including even trivial information within PII claims in the Matrix Churchill case – claims approved by ministers – they had ignored Osman's advice.

Arguments in favour of disclosure were given a boost in the case, reported in 1993, of Judith Ward, acquitted after serving 17 years in jail for bombing an army coach. The Court of Appeal said: "It would be wrong to allow the prosecution to withhold material documents without giving notice of that fact to the defence. If, in a wholly exceptional case, the prosecution is not prepared to have the issue of public interest immunity determined by a court, the result must inevitably be that the prosecution will have to be abandoned."

There were echoes here of a remark made before the trial by Cedric Andrew, a senior Customs official to Mark Gutteridge, Henderson's former colleague. Gutteridge was originally approached by Customs because of his knowledge of Iraq's links with British companies which he passed on to MI5. Gutteridge was worried that his links with MI5 would be disclosed in court. According to a secret MI5 memorandum, Andrew told Gutteridge that "In previous cases, HM Customs, in order to protect sources, had dropped proceedings altogether when the judge had declined to accept such a certificate."

The appeal court appeared to row back in 1993 in the M25 murder appeal (R v Davis and others) by stating that in exceptional cases – by implication, where police informers are involved – the prosecution need not even tell the defence about the existence of documents on which it was seeking PII.

But Lyell's position came under fire at the very time he gave evidence to the Scott inquiry. His assertion that ministers had a duty to claim PII and that such claims should be made automatically for whole classes of documents was challenged by the Law Lords, the highest court in Britain. "A rubber stamp approach to public interest immunity by the holder of a document is neither necessary nor appropriate," said Lord Templeman, as the Law Lords overturned a series of judgments protecting documents produced during Police Complaints Authority investigations. "It has been said," noted Templeman, recalling Lyell's claims, "that the holder of a confidential document for which public interest immunity may be claimed is under a duty to assert the claim, leaving the court to decide whether the claim is well founded. For my part, I consider that when a document is known to be relevant and material, the holder of the document should voluntarily disclose it unless he is satisfied that disclosure would cause substantial harm."

Ministers, notably Kenneth Clarke and Tristan Garel-Jones, dwelt at length on the threat to national security if the documents were revealed. In defence of their actions, Sir Nicholas Lyell and Sir Robin Butler insisted that PII certificates signed were not "gagging orders". It was up to the trial judge to decide whether or not the documents should be disclosed in the interests of justice.

But the courts have repeatedly made it clear that they are not in any position to judge whether, or to what extent, disclosure of information would damage national security. "National security," said Lord Diplock in the GCHQ union ban case in 1985, is *"par excellence* a non-justiciable question."

In 1994, the appeal court ruled that "When a Secretary of State signs a certificate claiming public interest immunity on the grounds of national security for documents before the court, the court should not exercise its right to inspect the documents. Although the courts should be vigilant to ensure that such immunity is properly claimed, the public interest in national security must prevail."

Rejecting an attempt by Andrew Balfour, a former FO official who worked closely with MI6 and claimed unfair dismissal, Lord Justice Russell said in the Court of Appeal that past judgments had held that national security is the sole responsibility of the Government who must have the last word, and it was undesirable for the courts to interfere. "I am bound to tell you," Russell remarked during the hearing, "I know nothing about national security."

Brian Smedley, the trial judge in the Matrix Churchill case, complained he was in no position to weigh the validity of the arguments put by Clarke and Garel-Jones. They were only the judges, he said. Pressed by Geoffrey Robertson, Henderson's counsel, to disclose MI5 and MI6 papers, the judge said he was being placed in an "invidious" position. "On the one hand, I have to protect national security, on the other, the interests of the defence in the interests of justice."

Revelations during the Scott inquiry of how the PII system had been abused prompted a warning from Lord Justice Simon Brown, the Government's former chief counsel in civil courts and president of the Security Service tribunal. In a speech to the Civil Service College in March 1994 – coinciding with Lyell's evidence – he criticised ministers for being too ready to sign PII certificates, and judges for being too willing to accept them. Certificates, he said in a pointed reference to the evidence of Treasury Solicitors, "should not be used merely as a convenience". He warned civil servants they would face increasing criticism if they tried to hold back whole classes of documents, regardless of their contents.

In particular, he said, it was not enough for the Government simply to fly the flag of "national security" as a reason for secrecy. "The very words, 'national security' have acquired over the years an almost mystical significance," said Simon Brown. "The mere incantation of the phrase itself instantly discourages the court from satisfactorily fulfiling its normal role of deciding where the balance of public interest lies ... Frankly, it is a nonsense to suppose that all risks to the national security are equal."

He added, "The courts should be less awestruck by the mantra of national security and readier to scrutinise the legitimacy and weight of these claims. For the courts to abdicate their role in the balancing exercise is to invite too cavalier an approach by Government to the assertion of this particular class claim." It would be quite wrong, Brown said, for Whitehall "to shelter behind the court's present reluctance to inspect documents by intentionally concealing in the language of the certificate the documents' likely impact upon the crown's pleaded case".

It was an unmistakable slap on the wrists of civil servants, government lawyers, and ministers.

CHARLES HASWELL, FO OFFICIAL FORMERLY RESPONSIBLE FOR BRITAIN'S RELATIONS WITH JORDAN/THE INDEPENDENT/EDWARD WEBB

16

An Amazing Gap

"Jordan has disappeared – well done." David Richmond, Foreign Office official.

Iraq was not the only country in the inquiry's sights, nor was Matrix Churchill the only controversial prosecution. Throughout the Iran-Iraq war, and later – even after Saddam Hussein's invasion of Kuwait – Jordan was used as a conduit for arms and other exports to Iraq.

Whitehall was alerted to Jordan's role as early as 1983 when three men were charged with trying to smuggle British sub-machine guns to Iraq via Jordan. In 1985, the Joint Intelligence Committee specifically tasked MI6, GCHQ, and the Defence Intelligence Staff with monitoring trade with Jordan.

In 1988, Jordan was placed on a list of countries suspected of diverting exports which could be used for nuclear, biological, or chemical warfare – the NBC list. According to British intelligence, Jordan is now host to more than a hundred Iraqi companies fronting for Saddam Hussein's procurement network. They include TDG, the Iraqi-controlled company which used to own Matrix Churchill.

Bin Shaker, a Jordanian field marshal, warned the MoD, in 1988, that Iraq wanted to use Jordan as "a front" to supply it with British arms. He gave his warning after a visit to Baghdad by Jordan's King Hussein. The warning was never passed on to Lt. Col. Glazebrook, the MoD officer responsible for vetting sensitive defence exports. According to Alan Collins, former head of the FO's Middle East Department, DIS warnings about Jordan also were not passed to the FO.

Astonishingly, despite mounting evidence in 25 separate intelligence reports, as well as concern expressed by ministers, of Jordan's role, the Foreign Office succeeded in taking Jordan off the NBC list. Documents passed to the inquiry showed that a member of the DIS, identified only as "Mr N", and another agent identified as "Mr J", came away from a Cabinet Office meeting in November 1991 assuming that Jordan would be on the list of suspect countries. Douglas Hogg, FO Minister of State, singled out Jordan as a country which was "irrefutably conniving in, or turning a blind eye to" trade diverted to Iraq.

But when the list was sent by Peter Lilley, then Trade and Industry Secretary, to John Major in November 1991 – and announced in Parliament the next month – Jordan was not included. David Richmond, a Foreign Office official on the Jordan desk, wrote to a colleague: "Jordan has disappeared – well done."

Simon Fuller, head of the FO's Near East and North African Department between 1990 and 1993, told Scott he believed the list should have applied only to countries where there was "firm evidence" Jordan was diverting products specifically designed for weapons of mass destruction. (In fact, there was clear evidence of Jordan's role.) Fuller also explained it was important not to publicly criticise Jordan, "an old friend" in a "highly-volatile area" of the world. It was better to apply pressure on Jordan "by means of vigorous demarches to top people".

The DTI noted a "general appearance of inactivity" among FO officials "because of a reluctance to ... upset the Jordanian authorities". Scott and Baxendale expressed their views rather more vividly. The way the FO dismissed a wealth of intelligence information giving warnings about Jordan was "potty" and "remarkably blinkered", they told Charles Haswell, a Foreign Office official formerly responsible for Britain's relations with Jordan. "If you think my view's bonkers, all I can say is that was my view at the time," replied Haswell, "I would like to think I'm not bonkers."

He later acknowledged it was "common knowledge" that Jordan was used as a conduit for illegal trade with Iraq before the invasion of Kuwait, and that a British company, Ordtec, tried to sell illegal arms to Iraq in 1988.

"I can't understand why you didn't check intelligence reports," said Baxendale. "Why on earth didn't you go back?"

Haswell replied, "I might have been remiss in not checking the files."

The decision to leave Jordan off the list was an "amazing gap", Baxendale told Peter Vereker, head of the FO's Arms Control and Disarmament Department. Scott suggested he was prejudicing the interests of his own department by what he called the "apparently glaring loophole".

The inquiry heard that a Cabinet Office memorandum, called "The Iraq Note", drawn up in July 1990, had warned: "It appears that Iraq systematically uses Jordan as a cover for her procurement activities, almost certainly with the connivance of senior figures in the Jordan administration." Yet in September that year, a month after the invasion of Kuwait, the Ministry of Defence cleared for export to Jordan more than 5,000 Royal Ordnance shells to Jordan.

On August 16, two weeks after the invasion of Kuwait, 42 wagons containing the Royal Ordnance shells were stopped by Customs officers at Hull dock. After a month of haggling between Royal Ordnance – a subsidiary of British Aerospace – and Whitehall, a Yugoslav ship set sail for Aqaba with the shells on board.

The explanation of the Government's refusal to take effective steps to control exports it knew were being diverted to Iraq lies in Britain's special relationship with Jordan, and with King Hussein in particular. Alan Clark said he was so angry when he learned that Jordan was being used to divert "illicit traffic" to Iraq that he helped to prevent King Hussein being invited to take the Sovereign's Parade at Sandhurst in 1991, "because I thought it wrong and insulting". He told the inquiry, "I never understood the level of trust which was reposed in Jordan, which seemed to me to over-reach an objective assessment of what was happening ... I was uneasy about it, but there were wider diplomatic considerations." Clark revealed that it was well known in the MoD that "There was a tendency for the trickier items to be consigned to Jordan ... Nobody seemed to do anything about it."

Indeed that seemed to have been the case. Asked if there was a "hands-off-Jordan" feeling in the FO, David Gore-Booth acknowledged, "I think it would be fair to say that, yes ..."

Douglas Hurd had a quiet word with the king in May 1990. But he told the inquiry, "We had other objectives, even in the Middle East. One

DOUGLAS HURD, FOREIGN SECRETARY SINCE 1989/THE GUARDIAN/ALAN REEVELL

of them is the preservation of the stability of Jordan, because it is a key country ... This is sometimes regarded as old-fashioned Foreign Office sentimentality for that dynasty, but that is absurd ... This Jordan point, where there was a problem about possible diversion, which we could not ignore, was a problem we had to handle in relationship to our other objectives as well."

"Jordan," said Thatcher, "always had a destabilising danger ... There was a possibility that this rather remarkable country and this very, very courageous king, who never flinched from personal danger, might be destabilised. That would not have done British interests any good at all. To destabilise Jordan would have been a very, very serious matter indeed. So we took the course of doing as much as we could and seeking what for the king was unusual – to give a personal assurance."

Lord Howe said he could not recollect, when he was Foreign Secretary, "being triggered [about Jordan] because I think one was so constantly exposed to the extreme courtesy and charm and genuineness of the people themselves".

He told a bemused audience at the inquiry, "I have never met a more courteous individual, and the most marvellous sight in the world is to see Mrs Thatcher and King Hussein dealing with each other, because they both sought to outstrip each other in courtesy, 'Your Majesty' and 'Ma'am' and everything. It was an amazing sight, and he was extraordinarily good at it. I had this impression of a man of huge integrity and certainly a man of great courage and admirable qualities."

The Dunk Case

The Jordan connection was the origin of a trial which was to have serious repercussions in Whitehall, with senior officials accused by a top judge of interfering with the course of justice. In 1985, Reginald Dunk, director of Atlantic Commercial, an arms dealing firm, and Alexander Schlesinger, a middle-man, were fined £20,000 after pleading guilty of trying to smuggle 200 Sterling sub-machine guns to Iraq via Jordan. A third man, James Edmiston, a director of Sterling, was acquitted.

Dunk and Schlesinger pleaded guilty after staff at the Jordanian and

Iraqi embassies in London reneged on their assurances to appear as witnesses for the defence. The diplomats had promised to argue that the guns were "a gift" from Iraq to Jordan. Their credibility before a jury was not the issue. The question was why they had suddenly backed down.

The answer came in documents reluctantly given to the Scott inquiry by the Foreign Office. They revealed that, at the behest of Customs and Excise, senior FO officials had "friendly words" with the Iraqi and Jordanian ambassadors persuading them to claim diplomatic immunity and prevent their staff from appearing as witnesses for the defence.

One document was a handwritten note from Patrick Nixon to an FO colleague, Carsten Pigott. "I confess," said Nixon, "to innocent reluctance to connive at impeding the course of justice!"

Asked by Scott whether he agreed with the adjective "disgraceful" to describe Whitehall's antics, Sir Stephen Egerton, a former senior official at the FO responsible for relations with the Middle East and ambassador to Saudi Arabia, replied, "I would say it was a bad show."

Armed with these disclosures, Dunk and Schlesinger appealed against their convictions. In July 1994, Lord Taylor, the Lord Chief Justice, delivered a severe indictment of the civil servants. After referring to the Scott-Egerton exchange, Taylor said he preferred "the plain adjective" used by Scott. "The machinations in this case," he told the Court of Appeal "to prevent witnesses for the defence being available coupled with the non-disclosure of what had been done, constituted such an interference with the justice process as to amount to an abuse of it."

Officials named in his judgment included Patrick Nixon, now High Commissioner in Lusaka, Zambia; Patrick Wogan, ambassador in Doha, Qatar; Carsten Pigott, deputy head of Mission in Addis Ababa; and Graham Boyce, head of the FO's Environment, Science and Energy Department. Customs officers named by Lord Taylor were Mike Knox, now in charge of the agency's European and International Division, and John Cassey, a special investigator.

After the judgment, Sir David Gillmore, then permanent secretary at the FO, sent a circular to his officials reminding them of the "need unfailingly to observe the law of the land".

Meanwhile, Edmiston wrote a book, The Sterling Years. He describes a visit to the Jordanian port of Aqaba in 1983. "I was rather taken aback," he recalled, "in a huge enclosure just outside the port area, stacks upon stacks of equipment – much of it British – that was plainly labelled as destined for Iraq, including military vehicles painted in Iraqi, not Jordanian, army colours."

Every major case relating to exports to Iraq that Customs have brought to trial has foundered – the Dunk case, the "nuclear triggers" case and the supergun affair. Meanwhile, the Ordtec case was referred to the Court of Appeal.

The Ordtec Case

In 1989, the MoD and the DTI cleared for export the sale, ostensibly to Jordan, of an entire assembly to produce large quantities of fuses for artillery shells. The deal was put together by Ordtec, a Berkshire-based company. Ordtec took over the deal from Allivane, a company based in Cumbernauld, near Glasgow which folded in 1989. Some of the directors of Allivane – which briefly changed its name to Aerotechnologies, or Aerotech, became directors of Ordtec.

The assembly line deal also involved SRC, the company set up by Gerald Bull, designer of the Iraqi supergun. An end-user certificate saying the equipment was destined for Jordan was signed by the Jordanian field marshal and chief of staff, Bin Shaker, who had earlier warned the MoD that Iraq had asked Jordan to be "a front" for Iraq. The assessment, backed by the FO, that the assembly line was truly destined for Jordan was wrong, according to Lt. Col. Glazebrook. Jordan, he told the Scott inquiry, was unlikely to need, or be able to afford, such equipment.

An export licence for a contract Ordtec placed with BMARC, a subsidiary of the defence compamy, Astra, for pellets for the shell fuses to be made in the assembly line was designated "Al Fao Organisation, c/o Jordanian armed forces". Al Fao was an arms factory near Baghdad.

(Chris Cowley, one of those arrested in connection with the supergun affair, has said that, in 1988, he saw Royal Ordnance shells at Hutteen, the Iraqi arms factory near Baghdad.)

Early in 1992, Paul Grecian, Bryan Mason and Stuart Blackledge, received suspended sentences at Reading Crown Court. They admitted trying to smuggle the equipment via Jordan to Iraq in plea bargaining on the advice of their defence lawyers. A fourth man, Colin Phillips, employed by a Poole-based trucking company, EC Transport, was fined. Their lawyers advised them to plead guilty after the Government prepared PII certificates signed by Kenneth Baker, then Home Secretary, and Peter Lilley, then Trade and Industry Secretary. The Government also refused to allow DTI officials, including Tony Steadman, to give evidence. The defence suspected that the Government were implicated in the deal and sought the disclosure of Whitehall documents to prove their case. The trial judge, Stanley Spence, ruled that these documents were irrelevant to the case.

One problem was that Paul Grecian had been feeding the intelligence agencies with information about what Saddam Hussein was up to. In February, Annabelle Bolt, the Customs lawyer, warned Stephen Wooler at the Attorney-General's office, "The ... area of difficulty concerns the defendant JP Grecian. For a number of years, he has been providing information to the Special Branch. The information did not cover any matters connected with the prosecution. However, in late 1989, he provided information on Iraq and in particular Operation Babylon. As a result of this information, he was introduced to the security services and had several meetings with them."

Sir Nicholas Lyell admitted at the Scott inquiry that the framing of the PII certificates in the Ordtec case was "over-wide", but he was not personally involved.

In light of the evidence of government complicity in trade with Iraq that emerged in the Matrix Churchill trial, the Ordtec 4 lodged an appeal. Andrew Collins QC, Customs prosecutor in the Ordtec case, maintained that the documents, which he had seen, were irrelevant. Lord Justice Scott had other views. After the Ordtec defence lawyers warned there was clear evidence of a miscarriage of justice, Scott decided to have a private meeting with Collins. The meeting took place in the Scott inquiry's room at 1, Buckingham Gate on June 16, 1993.

Transcripts of the meeting reveal a remarkable clash of views in exchanges which raise further serious questions about the Government's conduct. Scott began by telling Collins that if the defence wanted material "which shows that the Government had a very strong suspicion that a number of things that went to Jordan were destined to go on to Iraq, there is a stack of documentation to that effect. If [the defence] wants specific material showing that strong suspicions were held in respect of the Ordtec applications – that they were destined to go to Iraq – there is that too ... You did not say those were irrelevant, did you?" he asked.

"Yes," replied Collins.

"How could you?" asked the judge. The papers would "show [government] knowledge ... Surely this was relevant?"

In echoes of the Matrix Churchill case, Collins argued that the documents were not relevant because although they might show the Government had *suspicions*, it did not actually know for sure the assembly line was destined for Iraq, and anyway Ordtec was trying to deceive the Government whatever the Government knew.

"The powers that be knew that Jordan was being used to some extent ... More than suspicion. They knew it was happening," Scott exclaimed.

Collins admitted that "The Government knew what was going on."

"And turned a blind eye to it in circumstances where a little careful probing would have produced certainty?" suggested Scott.

Collins replied that that was "probably right", but that was not a defence.

At the Ordtec trial, Judge Spence told the defence that Collins had stated "perfectly clearly" if any documents existed showing Whitehall "acted in a manner to indicate double standards and in a devious or dishonest way", then Collins would drop the prosecution.

Collins, meanwhile, told Scott that the Government may have taken the view that what Jordan did with the assembly line was not its concern. "We are not talking about nuclear triggers or chemical warfare or anything like that. We are talking about things which blow people up which apparently are not considered to be all that unpleasant."

Collins, the son of Canon Collins, a prominent CND activist in the early days of the nuclear disarmament campaign, has since been appointed a High Court judge.

The inquiry also heard that Customs officers first visited Ordtec under the guise of a VAT inspection. Valerie Strachan, chairman of

Customs, told Scott that she would investigate Customs' pre-trial handling of the Ordtec prosecution. Meanwhile, the Ordtec defendants have joined the list of appellants – including Dunk, Schlesinger, and Daghir and Speckman (see below) – who have sought justice in the light of new evidence disclosed by the Scott inquiry.

● ● ●

The Government suffered further embarrassment in June 1994 when Lord Taylor quashed convictions against two exporters jailed for conspiring to export electrical equipment – described by the Government as "nuclear triggers" – to Iraq.

Ali Daghir, of dual Iraqi-British nationality and managing director of a company called Euromac, and Jeanine Speckman, his sales manager, were convicted in 1991 after after a 19-month sting operation conducted by US Customs with Thatcher's personal backing. Lord Taylor overturned the conviction on the grounds that the trial judge, Neil Denison, misdirected the jury. The prosecution had relied on the claim that the electrical capacitors – devices which store and release electrical energy – were specially designed for use in nuclear weapons. The judge explained to the jury they could convict if they found that the equipment had any military use.

A US Customs document reveals that "The British Prime Minister was advised of the status of this investigation and is very much interested in its progress and successful outcome." After Daghir and Speckman were arrested, Thatcher congratulated Customs. She did not refer to her involvement in the case in her evidence to the Scott inquiry.

Like the Matrix Churchill 3, Daghir and Speckman are seeking compensation for their treatment by Customs prosecutors.

Customs obtained a court injunction preventing the defence in the Daghir appeal from disclosing information about British equipment found by UN inspection teams at Iraq's nuclear sites. Customs was concerned that the UN found no evidence of Euromac's involvement and that Iraq had no need for the capacitors in its nuclear project.

A UN report drawn up in 1992 made no mention of Euromac, although it did say that Matrix Churchill machine tools exported to Iraq had "technical characteristics required for producing key components needed in a nuclear programme".

John Gordon, former head of the FO's Nuclear Energy Department, has suggested that the Government may have ignored its Non-Proliferation Treaty obligations by approving the Matrix Churchill exports. The International Atomic Energy Agency holds the view that the company could not have known whether they would be used by Iraq for the manufacture of shells, in a nuclear context, or for assembly lines.

● ● ●

There is evidence that other countries, in addition to Jordan, were used as conduits for Iraq with the British Government's knowledge. Frank Machon, a Glasgow-based transporter whose customers included Allivane and the Ministry of Defence, warned 10 Downing Street in 1988 that large quantities of shells shipped by Allivane to Saudi Arabia, Spain, and Portugal were destined for Iran and Iraq.

Sir Stephen Egerton recalled at the Scott inquiry how a Saudi prince gave him "a rocket" because of delays in Allivane exports to Saudi Arabia. Egerton refused to name the prince in public but handed it to Scott on a piece of paper. A former Allivane director later said the company had negotiated a contract for 155mm artillery rounds to Saudi Arabia with Prince Sultan Bin Turki Bin Abdulazziz, a nephew of King Fahd. Documents show that the MoD in 1988 suspected an Allivane contract of 155mm shells for Saudia Arabia may have been destined for Iraq. The prince may have been discussing a shipment for the use by the Saudis themselves.

There is evidence, too, that Royal Ordnance and Nobel Explosives, a subsidiary of ICI, were part of a European explosives cartel whose arms ended up in Iraq and Iran.

Cowley says he saw Royal Ordnance barrels for 155mm howitzers Iraq's Hutteen factory. Gerald James, former chairman of Astra, says that BMARC ammunition for the Skyguard 35mm anti-aircraft gun was shipped to Cyprus even though the country did not possess the gun. He says he was told the ammunition was destined for Iraq.

PAUL HENDERSON, FORMER MANAGING DIRECTOR OF MATRIX CHURCHILL/THE GUARDIAN/GRAHAM TURNER

17

The Unliked Spy

"There was misunderstanding by all parties at the meeting." Paul Henderson.

Paul Henderson gave evidence to the inquiry on July 7, 1994, to rebut testimony from Lord Trefgarne. At his request, he also gave evidence in secret about his contacts with MI6.

Trefgarne told the inquiry that he approved export licences only after Henderson assured him the equipment was intended for civilian use. "Mr Henderson gave me the plainest assurances the exports were for innocent purposes," he said, referring to a meeting between the two men on September 26, 1989.

At the inquiry, Henderson flatly denied the claim, saying that the meeting "concerned itself with generalities". He said Trefgarne never asked him about the intended end-use of the machines and he gave the minister "no assurances whatsoever". He insisted that specific licence applications were never discussed and that the meeting was devoted mainly to a general discussion about prospects for Iraq's industrial development after its cease-fire with Iran. He described Lord Trefgarne as "confused".

Reacting to Trefgarne's evidence, he said that nine licences were discussed at the meeting, only one of which was linked to arms. The one licence linked to weapons – part of a deal with Carlos Cardoen, the Chilean weapons manufacturer – was never mentioned. Henderson's argument is supported by documents disclosed to the defence at his trial in 1992. Eric Beston – a senior official at the DTI who was present at the meeting – said he "did not get an opportunity to raise the sales through a Chilean middle-man" – a reference to Cardoen.

Documents also say that at a meeting the same week with Rob Young, a senior FO official, Henderson "had been frank in admitting that he could not guarantee that the lathes would not be used for military manufacturing purposes". Asked why he did not refer to the Cardoen contract then, Henderson said the Government already knew about it as a result of information he had passed on to MI6. Asked by Baxendale whether that was a reason for not telling Rob Young, Henderson who had just had a secret session with MI6, replied, "It was the way the meeting was arranged."

It was not only Trefgarne who seemed "confused", Henderson also appeared muddled giving evidence which was less than fully convincing.

In a note to the DTI before the Trefgarne meeting, Henderson emphasised the dual, civil/military use of Matrix Churchill machine tools. He also pointed to a number of civil contracts with Iraq involving Perkins diesel engines, General Motors, and Mercedes Benz. "Any countries seeking to develop its industrial capacity must acquire machine tools. Iraq recognises this need and if machine tools are not supplied by [Britain], there is no shortage of other foreign suppliers."

An official DTI note of the meeting quoted Henderson as saying the machines "would be used for general engineering purposes, principally for production of automotive components. He understood they would be used for civil production only." Henderson denied he had said that. He also said that suggestions at the trial by his defence counsel, Geoffrey Robertson, that he had described the machines as going to Iraqi factories which were diversifying to industrial production were "mistaken" and were the result of Robertson misinterpreting his instructions.

A minute of the meeting by John Nosworthy, director-general of the Machine Tools Technologies Association, who was also present, also recorded Henderson as assuring the minister that the machine tools "were intended for industrial use at two factories previously involved in the war effort". That, Baxendale pointed out, tied in with the recollections of Trefgarne and civil servants. Henderson agreed, but insisted their accounts of the meeting were inaccurate. He added, "I think there was misunderstanding by all parties at the meeting."

Baxendale turned to Henderson's book, The Unlikely Spy. Henderson wrote that at the Trefgarne meeting, he acknowledged "That the machines had commercial and military uses." Yet in a prepared statement to the inquiry, Henderson had said: "I can say categorically there was no discussion either in general or specific terms of the end-use to which any of the [Matrix Churchill] equipment under consideration would be put." Asked to explain the apparent discrepancy, Henderson told the inquiry that he had a ghost writer for the book which was meant to give the "flavour" of the meeting and was not meant to be a *verbatim* record. Henderson said the meeting was largely devoted to future, potential contracts with Iraq, not the licences whose delay prompted Henderson's request for the meeting in the first place.

The other dispute was between Henderson and MI6. At issue was the date when MI6 first contacted Henderson asking for help in providing information about Iraq's arms procurement activities. Henderson's controller, "John Balsom", told the Old Bailey trial that he did not contact Mr Henderson until April 1989.

Henderson maintained he was first approached by Balsom in the autumn of 1988. He says in his book that Balsom telephoned him in late August 1988, and the two men met in early September.

Henderson also strongly disputes Balsom's pre-trial written statement in which the MI6 agent-runner said the Henderson passed on only "a certain amount of useful, though generally not high-level, information on Iraqi policy, operational activity, and a few technical snippets". Henderson comments, "I never expected Balsom to lie." He says he gave MI6 detailed information about Iraq's missile programme at a meeting at Carlton Gardens, near Buckingham Palace, in September 1989.

In secret hearings of the inquiry, MI6 officers have admitted there are no records of at least one crucial meeting between Henderson and MI6.

Henderson was described in court by Balsom as "a very brave man". His bravery and the personal risks he took in providing some information to MI6 should not prevent us from ignoring Henderson's personal and financial interest, as well as that of his workforce, in Matrix Churchill's arms-related trade with Iraq.

Henderson remains the target of smears by ministers and Whitehall officials. Senior Customs officers say they have no regrets about bringing the prosecution, and insist privately they were looking forward to

Henderson's cross-examination in the witness box and a jury verdict. And the Government continues to treat Alan Clark as a scapegoat for the fall of the trial.

But the more the inquiry delved, the more the documents disclosed, and oral evidence revealed, so it became increasingly clear that Henderson was merely a small cog in the arms-to-Iraq affair.

For Henderson, the survival of Matrix Churchill was at stake. The company collapsed after Iraq's invasion of Kuwait with the loss of some 700 jobs in Coventry. Its controversial exports to Iraq, valued at about £50 million in all, were crucial to the company's survival, as Henderson repeatedly reminded his MI6 controller. But this compares with over £2,300 million worth of British machinery and transport equipment exports to Iraq between 1981 and 1990, according to DTI figures.

Other companies were involved, including BSA, whose chairman, Keith Bailey (who took over Matrix Churchill) was also arrested and charged with illegally exporting arms equipment to Iraq even though Whitehall knew about the sales. His charges were dropped after the collapse of the Matrix Churchill trial. The MI6 report, dated November 1987, named several machine tool companies, including Wickman Bennett and Colchester Lathes, and the company which originally introduced them to Iraqi arms procurers – Meed International, a company formed by Anees Wadi, a businessman with Iraqi connections, and a British consultant, Roy Ricks. They took an Iraqi delegation, led by Safa al-Habobi, a senior official at Iraq's Ministry of Industry and Military Production and an Iraqi intelligence agent who later became chairman of Matrix Churchill.

With the exception of Paul Henderson and David James, the Scott inquiry did not hear evidence in public from other businessmen. Those who could have enlightened the hearings include: Sir John Cuckney, former MI5 officer, former chairman of the MoD's company, International Military Services, former deputy chairman of the TI Group which sold Matrix Churchill to the Iraqis; Stephan Kock, a shadowy figure with links to the intelligence agencies who was involved in the Midland Bank's secretive Defence Equipment Finance Department and later a non-executive director of Astra; Sir James Blyth and Sir Colin Chandler, successive heads of arms sales at the MoD; Sir

Peter Levene, former chief of Defence Procurement at the MoD and
now head of the Whitehall Efficiency Unit; and Sir John Bourn, former
senior arms procurement official at the MoD and now the Comptroller
and Auditor-General, Parliament's chief financial watchdog.

Some of these were contacted by the inquiry in writing, but the
message from the inquiry was that Scott's concern was in *government*
involvement in, and knowledge of, exports to Iraq in breach of official
guidelines. Private businessmen, according to the inquiry team, were
unlikely to volunteer to point the finger at the Government, or implicate
themselves in any way.

The British Government was not the only western government which
deceived its legislators by dealing in arms exports or credit deals with
Saddam Hussein. In the US, Judge Marvin Shoob presided over the trial
of Christopher Drogoul, manager of the Atlanta branch of the Italian
bank, BNL, accused of illegally arranging finance for Iraq (it was one of
Matrix Churchill's bankers). The judge told the court in October 1992
that Drogoul and BNL had been "pawns or bit players in a far larger and
wider-ranging sophisticated conspiracy that involved BNL Rome, and
possibly large American and foreign corporations and the governments
of the United States, England, Italy and Iraq".

Intelligence agencies knew from other sources – including Mark
Gutteridge – the use to which British machine tools were being put.
Gutteridge suggests that Henderson exaggerated his role in helping MI6,
and that MI6 may even have been misled. There seems little doubt
Gutteridge was giving detailed information to his MI5 controller before
Henderson began to pass information to his MI6 controller. Company
documents show Gutteridge was in a position as early as the summer of
1987 to tell the intelligence agencies that Habobi was ordering British
machine tools specifically required to make shells. The Government –
ministers and civil servants – knew the equipment was being used by
Saddam Hussein to make weapons, and did not care. If Henderson did
not tell MI6 everything he knew, the Government certainly did not tell
Parliament what it knew.

The DTI tried to stop a prosecution. It knew that, at one level,
officials would be shown up to be incompetent – even though they
would argue that they were simply too busy to cope with the export

monitoring work load. At a much more damaging level, they would be exposed as having known the destination of Matrix Churchill machine tools, but doing nothing about it. When Customs officers – who claimed they were originally tipped off, not by British intelligence, but by German Customs officers – civil servants withheld embarrassing information, signed incomplete witness statements, and then, by their own admittance, misled the jury. Ministers, meanwhile, signed PII certificates which would have denied crucial documents to the defence.

The inquiry was set up to investigate whether the Government had subverted its publicly-stated policy on exports to Iraq and ministers' use of PII certificates. It gave a unique insight into Britain's system of government, revealing incompetence, dissembling, cynicism, cock-ups, and an astonishing lack of co-operation between and within different Whitehall departments. In just one example, Lt. Col. Glazebrook was told in June 1989 that the new 1988 guidelines would lead to a "significantly softer" approach to Iraq, but was warned never to disclose the changes to anybody outside the ministry.

Mystique surrounding the work of the intelligence services proved self-defeating, with their reports either not getting to the right people or simply ignored. Customs seemed to be out of control, with suggestions during the inquiry that they did not even observe Police and Criminal Evidence Act (Pace) obligations during the supergun investigation. Customs blames other departments. "Customs are investigators, the DTI and the MoD are administrators. The two never get together, " according to a senior Customs investigator. But the inquiry heard that Douglas Tweddle, the head of Customs' investigation branch had no previous experience as an investigator. Asked by Scott who was responsible for supervising Customs, Sir Patrick Mayhew replied, "The short answer is nobody."

The relationship between Customs – which enjoys a unique role as both an investigating and prosecuting authority – and the Attorney-General had "never been defined", he said. Valerie Strachan, Unwin's successor as chairman of Customs agreed that the agency should be brought more closely under the Attorney-General's supervision.

The Scott inquiry also pointed the spotlight at individuals. Eric Beston, a senior DTI official with intimate knowledge of the Matrix

Churchill licence applications, acknowledged that evidence he gave from the witness box was misleading. Andrew Leithead, an assistant Treasury Solicitor, changed Tony Steadman's witness statement. Senior Foreign Office and Customs officials interfered in the Dunk case.

Sir Nicholas Lyell gave a personal assurance to Michael Heseltine that his reluctance to sign a PII certificate would be passed on to the trial judge via Alan Moses, the senior prosecution counsel. It never was. At the Old Bailey, Moses blamed the collapse of the trial on Alan Clark. At the inquiry, he said he would not have pursued the prosecution had he been aware of documents, including intelligence reports, showing the Government knew Matrix Churchill machines were being used by Saddam Hussein to make weapons.

William Waldegrave acknowledged his thesis that the export guidelines were not changed entailed "obvious difficulties". He was provided with a stream of intelligence reports warning how Britain was helping to build up Iraq's war machine. On August 24, 1989, Stephen Lillie of the FO's Middle East Department minuted that "Mr Waldegrave will be familiar with the background to Matrix Churchill ... Assuming the equipment has been used specifically for arms production, this is in contravention of our policy on defence sales to Iran and Iraq." He noted that MI6 had, by then, agreed to use its intelligence reports to justify blocking the machine tool exports.

Waldegrave did not query a briefing on the eve of a key meeting with Clark and Lord Trefgarne on November 1, 1989. The briefing said that MI6 was suddenly no longer sure that the machines were being used to manufacture arms.

Secret minutes of the meeting noted that Waldegrave had said, "Iraq was rebuilding its military capability, including CW (chemical warfare) and ballistic missile operations. Matrix Churchill's exports probably went into the Iraqi armaments industry." He nevertheless approved a new batch of Matrix Churchill exports, with Clark and Trefgarne agreeing to maintain at least some export guidelines and that "any PQs (parliamentary questions) or public condemnation arising from the issue of licences should be dealt with by the DTI".

Yet in September 1993, Waldegrave told the Scott inquiry in a prepared written statement that dual-use exports were not allowed "if it was believed they were to be used to make weapons". He later acknowledged the statement was inaccurate.

Lady Thatcher said she knew nothing about any change in the export guidelines, as did her predecessor, John Major. Sir Robin Butler, Cabinet Secretary and head of the Civil Service, defended secrecy for the sake of what he called "good government". Kenneth Clarke, who said he would resign if the inquiry found him "at fault", signed a PII certificate without reading documents about the case and not knowing that Henderson had connections with MI6. After Geoffrey Robertson had explained why they were relevant, it took only a 15-minute telephone call between Moses, the prosecution counsel, and Whitehall for them to be released.

The arms-to-Iraq affair was one of the most seedy, dishonest, buck-passing episodes in the history of modern British government. Had the Matrix Churchill trial not collapsed, and documents, ministers wanted to suppress, not been disclosed, three men could have been jailed in a miscarriage of justice in which ministers and civil servants would have connived.

Despite Sir Robin Butler's concept of being "blame-free", we are repeatedly told that in our parliamentary democracy, ministers are responsible for the actions and failings of the Government.

The Scott report will be a seminal – and extremely lengthy – treatise on the state of Whitehall, going well beyond the specific, though important, issue of how the government machine sabotaged its own publicly-stated export guidelines. Although Whitehall mandarins, some ministers and Tory MPs are trying to smear Scott, they are also giving him the greatest compliment – they are unable to disguise their anxiety about what his report will say.

Several clear issues emerged from the inquiry. One is Whitehall's culture of secrecy – described by Scott during Lord Howe's evidence as the "Government-knows-best approach". The inquiry, and the Scott report, should support those demanding a fully-fledged Freedom of Information Act along the lines adopted in some of Britain's oldest allies – the US, Australia, Canada, New Zealand. It will also provide ammunition to those civil servants demanding a statutory code of ethics.

Never again will the system of Public Interest Immunity certificates be used in such a cavalier way – certainly not in criminal cases – with ministers signing "gagging orders" covering whole classes of documents, regardless of their contents. Lyell was criticised not only by Scott, but by the Law Lords themselves, for insisting that ministers had a duty to sign PII certificates which could not be waived. The term, "national security" will no longer be treated with the awe it has been in the past.

Another central theme was the failure of intelligence reports to get to the people who needed them. Scott and his team took a keen and deep interest in the activities of the intelligence agencies, notably MI6 and GCHQ. Scott did not hesitate to recall MI6 officers when he was dissatisfied with their initial evidence. He had a private session with Dennis Mitchell, a former senior GCHQ official who left the agency in protest against the Government's 1984 ban on trade unions there.

Mitchell left on conscientious grounds, unhappy both with the union ban and with the use to which the Government put information about allied and hostile countries intercepted by GCHQ. So concerned was Sir Robin Butler when he heard Mitchell had given evidence that he wrote to Scott insisting it should remain secret.

Whitehall deployed its traditional weapons to hinder the inquiry. Departments, notably Sir Robin Butler's Cabinet Office, delayed passing on documents. They gave the inquiry misleading figures about the amount of arms-related exports approved for Iraq. It fought to the end to try to persuade Scott to suppress embarrassing information contained in thousands of documents not read out in the public hearings. Scott reminded Whitehall that the Prime Minister had given him "unfettered discretion" over what to publish, and promised to take a "robust" view in arguments with Whitehall.

The Government will try to say that many of the criticisms identified by Scott have been recognised and put right. It's all past history, it will say. It is not – the Whitehall machine and the Whitehall culture, embracing civil servants and ministers alike, does not move, or change, that quickly.

The bubble burst and our system of Government will never be the same again.

Half the Picture

Half the Picture

Original art: Sue Gell

Adapted and redacted by
Richard Norton-Taylor

with additional material
by John McGrath

First performed at the
Tricycle Theatre
on June 14th, 1994,
directed by Nicolas Kent.

starring
Margaret Thatcher and John Major

with
Sir Nicholas Lyell
Michael Heseltine
William Waldegrave
Alan Clark

and introducing
Presiley Baxendale QC

With the exception of a very few phrases added only to clarify points of fact and identify individuals, the words are those exchanged between Lord Justice Scott and Presiley Baxendale QC and the witnesses.

Half the Picture

Act I

Enter a 56-year-old woman, smart, attractive: Colette, who worked in the office at Matrix Churchill. She faces audience.

Colette: I worked in the office at Matrix Churchill, Coventry. I saw what was going on. The machine tools Matrix Churchill were selling to Iraq were undoubtedly designed for making artillery shells and mortar-bombs. So when I wrote to Geoffrey Howe, the Foreign Secretary, telling him this, they said I was just being menopausal. I swallowed the insult to women in general, and thought quietly about the tens of thousands of women and their babies being killed among the Kurds and the Marsh Arabs in Iraq. I felt a great sense of identification with them.

So I wrote to the Foreign Secretary, so he would know, and couldn't say he didn't, about what we were being asked to do. But, of course, he was a man. I believe he sent copies of my letter to other men, in the Ministry of Defence, in the Department of Trade and Industry, and in MI6. What I didn't realise was that, of course, they all knew. Mr Henderson had been telling MI6 all along. They all denied they knew, but my letter I suppose they couldn't avoid. Anyway, when Mr Henderson was arrested and put on trial, the judge eventually had to admit they knew. God bless him. He must have been a bit ... menopausal.

He dismissed the case against Mr Henderson, but now what I wonder is: does this mean it's all right to sell machine tools for horrible weapons to people like Saddam Hussein as long as you tell the Secret Service? Or as long as we ordinary people don't find out? The

Government said it *wasn't* doing what it *was* doing and it helped to kill all those people. Why? We're all out of work now anyway ... Does this mean I shouldn't have written to Geoffrey Howe?

I've got three children, all boys, growing up. I wonder what I should be teaching them. What they're learning.

[She goes off, thoughtful.]

sc ii
Evidence of John Major

Bax: 10th November 1992. You are answering this question in Parliament, a question from Mr John Smith: "Does the Prime Minister recall assuring the House in January 1991 that 'For some considerable time, we have not supplied arms of Iraq'? How does the Prime Minister reconcile the assurance with the revelation in the government documents produced at the Matrix Churchill trial, that as late as 27th July, 1990, only six days before the invasion of Kuwait, machine tools, known to be intended to make fuses for missiles and artillery shells, were supplied to Iraq?"

Then your answer: "The Right Honourable and learned Gentleman knows that from 1985 until the Iraqi invasion of Kuwait, the Government operated under guidelines first set out by then Foreign Secretary." And then you refer to the full embargo since the invasion.

Major: The question I was specifically asked, of course, was about supplying arms to Iraq, and, of course, arms are self-evidently lethal. I was responding to the fact that those arms were banned, and that the embargo was clear-cut.

Scott: One of the problems is that not only in questions, but also sometimes in answers, the expression "arms" is used in its correct sense.

Major: I agree.

Scott: And sometimes in a broad sense, including also just defence-related equipment. It is often not quite clear in what sense it should be read.

Major: I agree. Here, there was no doubt, I think, in terms of the question, that it was referring to arms. I responded to it entirely accurately.

Bax: You are saying that the original question was: "We have not supplied arms to Iraq", and so, although –

Scott: The original question was talking about machine tools.

Major: The question here is: "Does the Prime Minister recall assuring the House in January 1991 that "For some considerable time we have not supplied arms to Iraq'?"

Scott: It goes on to refer to machine tools. He – John Smith – wants to know whether that assurance is consistent with what he says has been happening in regard to machine tools.

Major: If it is thought that machine tools were likely to be used for lethal weapons, and that is, of course, why we have the guidelines. One of the points you have to consider, of course, is whether there was a change in 1988. I had no knowledge of any discussion of the change in 1988. It was on that basis I replied to the question in the House.

Scott: Did you regard your answer as dealing with arms strictly, or with arms and things like machine tools?

Major: In the heat of Prime Minister's question time, it is difficult to recall at this distance, but, by that, you mean did I think I was making a clever and cunning distinction between the two in order to hide something that I knew and did not want to reveal, the answer is no.

Scott: I did not mean that. I wondered ... I wondered were you interpreting the question as being directed strictly to arms?

Major: I was responding to the fact that, in my judgment, and on the basis of the information available to me, we, that is to say the Government, had followed the guidelines strictly, from their inception and thereafter.

Bax: I would like to go on, we can now carry on with the chronology. Three days later, on 13th November, 1992, you received a minute from your private secretary, Stephen Wall, saying: "The Cabinet Office and other departments will be working through the weekend to produce as comprehensive a chronology as possible on the Matrix Churchill issue. There are a lot of simple questions, but very few simple answers. It emerges, for example, that the Howe guidelines of 1985 were amended by ministers in December 1988, but the amendment was never announced in Parliament."
I see a cross against the bit about the amendment. Is that your cross? Is that not your writing up at the top of the page?

Major: Yes, it is my cross because Mr Wall's note of 13th November 1992 was the first I knew about it.

Bax: There is a tick against documents that you had seen, the bit about "there is no evidence"?

Major: I have ticked the sentence here which says: "There is no evidence that, as Foreign Secretary, you saw the documents." In retrospect, one can never be certain of those things. I asked to check what I had actually known in the welter of papers that crossed ministers' desks, and there is the response from the Civil Service that I had not seen the documents.

Bax: If we go over the page, there are suggestions about the accusations that could be made against you.

Major: That is correct. One of the charges at the time, of course, was that, in some way, I must have known, because I had been the Chancellor, because I had been Foreign Secretary, because I had been Prime Minister – that, therefore, I must have known what was going on ... I was asking precisely what I had known and I asked for all the documentation to be checked. What you have read is the response that came back checking over again what I knew.

Bax: Going back to the beginning of this document, you have marked the bit about the amendment was never announced to Parliament. It is only a very short time after the answer to Mr Smith in the House of Commons. In the light of the evidence you have been giving us, did you consider at this stage, "Gosh, perhaps I should be clarifying that answer and saying, 'The guidelines *were* amended' "?

Major: I did – you will see why I did not – you can recall the atmosphere at the time. There was a great deal of high profile publicity. It was a very interesting few days. I asked for further inquiries to be made.

Bax: Some days later, on 23rd November, 1992, Mr Heseltine made a speech in the House of Commons. He said, "A change in the wording of the guidelines was obviously necessary to reflect the fact that there had been a ceasefire in the Iran-Iraq war." So at this stage, Mr Heseltine was saying there *was* a change.

Major: He thought there was. Two days later further research suggested that there was not.

Bax: Do you have the document sent to your private secretary – copied to

Sir Robin Butler, the Cabinet Secretary, from Miss Neville-Jones, on 25th November, 1992?

Major: Yes.

Bax: Wonderful, good. If we could go through it. She refers to a further element "that has come to light since I last minuted you. Further research in files obtained from the Foreign Office show that a group of junior ministers which considered a change in the guidelines subsequently decided not to do so. There was, therefore, no cause for a statement in the House of Commons and it is absolutely true to say that the guidelines were not changed, and, therefore, the House was not misled". Your cross is against that part of it?

Major: That is correct. There was a great deal of uncertainty over what had actually happened ... we were in a very frenetic atmosphere.

Bax: Then a few days later, we get a comment from Mr Heseltine: "Mr. Heseltine accepts the Cabinet Office conclusion that the guidelines themselves were never formally changed, and that it was in their interpretation that the ceasefire was reflected."

He goes on to say: "It seems clear that ministers involved at the time intended the change of approach to represent a more liberal policy towards defence exports to Iraq ... It would be extremely disingenuous for us now to say that there had been no change. It underlines the unstable nature of the ground beneath ministers' feet."

Major: I agree with the conclusion of Mr Heseltine's letter. I have to say I did not necessarily accept all his phraseology. What Mr Heseltine was seeking to do in that letter, and sensibly seeking to do, was the same point I referred to a moment ago: to look for a way to avoid misleading or confusing people. At that stage, of course, Mr Heseltine had not seen all the documentation, which has subsequently been submitted to this inquiry.

Bax: I am now going back a month to October 1992, just before the Matrix Churchill trail. It is a minute from the Foreign Secretary's office to 10 Downing Street. "The trial may be embarrassing for the Government because it will involve the disclosure of documents which reveal discussions between ministers and officials. The press may use the disclosures in an unhelpful sense to suggest that ministers knowingly broke their own guidelines."

Major: I do not remember this specifically, but I clearly did not agree to drop the prosecution.

Scott: Prime Minister, that, I am sure you will be glad to hear, brings to an end the questions which we wanted your help about. If you want to make any additions or corrections, of course we will be very glad if you would.

Major: Sir Richard, thank you very much indeed.

sc iii
Evidence of Mark Higson

Bax: Mr Higson, please can I confirm that from 23rd March, 1989 until January 1990, you were desk for Iraq at the Foreign Office?

Higson: Yes. Under David Gore-Booth who was the assistant under-secretary responsible for Middle Eastern affairs, it involved input into other departments' work with Iraq, and political input. That could be anything from answering letters to an awful lot of work on political hostages or prisoners (depending on what you want to call them) and lobbying or drafting lobbying papers for ministers and senior officials.

Scott: Lobbying papers? What sort of lobbying papers?

Higson: Lobbying other possible intermediaries for the release of the likes of Mrs Parish and Ian Richter.

Bax: Were you the person who was principally responsible for drafting the letters that were directly related to Iraq? How did it work?

Higson: How it worked was that a particular room in the Middle East Department had two sides and both had flags up at either end, one which was Iranian and one which was Iraqi.

Bax: So you would remember which side you were on?

Higson: Yes, I certainly do. I was very partisan.

Bax: I want to go to a Foreign Office document dated 6th October 1989. There is some handwriting on the left-hand side of it. Rather than squint and try to work out what it says, if you turn over the page, you have a transcription of it. That is a handwritten note by Mr Waldegrave, is it not?

Higson: Yes.

Bax: Could we just look at it for a minute? "I doubt if there is any future market of such a scale anywhere where the UK is potentially so well placed if we play our diplomatic hand correctly, nor can I think of any major market where the importance of diplomacy is so great on our commercial position. We must not allow it to go to the French, Germans, Japanese, Koreans etcetera ... The priority of Iraq in our policy should be very high: in commercial terms, comparable to South Africa in my view ... A few more Bazofts or another bout of internal repression would make this more difficult." What I wanted to ask you about was did those comments of Mr Waldegrave sum up, so far as you were aware, the Foreign Office view of Iraq at the time?

Higson: Yes.

Bax: It was seen that it was a very important commercial market?

Higson: The Iraqi market, after the end of the Iran-Iraq war, was summed up as being "the big prize". However distasteful we found the Iraqi regime, we could not afford to be left behind in developing trade links, and we were in prime position, to use a motor racing phrase.

Scott: Everybody recognised the big prize, but the Foreign Office was not prepared to go as far as other ministries to try to achieve it and to try to capture it?

Higson: We needed – this my opinion, which you have asked for – to sort out other problems as well. The fact that we were the Ministry tasked with all the other questions, such as gassing of Kurds, removal of the marsh Arabs, etcetera, from the south of the country, to the execution of Bazoft, etcetera, meant that, yes, we took a slightly more reserved position.

Bax: In your statement, you say you were aware of changes to the guidelines through the discussions between Mr Waldegrave, Lord Trefgarne, and Alan Clark in 1988. There was a relaxation, was there not?

Higson: Yes, and it was not announced – we continued to churn out the same old line.

Bax: On 7th February, 1989, there was a letter from Mr Waldegrave's private secretary to Alan Clark's private secretary, where he says: "Mr Waldegrave is content for us to implement a more liberal policy on defence sales without any public announcement."

Did you know why at that stage it was preferable not to have to announce publicly any change in the guidelines?

Higson: To be quite honest, I was simply advised that it was preferable not to make any public announcement, so I continued to use the old guidelines in response to members of the public and to MPs.

Bax: Did anyone tell you why it was preferable not to announce them? What was the reason? What was the Foreign Office's view about it?

Higson: I am very much ex-Foreign Office. It was an issue at the time that we officially kept a position of neutrality officially between the two countries. There was obviously a swing towards Iraq. Iran was still being seen as a complete pariah, and we wanted to allow greater flexibility towards Iraq which was going to be potentially very lucrative indeed.

Bax: No one wanted to announce this?

Higson: You will have to ask ministers about that.

Bax: I just wondered what –

Higson: I just did what I was told ... Can I just come back to that last point, when I listed what I was told? The answer is obviously that public perceptions of both regimes would have been that they were as vile as each other and we had particular problems with both. Yet the potential for Britain in relation to trade was with Iraq, but this would have been seen as unacceptable.

Scott: You mean the public would not stand for it?

Higson: We were getting, you know, tens and tens of letters about gassing of the Kurds and political prisoners or hostages and whatever. It would have been unacceptable to have announced the fact that we were relaxing a policy in favour of Iraq.

Scott: Unacceptable because of the public reaction?

Higson: Public and parliamentary reaction.

Bax: Unacceptable to members of the public and Members of Parliament?

Higson: Yes.

Bax: Would there have been a lot of trouble?

Higson: There would have been a lot of unanswered letters sitting around. There would have been trouble from the public and Members of Parliament if we had announced publicly that there was a relaxation in favour of Iraq.

Bax: You have been saying you have been giving your view. What I want to know is: at the time, is that the reason you understood why it was not being announced publicly?

Higson: We were doing a juggling act. There was a lot to gain and there was also a lot to lose. As Mr Waldegrave said in his letter to Mr Clark, he was satisfied with going along that line provided that, if it came out into the public domain, the Department of Trade would take the responsibility, the onus.

Bax: I want to make quite sure about this. Are you saying that the position was that Parliament was not to know, because otherwise Members of Parliament would have disagreed and wanted to discuss it?

Higson: Personal view – yes.

Bax: Members of the House of Lords did not leave it there. They picked it up. The answer that you have drafted: "British arms supplies to both Iraq and Iran continued to be governed by very strict guidelines", does not set out the true position, does it?

Higson: No.

Scott: If one was looking for an adjective to describe the answer as compared to the then current practice, what one would you choose?

Higson: I am not allowed to swear, am I?

Scott: Without swearing, how would you react to the adjective, "misleading"?

Higson: It was certainly misleading.

Bax: This was not telling the truth, was it?

Higson: It was one of the contributory reasons for why I actually left the Foreign Office.

Bax: Had you at any time been told, when you were at the Foreign Office, whether it was important to tell truthful answers to the House of Lords or the House of Commons.

Higson: Well, any civil servant's job is going to be, to quote somebody else, "economical with the truth". Sometimes, for reasons which obviously were not in the public domain, we had to sort of give only 75 per cent of the story and not 100 per cent.

Bax: Less than 75 per cent?

Higson: Fifty.

Scott: There is a distinction between a half truth and an untruth. Your 75 per cent is not a half, it is a three-quarter truth. Then there is an untruth, which is just not true. It is not a question of just being true to a point.

Higson: I will have to think about this one.

Scott: Just tell me ... If someone in the Foreign Office asks for information from another department, either he gets answered or he is told to go and mind his own business.

Higson: The moment you enter a ministry, you are indoctrinated with "need-to-know". I find it as risible and unacceptable as I think you both do ... We were lying to each other.

sc iv
Evidence of David Gore-Booth

Scott: Mr Gore-Booth, good morning. Thank you very much for sending us your statement which we have of course, read with great interest. Miss Baxendale, on my left, will mainly be asking you some questions arising from it, and I may ask some myself.

Bax: Can I ask you about asking questions in Parliament? If there is a question, it should be fully answered, should it not? The answer should be sufficiently full to give a true meaning?

G-Booth: Questions should be answered so as to give the maximum degree of satisfaction possible to the questioner.

Bax: I am not sure you really mean that, because that is rather like people just giving you the answer you want to hear, I think is what you have just said. I do not think you quite mean that.

G-Booth: No, it might be the answer you do not want to hear.

Bax: That does not give you much satisfaction. Should the answer be accurate?

G-Booth: Of course.

Bax: And they should not be half the picture?

G-Booth: They might be half the picture. You said, should they be accurate and I said yes, they should.

Scott: On a more broad approach to answering questions, there would be nothing the matter with an approach which proceeded on the footing

	that you would in every case be as forthcoming as you could?
G-Booth:	Correct. But there are often cases in which you cannot be so forthcoming, for reasons of what are called foreign policy.
Scott:	It is a question of where you start from. If you start from the view that you are going to be as forthcoming as you can, you will have a very good reason for holding something back.
Scott:	It is very much for a minister to decide how to answer a parliamentary question and then the civil servants draft it. So the extent to which an answer should be full, half-full, or empty, is very much a ministerial decision.
Bax:	Lord Glenarthur's answer in the House of Lords on 20th April, 1989, does not really set out the full picture, does it, with the sentence: "British arms supplies to both Iran and Iraq continue to be governed by very strict guidelines preventing the supply of lethal equipment to either side"?
G-Booth:	That is a correct statement.
Scott:	Notwithstanding the decision to be more liberal in the approach for applications for exports for Iraq?
G-Booth:	I think the statement as made by Lord Glenarthur is absolutely correct. Given that it had been decided that there would be no announcement of the modification of the guidelines, that seems to me to be an entirely appropriate response.
Bax:	You say that the original guideline 3 is still in place?
G-Booth:	It is kept under constant review and applied on a case by case basis in the light of the prevailing circumstances, including the ceasefire.
Bax:	That is completely ridiculous, is it not, in the light of the fact that it has been amended for Iraq, to completely different words?
G-Booth:	I do not think so at all. We come back to the point of whether you think the British public and parliament are so dumb as to realise that there has not been a ceasefire.
Scott:	They certainly cannot have known what the revised wording was.
G-Booth:	Indeed not, but it had been decided not to make a public announcement.
Bax:	It is not completely misleading?
G-Booth:	I do not think so at all.
Bax:	Can I ask you about something? It is a document put out by the

Ministry of Defence. It is about guidance on answering parliamentary questions: "Ministries generally prefer to give parliamentary answers that are factual and straightforward. Answers must be meticulously accurate and worded in clear and unambiguous terms. An error of fact or an answer that misleads the House can be dreadfully embarrassing to the minister."

Do you think that what we have just seen in relation to Lord Glenarthur would have complied with the Ministry of Defence guidelines that we have just been looking at?

G-Booth: Yes.

Bax: In your view, is it factual, straightforward, meticulously accurate and in clear and unambiguous terms?

G-Booth: Yes.

Bax: Can I suggest that, in fact, for various policy reasons, there was a view that the House of Lords should not be told that a more relaxed attitude had been adopted in respect of Iraq?

G-Booth: Yes, it had been agreed that there should be no public announcement ... and that is what happened.

Scott: Why should that have not been announced?

G-Booth: Because there are all sorts of reasons why Iraqis were not very popular, even though they were slightly more popular than the Iranians.

Scott: There would have been domestic upset because of the chemical warfare.

G-Booth: Kurds, chemical warfare and so on, on the one hand; and also that we were trying, rather unsuccessfully I admit, to establish and maintain a relationship with Iran. Of course, one of the factors that would have complicated that would be the Iranians knowing that we were giving the Iraqis a slightly better treatment than the Iranians were getting. There was a myriad of foreign policy reasons tucked away.

Bax: Rather like you were saying that the British public are not idiots; presumably neither are the Iranians ...

G-Booth: That is a very hazardous statement.

Bax: I would not have thought so. If they had just issued a *fatwa* against Salman Rushdie, there is enormous political upset going on about it. Would they not be surprised to discover that maybe the British

Government was favouring to some extent the Iraqi government?

G-Booth: The Iranians are not people who think in very logical terms. They thought the *fatwa* was perfectly justified and we should not have reacted to it at all.

Bax: I am now going to the consideration of the Matrix Churchill export licence applications at the beginning of 1989. What you need is MoD 24, Volume 1. It is page 72A. This document sets out the view of Defence Intelligence. Then the document refers to Hutteen, described as the main ammunition manufacturing plant in Iraq, and to Nassr, capable of producing 500,000 artillery rounds of assorted calibres annually. Defence Intelligence says that if this information had been available originally, the export licences would not have been granted. Do you think it would have been useful to have known about this intelligence?

G-Booth: When I was discussing my travel plans with a doctor in Riyadh before coming, he referred me to something called a retrospectrascope, which you stick into people and it enables you to look backwards. You are drawing me down the track of trying to look backwards in the light of information which we now have and which we did not have at the time. I am reluctant to get drawn too far down that track.

Scott: I think you have a rely on me to make a fair use of your answers. Of course, I understand you are being asked to look back. Can you answer the question?

G-Booth: If we had known then what we know about Iraqi arms procurement programmes now, and if we had known then that Saddam was intending to invade Kuwait, I dare say the decision would have gone differently. Of course, my own view at the time was that it should have gone differently.

Bax: I was going to move ... you'll be delighted to hear we're moving on to another section. We are whizzing through sections now. We are going on to FCO 230, page 48. A Foreign Office official wrote a note saying: "We need to know if Matrix Churchill cheat, by not returning to the UK the equipment on display at the Baghdad Trade Fair." Then it refers to a letter from DTI to FO, Middle East Department, about a request from Matrix Churchill to have made permanent a temporary export licence issued for two lathes, taken to the Baghdad

Trade Fair last year: "The company now has a firm order from Iraq for these lathes, but the end user was known to be the Iraqi missile programme."

Do you think you should have known about it?

G-Booth: If I had not seen it, how do I know if it existed?

Scott: You are seeing it now and you are being asked now whether you think this ought to be brought to your attention.

G-Booth: Again this is not the line of questioning that I think is appropriate, the retrospectrascopic line of questioning.

Bax: I would now like to ask you about a parliamentary question. It is directed to DT1 Ministers, sent to the Foreign Office for clearance. It is MoD 40/3, page 293, 7th November 1989: "To ask the Secretary of State for Trade and Industry what investigations his department has undertaken into the Matrix Churchill company and the possibility that the company is supplying parts to Iraq which could be used in ballistic missile production." The answer given is: "I have no reason to believe that the company has contravened UK export controls." The response is not an answer to the question, is it?

G-Booth: I thought you were going to ask me whether this was an accurate and sufficient answer to the question to which I say, "Yes", in the light of information available at the time.

Bax: Give yourself a chance to think before you say something like that. Look carefully at the question. The answer: "I have no reason to believe that the company has contravened UK export controls", is not an answer to the question, is it?

G-Booth: I think you must put these questions to those more concerned.

Scott: It is not an answer to the question, is it? It is an evasion of the question, and the answer to the question would have been an extremely embarrassing one?

G-Booth: It must eventually be for ministers to decided the terms in which they answer parliamentary questions.

SC V

Enter Mustafa, a Kurd, in Kurdish costume. He sits and talks to the audience.

Mustafa: To be a Kurd is to be at war. Our country and our people live up in one big mass of mountains, but foreigners have drawn lines, have divided the home of the Kurds between Turkey, Syria, Iran, Russia, and Iraq.

Our legend says the Prophet called all the princes of the world to embrace Islam. Oguz Khan, the Prince of Turkestan, sent a Kurd to represent him. When the Prophet saw this giant, with his piercing eyes, and learnt he was a Kurd, Mohammed prayed to God that such a terrifying people will never unite as a single nation.

So far, his prayer has been answered.

Sometimes it seems every nation in the world takes it in turn to try to destroy us. This is maybe lucky – when they stop for a week, we try to destroy each other.

There was a time when we came to realise that whenever Turks fought Persian, Iraqi fought Turk, it was always Kurdish blood that was spilt. We tried to stop fighting each other, and to stop fighting as mercenaries in other people's wars. We began to unite, to behave like a nation.

What we needed was to have some self-government in Iraq. In 1968, Saddam Hussein came to our mountains to promise exactly that. But he was, of course, lying, playing games with us. Then the Shah of Persia, and the CIA, said they would support us if we fought against Saddam. We did. But after three years, no more. They were playing games with us. When Saddam went to war with the Ayatollah, of course, we fought against Saddam again. We were not prepared for what came next. Perhaps we are aggressive, perhaps we trust no one but ourselves, but we have reason. We do not deserve genocide.

From 1985, Saddam tried to wipe us out. In Suleimaniyeh, 300 children were rounded up and tortured, 23 people shot, eight buried alive. We demonstrated: 200 more were shot. In 1987, Saddam sent his cousin, Majid, the one he later sent to govern Kuwait. He was to "Arabize" Kurdistan. Four thousand villages were demolished, half a million Kurds sent to protected camps, many out of our country, whole areas were prohibited, emptied, any person or animal in them was shot, artillery, helicopter gun-ships, jet planes were used against us. Then Majid ordered chemical warfare against us – sulphur mustard gas, and nerve gas, the worst of all. Men, women and children are left with a film over their eyes, out of their nose and mouth comes a horrible slime, their skin peels, it bubbles up.

On 16 March, 1988, Iraqi planes flew over Halabja. They dropped cyanide, mustard, nerve gas. Five thousand people died this horrible death. Nearly all of them were civilians. They died because they were born Kurdish.

Your Government knew about this. Yet your Government allowed your countrymen to help these unspeakable people to make the shells they fired, even the bombs they dropped the chemicals in.

They found out, as we found out, what a friend they had in Saddam after he defeated the Ayatollah's people. He turned on us with even more cruelty. Then he turned on you: he took Kuwait.

And you may think you have won. But he is still there. We know he is still there. And we are still there.

[He goes.]

sc vi
Evidence of William Waldegrave

Bax: Mr Waldegrave, please can I confirm that you were Minister of State at the Foreign Office from July 1988 until November 1990?

Walde: That is right.

Bax: You say in your statement to us that: "It was important that the policy of restraint in defence sales to Iran and Iraq, and indeed other countries in the region, was understood and, if there had been a change in the policy, Parliament should normally be told." Did you think it was important that Parliament, and through it, the public, should know about the guidelines?

Walde: Yes.

Scott: There had been, for very many years, within the Foreign Office internal guidelines as to the manner in which export applications relating to defence equipment should be dealt with, indicating the importance to be given to the human rights record of the country concerned, the military capability of the country and so on. What was the difference that prompted the 1985 guidelines?

Walde: I guess – I am now out of my period – but I think the Iran-Iraq was turning out to be a really major war. It was not just an incursion. Persians and Arabs had been squabbling with each other for 8,000 years, but this was turning out to be a very major war with hundreds of thousands of people killed.

Though it is notable that there is not much debate. There is understandable concern when there is an atrocity on one side or the other. But I think Parliament took the realistic view there was not actually much we could do about it. In terms of, I remember, parliamentary interest, there were far more debates, for example, about Cambodia and there was not much we could do about that either.

Scott: There were quite a number of questions arising out of the atrocities?

Walde: I am not saying there was not interest. When there was some frightful horror, like gassing of Kurds, like a variety of horrors that went back beyond my time, actually in the conduct of the war and in the awful things that happened immediately after the war, there was indeed interest.

Bax: That is one of the reasons why Parliament should be told. If MPs do not agree with the policy, it can be discussed, it can be debated in Parliament?

Walde: I guess so.

Bax: There was a paper prepared by the Foreign Office, the intention was it should go to the Prime Minister. Subject: "Implications of a ceasefire for defence sales to Iran and Iraq."

Scott: This seems to me contemplating relaxing restrictions, letting through things that otherwise would have been refused.

Walde: The Foreign Secretary, Sir Geoffrey Howe, says, "We do not want to have a great shaboozal in public, which is then going to cause a bad signal to Iraq, which has been behaving extremely badly."

Bax: If we go to the Foreign Secretary's comments on defence sales – he says he is "reluctant to put this paper forward". He feels it would look

"very cynical if so soon after expressing outrage over Iraqi treatment of the Kurds, we were to adopt a more flexible approach on arms sales". It is clear the Foreign Secretary did not think the paper should be circulated.

Walde: Right.

Bax: Then there is a letter of 4th November from Mr Clark to you. It says: "Concerned about a large number of licence applications, for exports of dual use equipment for Iraq and Iran." He refers to the harm that is being done to British Industry. Then he says: "I recognise, of course, that whatever is agreed between us will require the Prime Minister's approval."

Walde: Yes.

Bax: All this correspondence between you and Alan Clark is copied to the Prime Minister, is it not? That is presumably because of an earlier comment from her private secretary saying that the Prime Minister wanted to be kept closely in touch with it?

Walde: Sorry, I do not expect you to understand this extremely well, but silence is an important event when you are circulating things to other ministers, and I think that the lack of comfort from on high means something too.

Scott: I am not quite sure what that means. If ministers' correspondence goes to the Prime Minister and there is silence, it does not mean anything at all?

Walde: All that it can be taken as meaning is that the argument will continue.

Scott: The point remains open?

Walde: The point remains open

Bax: Are you saying the new wording covering exports to Iraq was never used, or are you saying, because it never went to the Foreign Secretary and the Prime Minister and it was not announced, the guidelines were never changed?

Walde: It is perfectly clear the guidelines were never changed.

Scott: There is a problem about this, which has been keeping me awake at night. The proposition that seems to come from your paper to the inquiry is that the guidelines were announced in 1985. The guidelines could not be changed without the proposal going to senior ministers, the Prime Minister, and being announced in Parliament. None of

	these things ever happened. Ergo, the guidelines were never changed.
Walde:	To accept that is the only argument, you have to believe that Whitehall is basically honest, which I do believe.
Bax:	Surely the most important thing is what they are doing?
Walde:	Absolutely.
Bax:	The policy you are operating is not what you say, it is what you do.
Walde:	We kept saying to each other, "You cannot agree these revised guidelines until they have gone to Number 10 and goodness knows what."
Bax:	What happens next is the *fatwa* on 14th February 1989.
Scott:	There was a tilt in favour of Iraq as a result of the *fatwa*.
Walde:	There was, indeed, but not derived from any change in British policy about the neutrality that we had in the Iran-Iraq conflict.
Scott:	That conflict, of course, at this stage being at an end?
Walde:	Being at an end, but still fragile. I do not know whether I can just say a word about the extraordinary capacity of people in the Middle East to believe peculiar things about Britain. There is a story which I believe is true that the Iranians say that if you lift up the beard of the Ayatollah, you find "Made in England" written underneath because we had clearly put the Ayatollah there because we wanted to get rid of the Shah, because the Shah was too pro-America. It is quite difficult to redress that kind of public opinion.
Scott:	It is something you should try?
Walde:	I think the Foreign Office came to be conclusion it was doomed sometimes.
Bax:	You said that, after the *fatwa*, I think you said no one referred to the revised wording of the guidelines again.
Walde:	You have clearly shown me from the documents that this is wrong. If you, Sir Richard, have been worrying about this at night, you can imagine that I have, because it is jolly important to me, and I have come to the conclusion that we did not do wrong.
Bax:	There was a Ministry of Defence paper form Mr Barrett saying: "Mr Waldegrave is content for us to implement a more liberal policy on defence sales without any public announcement on the subject."
Walde:	It is not the most brilliantly drafted note.

Bax: It fits very nicely. I do not understand any problems with it.

Walde: The letter should have said something like: "Mr Waldegrave is content for us to implement the more liberal *interpretation* of the *existing* guidelines."

Scott: Why can you not tell Parliament what [formula] is being used [even] on a trial basis?

Walde: We did not want to stir up a hornet's nest. I will say again, when Sir Richard said he had sleepless nights worrying about this and I subsequently said I had sleepless nights too. After the collapse of the Matrix Churchill trial and all this comes right to the fore. I looked at this and I remember talking to Sir Robin Butler, the Cabinet Secretary, about it at the time saying I do not remember changing the guidelines. Into the papers we dived and find actually that is not what happened.

Bax: You dive into the papers and you find it is not what happened. We have dived into the papers and we have seen that in practice that *is* what happened. I was now going to move on to what was said publicly. Lord Glenarthur says, "We should continue to scrutinise rigorously all applications for export licences for the supply of defence equipment to Iraq and Iran."

Scott: Why is not the right answer to say there is the flexible interpretation, the flexible policy, call it what you like, in relation to Iraq?

Walde: Because it was judged that there were overriding reasons for giving misleading information about tilts to one side or another, to put British citizens there at risk, and all the rest of it.

Scott: It is not a very healthy feature of a mature democracy that serious issues of this sort can be debated.

Walde: But it is also, Sir Richard, a definition of what a mature democracy means. I think, that it knows from time to time, in relation to foreign affairs, it is going to be necessary not for everything to be said in detail. There is in this country a certain ambivalence. We are, after France, the free world's second trader in arms-related goods. People want the jobs they do not always want to think about. Whenever Mrs Thatcher or Mr Major comes back, having batted for Britain and won a great deal, everyone says, "Hooray!" They are heroes on the front page.

Sc vii

Enter a distinguished North American economist: KENNETH GALBRAITH.
He reads from his own book to the audience.

Galbraith: Because it is so visible, there has been some error of emphasis in identifying the true locus of the military power. In the seemingly sophisticated tradition that associates power with industrial enterprise – in reality, a holdover of Marxist thought and the dominant critical attitudes of that last century – military power is extensively assumed to be associated with the defence industries. The military industrialists are the deus ex-machina; they both procure and profit from the military budget. There is no doubt that the power thus exercised is great: the submission of scientists, engineers, executives is great: the submission of scientists, engineers, executives, workers, and the defence-dependent communities is won thereby. Of this power legislators are made acutely conscious, and campaign contributions from the corporations involved add to their awareness. But the defence industries are only an extension of a larger structure, the heart of which lies in the autonomous processes of government.

sc viii
Evidence of Alan Barrett

Bax: Mr Barrett, you were in post at the Defence Export Services Secretariat from June 1987 to September 1990. A Treasury official reported that the Ministry of Defence's defence export services organisation was gung-ho to support sales of military equipment to Iraq and almost anywhere.

Barr: I think that is totally unjustified.

Bax: Also, Colonel Glazebrook of the Ministry of Defence had written to you commenting that Alan Clark was "gung-ho for defence sales!" You agree you may have said something that implied that meaning, is that right?

Barr: Yes, I do not dispute that at all. I cannot remember using those precise words. what does "gung-ho" mean?

Scott:	I would take it as meaning very, very enthusiastic – perhaps double the "verys" – very, very, enthusiastic?
Barr:	Yes, very enthusiastic.
Bax:	What I would like to do now is to come to your briefing for the ministerial meeting of 23rd December, 1988: "The Prime Minister agreed that, in order to protect the intelligence source, the licences already granted should not be revoked." The point is picked up again at Page 45. "More disturbing intelligence coming to light. Press for a separate submission to go to the Prime Minister, as she was involved last time." At that time, you clearly thought the Prime Minister had been involved in the initial consideration of the Matrix Churchill lathes?
Barr:	That is what I wrote at that time, yes.
	I would like, at this stage, to read what I have actually written in my present submission to you: "I cannot now find any papers to corroborate the statement in the aide memoire I drafted then. I can only assume now that I was mistaken."
Bax:	In the 1988 aide memoire, you have referred to the Prime Minister twice in one paragraph. This is no casual dropping of the name in. I cannot imagine you would casually drop the Prime Minister's name in. It seems to me that would have been a rather peculiar thing to do?
Barr:	I certainly did not make it up.

sc ix
Evidence of Alan Clark (1)

Scott:	Mr Clark, thank you very much for coming here today, and thank you for your extremely helpful statement that you provided us with. Presiley Baxendale on my left asks most of the questions, but I may ask a few myself arising out of it.
Bax:	Mr Clark, we asked you to provide a general statement describing your role as a minister at the Department of Trade and Industry and the Ministry of Defence. You say: "My general understanding, coloured possibly by some personal prejudice, is that it was my duty to promote, facilitate and give impetus to British exports and the

industries from which they emanated."

Can I then move on the guidelines? You compare them to a Cheshire Cat, and then you go on to say: "They were high-sounding, combining, it seemed, both moral and practical considerations, and yet imprecise enough to be overridden in exceptional circumstances."

Clark: Yes. I would argue they illustrate the – and this is the kind of thing you could say about them – the constructive tension between positivism and ambiguity, a doctoral thesis of Professor Ayer.

The whole of guideline 3 is magnificent – "We should not in future sanction any new orders which, in our view, would significantly enhance the capability of either side to prolong or exacerbate the conflict." It is a brilliant piece of drafting, because it is far form being restrictive. It is open to argument in respect of practically every one of its elements. I regarded the guidelines as being so imprecise and so obviously drafted with the objective of flexibility in either direction - elasticity, shall I say - as to make them fair game. It denies the ordinary meaning of the English language to say that the guidelines were not changed.

Bax: You say [in your statement]: "It must be understood that the guidelines were an extremely useful adjunct to foreign policy, offering a form of words elusive of definition. There was an understandable reluctance in Whitehall to stir up Parliament."

Clark: Yes. The House of Commons is a very volatile place and you get rows and scenes and "ooh-err" on tape, and ministers have an aversion to this unless they are exhibitionists and like participating.

Can I just add a small postscript? You must not ever lie to the House of Commons. If you do lie, what I find is, normally, your resignation should follow immediately.

Bax: You say, "It is a matter of record" that guidelines 3 remained, I am not quite sure what you are saying.

Clark: One is back now to the slightly Alice in Wonderland suggestion, where I remember my former colleague, Mr Waldegrave, said, "Because something was not announced, it had not happened." He was arguing that because it had not been announced, it could not have happened, a sort of Berkeleyan philosophy.

Bax: Can I go to your statement. You say: "The Prime Minister most certainly was informed of the new approach and indeed included it in her parliamentary answer to Harry Cohen MP."

Clark: She must have had something, because otherwise we would not have tagged onto the answer: "'and in the light of developments in the peace negotiations with Iran.' That indicates a loosening, you see, that was the agreed form of words. The trail was laid.

SC X
Evidence of Lady Thatcher

Bax: Lady Thatcher, I should like to start with the establishment of the guidelines in December 1984 ... The document is Lord Howe's minute to you of 4th December, 1984.

Thatch: I have it.

Bax: Some of the witnesses we have had have described these guidelines as a framework, within which they had to work, or as a hurdle which exporters had to cross in addition to other existing constraints on exports. Does that fit in with how you saw the guidelines?

Thatch: They are exactly what they say, guidelines, they are not law. They are guidelines.

Bax: Did they have to be followed?

Thatch: I beg your pardon?

Bax: Did they have to be followed?

Thatch: Of course they have to be followed, but they are not strict law. That is why they are guidelines and not law and, of course, they have to be applied according to the relevant circumstances.

Bax: They are expected to be followed?

Thatch: Of course, they need to be followed. They need to be followed for what they are, guidelines.

Bax: The Ministry of Defence Working Group assesses ... and decides that the equipment would significantly enhance the capability of either Iran or Iraq to wage war. In those circumstances, can the equipment be granted a licence for other factors, for example, encouraging exports?

Thatch: We would not, I think – I say, "*We* would not" – I was not involved in the actual application of these guidelines. I was involved in the policy ... The precise question was, Miss Baxendale? I am sorry, you are more familiar with this. I have seen so much paper that I have never seen before. I was concerned with the policy, not with the administration.

Bax: What I was asking you about was, if you have the Ministry of Defence Working Group saying, "This equipment will significantly enhance the capability of either side", can other factors, such as employment in the United Kingdom override guideline 3?

Thatch: I do not believe you would ignore the guidelines solely for exports.

Bax: If there was going to be exceptional overriding, would you expect that to go up to ministers and maybe the Cabinet and perhaps even to yourself?

Thatch   If there was an exceptional case. And the only one that came to me that I recall was the question of the export of the Hawk trainer, which was a big order, a big issue. The big things would come up ... Only one came up, as I recall or have been able to identify in that way. That was the possibility of supplying the Hawk trainer to Iraq.

Bax: If you go to page 49, this is a memo from the Secretary of State for Defence.

Thatch: I think it is to the Foreign Secretary. I do not think I saw this document at the time. It has not got my initials on it anywhere.

Bax: Would it not go to you if it says: "I am sending copies to other members of the Cabinet's Overseas and Defence Committee, then the Cabinet Secretary"?

Thatch: Miss Baxendale, if I had seen every copy of every minute that was sent in Government, I would have been in a snowstorm.

Bax: If we could go to "Questions of Procedures for Ministers". I think it is attached to the letter we sent you yesterday. I am sure you know the document anyway.

Thatch: All ministers are very familiar with their accountability to Parliament.

Bax: I would like you to look at the Cabinet Secretary's minute. It starts: "The Government believes that Ministers are well aware of the principles that should govern their duties and responsibilities in relation to Parliament and in relation to civil servants. They include the duty to give Parliament and the public as full information as

	possible about the policy decisions and actions of the Government and not to deceive or mislead Parliament or the public." Yes?
Thatch:	Indeed. I would not quarrel with a word of that.
Bax:	I was presuming that would be the basis on which you and your Government, the Ministers, were working?
Thatch:	Yes, indeed, but the advice to me, and I think there is a document about it, is it is quite unusual to reveal guidelines.
Bax:	If we go to the comments of officials concerned at the time the original guidelines were published.
Thatch:	Is there more paper? I have never seen so much paper.
Bax:	That is only part of it. There is much more.
Thatch:	The majority of it I have never seen as Prime Minister. I find a lot very interesting now that I never knew before.
Bax:	Can we go to another bundle? If we go to FCO, 13/1 Page 29. This is a document of the 4th July, 1986 written in the context of the licensing of small boats.
Thatch:	Miss Baxendale, I did not see this document at the time. I have no knowledge of it. It is the comment of an official to a minister on how the policy should be administered. I was concerned with the policy. The administration was by officials under another cabinet minister. I could not possibly have got involved in these things. I could never have done my job as Prime Minister on policy if I got involved in all of these things.
Scott:	The purpose of putting some of these notes and minutes to you is because you were head of the administration at the time. You have an almost unparalleled experience in government. I do not think Miss Baxendale has actually asked the question. Could we leave her to ask it, and then see whether you would be able to help with an answer to it?
Bax:	I was going to ask you about a comment from a senior official in the Foreign Office. He says, "The guidelines should be regarded primarily as a set of criteria for use in defending against public and parliamentary criticism, whatever decision we take on grounds of commercial and political interest." So you take the decision on the basis of commercial and political interest, and you use the guidelines as a defence against public and parliamentary criticism?

Thatch:	Does your export policy override the guidelines? The answer is no, it does not.
Bax:	I would like to move on to 1988/89. It is page 6 of the questionnaire. Where we are now is there has been the Iranian acceptance of the UN Security Council Resolution, and the Foreign Secretary minuted you with this paper, "The Economic Consequences of Peace in the Gulf". It refers to relaxing control.
	Then your advisor, Mr Powell's response to the Foreign Office: "The general strategy will obviously require decision on a number of difficult and sensitive issues, such as the guidelines for defence sales to Iran and Iraq. The Prime Minister will wish to be kept very closely in touch at every stage and consulted on all relevant decisions."
Thatch:	Policy changes, I think, would have to come to me. It seems to me abundantly clear that, when ministers proposed this change, they did not regard it as a change of policy, but a change of circumstance. That would explain why certainly it may well be that I was just told there had been a change without a different policy.
Scott:	What is your view? Plainly, there was a change in circumstance. Plainly, the original guidelines 3 was formulated to deal with the then continuing war, so there was a change in circumstance and a new formulation was needed. Is this the sort of thing you would have expected to have been referred to you?
Thatch:	If they regarded this as a change in policy, yes, it should have come to me. It may have been mentioned to me by one of my secretaries. I have no recollection if it was.
Bax:	There is a letter from Mr Clark to the two other ministers, suggesting there should be a revision to the guidelines.
Scott:	This is a proposal for a change of policy. Would that not come to you?
Thatch:	I just cannot keep tabs on all this. It just has to be delegated.
Bax:	10th January, 1989. Mr Clark to Mr. Waldegrave: "The recent telegram from Washington implies their acceptance of the proposed revision ... With so many conflicting interests, any change would be likely to upset someone. We would, therefore, favour the implementation of a more liberal policy, without any public announcement."

Thatch: These were not submitted to me formally. Whether they were just mentioned to me, I have no recollection.

Bax: Mr Waldegrave was seeing this as implementing a more liberal policy?

Thatch: On a trial basis. And I do not like the use of the word "liberal".

Scott: Lady Thatcher, what I do think you can help me with is giving me an indication as we go through these letters, of whether you think the point had arrived at which you ought to have been informed.

Thatch: If there is a material change in policy, I would have preferred to have been informed. And if I am informed, I must be informed in a letter to me. Of course it would have been easier if I had been informed of any change. I assume that the reason that they did not inform me was that they thought there was not a change of policy, but a change of circumstances to which the policy applied.

Scott: References to a more liberal policy does not fit easily with the concept of there being no change in substance.

Thatch: "Liberal" is not a word I would have adopted.

Bax: I would like to go to an answer that you gave to a parliamentary question from Harry Cohen on 21st April, 1989. "To ask the Prime Minister whether Her Majesty's Government propose to change their current policy of prohibiting the export to Iraq of any weapon which could enhance its offensive capability or will agree to granting export licences for weaponry to Iraq to accommodate the United Kingdom exhibitors at the Baghdad fair and if she will make a statement'.
Your reply was: "The Government have not changed their policy on defence sales to Iraq." Do you think this answer is correct?

Thatch: It is a mixed question, is it not?

Scott: It is a mixed answer.

Thatch: Yes, indeed. It was a mixed question and it may require a mixed answer.

Scott: It is the shift from "weapons" in the question, to "defence sales" in the answer. That is the problem.

Thatch: It would, I am afraid my Lord, come back to the same point we have been concerned about for quite a long time – was it a change of policy, to which my advisers would say no. It was a change in circumstance.

Bax: Do you think that the fact that a different wording [in the guidelines] is being used should have been announced to Parliament?

Thatch: They did not think it was a change of substance.

Bax: What I do not understand is why you say ministers thought that it should not be announced because it was just a technical matter, because the documents that we have looked at show they thought it should not be announced because it was going to cause trouble.

Scott: It seems to come across that, if a policy of a more relaxed approach to Iraq had been publicly announced, there would have been some degree of public outcry against it because of revulsion at what Iraq was doing to the Kurds. Is that a matter which could properly play any part in a decision whether or not to make an announcement to Parliament?

Thatch: Anything to do with the gassing of the Kurds – as you see what happened when the Hawk decision came up – what decided us not to do it, was we simple could not supply *that* kind of weapon, the Hawk trainer, to a government that did the gassing of the Kurds.

Bax: What I would like to do, Lady Thatcher, is to move on to Matrix Churchill. Mr Barrett, an official in the Defence Export Services Secretariat, is dealing with specific cases: "Intelligence sources indicated that the lathes were to be used for making shells and missiles. The Prime Minister agreed that, in order to protect the intelligence source, the licences already should not be revoked."
Do you have any idea at all why Mr Barrett should have thought you were involved?

Thatch: No. I understand that he retracted afterwards.

Scott: He did not quite. He could not recall why he had thought you were involved, but he just thought there might have been a reason.

Thatch: I have no recollection, which is why I asked for minutes to see if there was something which I had not recalled.

Bax: I wanted to ask you briefly about the use of diversionary routes for to Iraq. We know that after the invasion of Kuwait, you were personally involved in discussions with the King of Jordan, but I want to ask you about the period before the invasion of Kuwait and the period before sanctions.

Thatch: When I saw the king there were many matters to discuss with him, the one being that he appeared to be on the side of Iraq, which was horrific. Jordan always had a destabilising danger. I had visited PLO camps in Jordan. There was a possibility that this rather remarkable country and this very, very courageous king, who never flinched from personal danger, might be destabilised. That would not have done British interests any good at all. To destabilise Jordan would have been a very, very serious matter indeed. So we took the course of doing as much as we could and seeking what for the king was unusual to give a personal assurance.

I hope, therefore, that I have explained what was in our minds. Life is a question of alternatives. Possibly with the alternatives that you face, neither of them are very palatable.

Scott: I am very grateful to you for coming. There will be a transcript prepared of everything that has been said in the course of today, which we will supply to you as soon as we can, and, if you have time to read it, and if it occurs to you that there is anything that you wish you could add or that you would wish to correct, then we would be very grateful if you would do that.

Thatch: I fear there will be much grammar to be corrected.

Scott: Never mind grammar, that is the least of the problems.

Act II

sc i
Enter Paul Henderson

Hend: Sometimes, on very rare occasions, I think about myself, and I suppose on one or two occasions, I don't quite know what to feel about myself, but really (*laughs*) can a salesman afford to gaze at his navel, does the Pope shit in the woods? As MD of Matrix Churchill I had a job to do. If we went under, who was to blame? Paul Henderson was to blame. I can't afford the luxury of a conscience. Look, I inhabit a wicked, sinful and highly competitive world, and I deal on a daily basis with hard, hard men, and I will do whatever I can to succeed.

That doesn't mean I'm immoral, or do anything immoral. I do what I do, I sell what I sell for excellent reasons. I'm not one of your public school, Oxbridge types creeping into business not knowing anything about the work, the people on the shop floor, the engineering, how it all comes about. I went in at 15, did my apprenticeship, did my engineering, my City and Guilds. I worked the lathes, and I know the people on the shopfloor – I was one of them.

And I've seen what happens to those people when a plant closes. I've seen too much of that in Coventry! I've seen what can happen – did happen – at Alfred Herbert's to the livelihood of hundreds of skilled, dedicated toolmakers. That's why I go all over the world to get orders for our machine tools, and why I'll sell them to whoever wants to buy them even if they are going to use them to make armaments, and why when the moment came, I went along with the Iraqis buying into Matrix, to stop some competitor buying us in order to close us down.

Sentimental? Not exactly. As I say, you simply don't think too hard about the morality of it all, you're in business, and business is business, competition is competition, and success is success. And if I succeed, I expect a reward – a personal reward of course, but above all, the reward of seeing my company busy, growing and profitable. There's no way I will apologise for that. After the mess of the Seventies, that's what the Eighties was all about. The self-interest of the managers harnessed to bring about the well-being of the workforce. That's what Thatcher was all about: real jobs, they called them.

If there had to be rules to their "game" of selling what I was selling, if there had to be prohibitions on who I could sell to, what I could sell, I certainly wasn't going to make them up: it's hard enough beating off the French, the Germans and the Japanese without tying one hand behind your back. If there was to be regulation, that was the Government's job, not mine.

Fortunately, they didn't want to close Matrix Churchill down any more than I did. And if ancient regulations inhibited my chances against the French, then as Lord Nelson said, putting his blind eye to a telescope, I see no Iraqi arms factories. This Government are all business men – they understand business – business is business.

Besides, they owed me a one. For years I'd been travelling behind the Iron Curtain, gaining the confidence, the friendship of the arms makers. And for years, I'd been filling in our Secret Intelligence Service on exactly where I'd been and what I'd seen. Risky, but interesting.

Then, when it came to my dealings with Iraq in the Eighties, they came back to me, "Spy for us." Saddam Hussein has the most efficient and ruthless counter-intelligence people in the world. I was supposed to go into Baghdad, off into arms plants, highly-sensitive Iraqi military installations, and spy for Britain, the hated imperialist power. And I did.

Not out of self-interest, nor for reward, certainly not. I happen to believe in my country.

Sentimental? Yes, but I did my bit. For Britain. I reported every single thing I saw, and did. They knew exactly what I was doing. It was a touch dicey at times. But I did it. What thanks did I get? A VC? I'm

afraid not. They humiliated me. They arrested me, put me behind
bars like a common criminal.

Of course the trial collapsed. But by then, my business was ruined, my
plant closed down, and 600 hundred more jobs went in Coventry –
good jobs, good people.

What was wrong was that they let this prosecution go ahead. And
when it did, they tried to say they knew nothing about it, that it all
came as a complete shock to them and what a wicked person I was to
give comfort to the enemy.

I'm going back into business now. Those 600 engineers aren't. That's
what annoys me. And my pride, of course.

sc ii
Evidence of Alan Clark (2)

Bax: Mr Clark, I would like to go now to the note of your meeting with the
Machine Tools Technologies Association in January 1988. "Choosing
his words carefully and noting that the Iraqis would be using the
current orders for general engineering purposes, Mr Clark stressed it
was important for the UK companies to agree to a specification with
the customer, in advance, which highlighted the peaceful – i.e. non-
military – use to which the machine tools would be put."

Bax: Yes.

Bax: The members from the Machine Tools Technologies Association
knew there was a concern that the machine tools are going to be used
for military purposes?

Clark: Yes.

Scott: You refer to "general engineering" purposes. But given that the
meeting had been called because of a known concern that the actual
use was going to be military, does not the use of that phrase carry the
implication that, provided the "general engineering" heading can be
relied on, the Government will not mind about the exports?

Clark: Yes, that was the impression I wanted to give, certainly. If you like, I
had to indulge in a fiction, and invite them to participate in a fiction.

Bax: The way of communicating that you were using at the time was you were entering into a fiction, and you were choosing your words carefully, you were deliberately using neutral words, which could encompass both military manufacture and civil manufacture?

Clark: Yes.

Bax: I think now we ought to look at your witness statement for the prosecution at the trial. "At the same meeting I was advised that the machine tools were intended for general engineering purposes." Is that right?

Clark: There was an implied invitation to them to participate in a fiction.

Bax: Were you concerned, though, when you were signing this witness statement for the trial that it did not actually set out what happened at the meeting?

Clark: It set out what happened at the meeting. It omits my knowledge.

Bax: That is right. It omits government knowledge, does it not?

Clark: Yes. I suppose I should have insisted that I – I do not know what …

Bax: You met officers from Customs and Excise. You say, "Their principle objective seemed to be to persuade me that the defendants had been grossly misleading in the description which they had tendered [in the licence application]."

Was there any in-depth discussion or any discussion at all with you about evidential matters that you might know about, rather than officials giving their reasons why they wanted to run the prosecution?

Clark: No. The whole thing was so dotty really. I do not see why it should be followed by this whole paraphernalia of a prosecution, unless real damage had taken place over a long period. If it did, it seems to me the prime responsibility for that lies with those charged with the duty of scrutinising and inspecting machines.

Bax: Did Customs and Excise tell you that it was thought likely that the defence wold be that the Government had known at the time that the licences were issued that the likely use.

Clark: No.

Scott: The proposition is that you, as the relevant minister, were being misled, because you thought these things were going to be used for civil application and, hey presto – they are not, they are being used for military purposes. The minister was deceived, so were all his officials deceived.

Clark: There may be an element of sleight of hand in it, I suppose. The trouble about this situation is, I am defending a position, defending conduct, which I am satisfied is defensible, but because the sails are right over and almost touching the water at times, if you understand the analogy, I have to choose my words carefully.

My attitude, I am satisfied can be defended, but I recognise that it has involved periodically a certain amount of dissimilation.

Bax: If we look at page 6 of your reply to our questionnaire. You say, "I was still doubtful about the wisdom of prosecuting them" – and that was without, at the time, knowing Mr Henderson was an intelligence source – "and I suppose this irritation or scepticism may have shown".

Clark: Yes, but the Customs and Excise investigator has not recorded that. He has not recorded my scepticism.

Scott: Is it possible that you made your opinion clear, that the prosecution was not one which you thought was very sensible?

Clark: Not very sensible, yes, certainly.

Bax: I would like to go to the trial itself. Can we go to page 82 of the transcript of your evidence. At page 82, between D and E, Mr Robertson, counsel for Mr Henderson, puts to you: "The writer of the minute of the meeting of the Machine Tools Technologies Association is attributing to you a statement that the Iraqis will be using the current order for general engineering purpose. That statement cannot be correct to your knowledge."

Your reply: "Well, it is our old friend, being economical, is it not?"

Clark: Because you are not extending it into the other potential.

Bax: That is what you then referred to, in the next bit of evidence?

Clark: Yes. All I did not say was "and for making munitions".

Bax: Yes, exactly.

Bax: Then it is suggested to you by the defence: "So the signal you are sending to these people is: 'I am a Minister. I will help you through these orders and follow-ups through the rather loose guidelines and the rather Byzantine ways of Whitehall. Help me by keeping your mouth firmly shut about military use.'"

Your answer: "That is too imaginative an interpretation. I think it was more at arm's length than that. I do not think I said 'nothing military'."

The defence's question: "They got it by implication"?
Your answer: "Yes, 'by implication' is different. By implication they got it."
That sound as though you were accepting that the implication, from what you said, that the exporters would receive was: "Do not say anything about military use"?

Clark: Yes.

Scott: Mr Clark, that finishes all the questions we wanted to ask you.

Clark: Sir Richard, thank you very much, and I have enjoyed it and found it enlightening.

Sc iii

Enter noisily, through the audience a PALESTINIAN ARAB. He is angry.

Siddiqi: Long life to Gamal abd al-Nasir. Long life to Saddam Hussein. My name is Abdul Siddiqi. I am an Arab. My home is in Palestine. In Saffed, what the Israelis call Zfat. My beautiful house is still there, looking out from Saffed to the peaceful mountains of Lebanon. But I live in a camp, with ten thousand others, outside Beirut. In my beautiful house, the son of a bank manager from Hendon. If I had a knife I would kill him, or any Israeli, or you.

In Arabic, we do not use words from the West. But there are four foreign words we have not avoided: a car – tumubil; telephones – tilifun; television – tilivisiun; and democracy – demokratiyyah. We embrace: cars, telephones, television. Democracy we spit on. What does it mean? America. Germans. Japanese. They say – democracy needs a free market with open borders; and who has the capital to dominate these free markets? America. Germans. Japanese. In fact we do not mind buying their cars, their computers, their technology. It is everything else that comes with them that we hate: American imperialism, German efficiency, Japanese brain-washing of their workers. Look at eastern Europe. Look at yourselves.

We live in our world. There are many things wrong with the Arab way of doing things, but it is our way, and it is for us to make it better. We will not sell it to the imperialist for a taste of democracy, because

it is precisely what real democracy stands for – the right to control our
own destiny – that imperialist democracy takes away. In the name of
a Christianity you did not practice, you tried to take my Palestine, for
centuries we fought you. Now in the name of a democracy that you
do not practise, you are trying to conquer the Arabs again, we will
fight you.

Why so many fundamentalists? Because so many Arabs are afraid.
Afraid to lose our world, and to be swallowed up into your world.
And how can we fight you? My uncles and my grandmother hijacked
aeroplanes, shot Israeli schoolchildren, drove you English out of Iran,
Iraq, Jordan, Egypt, Libya, the French out of Algeria, the Lebanon.
They got rid of King Farouk, the Shah, all the crooked, cruel men
you kept in power to look after your interests. We found ways to win
those fights. Nasser was our hero. Long life Gamal abd al-Nasir.

But still you tell us we are weak, we cannot win, you have airplanes,
tanks, rockets, you have nuclear bombs to wipe us out. America has
everything, of this and more, bombs that can find a house, find a
chimney pot, do down the chimney and explode in the fireplace!
How can we hold up our heads, how can we even talk to you at the
same table, without these things? Israel is our enemy, the Israelis took
my house, my country, by force, they keep them because they have
these terrible things, and we don't.

Gadaffi in Libya can't get them. Mubarak in Egypt is becoming the
new Farouk, he doesn't need them. Hussein in Jordan, no way. No,
my friends, it is Saddam Hussein in Iraq who has shown the Arabs
what to do now, today. He bought your technology, with money from
oil: from France, from Germany, from Austria, from England. He
even bought banks to finance it all, he bought the people, he bought
Matrix Churchill in Coventry.

Who is our hero? Saddam.

You may say, "Ah, but he is cruel." To be a leader, one must be cruel,
ruthless, even criminal. We Arabs have always suffered. There was a
time when mothers had to bury their girl-children alive, so they would
not have to suffer. But that is not the point. The Kurds are not the
point. Chemical warfare is not the point. The point is for an Arab to
have power in the world – the point above all is what he will do with

his power. Will he make himself rich, with places of gold – or will he
fight for his brother Arabs, stand against the evil forces of imperialist
democracy, and give us our own lives, and our own voice in the world?
That is what Saddam has done. That is why when he defied the
imperial powers and took back Kuwait, taken from Iraq by the trick
of a British diplomat, there was rejoicing all over the Arab world.
That is why when he fired Scud missiles into Tel Aviv, we Palestinians
rejoiced because we had at last an ally with power to attack Israel. In
our minds we can see what you can see, but in our spirits we need
Saddam. I know you don't listen to your spirit very much in England,
so there we are different. Saddam is what our spirit is looking for.
Long live Gamal abd al-Nasir.
Long life to Saddam Hussein.
[He goes.]

sc iv
Evidence of Tony Steadman

Bax: Mr Steadman, you drafted briefing papers before the meeting on the
20th January, 1988 of the Machine Tools Technologies Association
with Alan Clark, who supported sales of machine tools to Iraq?

Stead: Yes.

Bax: You see on the first page of the association's record of the meeting, it
is quite hard to read, but you see in the middle of it: "There was no
doubt, by persons attending this meeting, that we were being advised
to cloud the truth." Did you see that reference?

Stead: Yes, I would have done.

Bax: Then, you say: "Difficulty for DTI witnesses if he was asked at the
trial when we first knew the exports could be for arms manufacture.
Then there was an accusation that the Department of Trade and
Industry encouraged the company to falsify end use."

Stead: Yes.

Bax: Then paragraph 8 reads: "In December 1988, MoD, DTI, and FO
ministers met to agree a revised but unpublished interpretation to the
Iran/Iraq guidelines."

Stead: Yes.

Bax: I would like now to go to your prosecution witness statement for the trial. I want to look at the deletions. That sentence: "This was a result of information received. There was, however, no hard evidence as far as I am aware" – has been crossed out.

Stead: Yes.

Bax: Were you concerned that after the deletion, it now did not refer to the knowledge or the information that the Government had received?

Stead: I assumed there was good reason why that had to be deleted.

Bax: Were you not concerned that it did not accurately reflect what had occurred?

Stead: I do not think I was concerned, because I had been advised that it should be deleted. So there must have been good reason for that.

Bax: At the time, did you read it and think, "This is not representing the truth"?

Stead: It is not that it was untrue, but it did not go as far as obviously the previous witness statement had.

Bax: It is more than that, is it not? You knew those licences were going to make munitions?

Stead: Yes.

Scott::   To say: "We accepted their assurances" is more than not accurate. It is just not true.

Stead: Yes.

Scott: Is that not right?

Stead: Yes.

Scott: Why did you let it stand like this?

Stead: I had legal advice, and I assumed that the legal advice was correct.

Scott: It is you who has to sign things to swear that it is true.

Bax: I am looking at your witness statement for the trial. We had noted that your references to briefing ministers have also gone.

Stead: Yes.

Bax: I am now looking at page 16 of your witness statement. You knew, did you not, that the defendants were likely to run a defence that the Government knew?

Stead: Yes.

Bax: And were encouraging them?

Stead:	Yes.
Bax:	From what you have told us and what you have written, you could see that the company could have drawn the wrong conclusions from the Machine Tools Technologies Association meeting with Alan Clark?
Stead:	They could have done, yes.
Bax:	You could see their point? Is that a good way of putting it?
Stead:	It was a point of view.
Scott:	I think you said it was a "reasonable" point of view?
Stead:	It was a reasonable point of view, yes.
Bax:	There is no suggestion of anything like that in your witness statement, is there?
Stead:	No.
Bax:	There is no reference to intelligence information, is there?
Stead:	No.
Bax:	Did it worry you a bit that things were being taken in and out of your witness statement at will?
Stead:	I assumed that people were acting in good faith.

SC V
Evidence of Andrew Leithead

Scott:	Mr Leithead, thank you very much for coming this morning, and thank you for your statements. You have obviously very carefully prepared them. Most of the questions Miss Baxendale will be asking. I may be asking some myself.
Bax:	I am going to TSD27, TS1, page 3. Mr Steadman's witness statement for the trial. Mr Steadman was saying: "I recall there was concern by ourselves and departments involved in advising on licence applications as to whether these machine tools might actually be used by the Iraqis for military production." Then he had written: "There was no evidence as far as I am aware to support these suspicions." You had crossed that out?
Leit:	Yes.
Bax:	Why did you suggest that deletion?
Leit:	It did not seem a sensible course – there must have been some

evidence, if there were some suspicions. You know, it is precisely the sort of thing a witness gets caught out on when being cross-examined in a witness box.

Bax: Then on page 12, where he said: "The background briefing that I gave to the minister was on the basis that, despite our concerns, these machine tools could have dual-use civil/military." Right?

Leit: Yes.

Bax: You have crossed out both these bits.

Leit: Yes.

Bax: Then: "I was aware of suspicions; but in the face of assurances from Matrix Churchill, we relied on statements in the licence applications." Do you think, looking back at it, that it might have been sensible to discover what Mr Steadman could say about what he was relying on in the assurances he had had?

Leit: I am sorry. I have the greatest difficulty remembering what happened.

Scott: The point is a broad one. It is what are the officials doing, including the lawyers of whom you were one, in drafting what Mr Steadman is going to say in his witness statement? What business have officials got to be drafting something like that?

Leit: Well, it is merely suggesting to Mr Steadman what the correct position would be.

Scott: Suggesting what?

Leit: Suggesting to Mr Steadman what the correct position would be.

Scott: His evidence in a criminal case, or perhaps a civil case too for that matter, is evidence as to the truth as known by the witnesses, is it not?

Leit: Yes.

Bax: Do you remember, there would be two strands of defence?

Leit: Yes.

Bax: Firstly, that the DTI turned a blind eye to the military possibilities and, secondly, that since Mr Henderson of Matrix Churchill had been involved with the security services, the Government were in any event aware of the full facts?

Leit: Yes.

Bax: You know that those were possible or likely defences. Did you still consider that you were going to suggest that all the documents were irrelevant? I am going to the Public Interest Immunity certificate.

Leit:	When one is dealing with PII claims, one tends to take a rather generous sort of view of the –
Scott:	Take what sort of view?
Leit:	A generous view.
Scott:	Generous to whom?
Leit:	Generous to the government departments. Anything that involves advice to ministers is considered to be within that class. That is why PII tends to work.
Scott:	The way Government tends to work PII?
Leit:	Yes, that is right.
Scott:	Who regards it as damaging to the public interest that any of this decision-making process should be exposed? Who?
Leit:	I think it is a general view of people who deal with this subject.
Scott:	I did not hear, I am sorry.
Leit:	It is a general view of people who deal with this subject.
Bax:	The Government?
Leit:	Yes.
Bax:	Not necessarily the ministers concerned?
Leit:	No.
Bax:	It is not the minister's view, is it? We are going to come to one case where it certainly was not the view of the minister concerned.
Scott:	Is this approach bred of a desire for convenient administration?
Leit:	I think so, yes. We go back to the point that the policy and advice is worthy of the protection ... It is this whole process of confidentiality.
Scott:	Confidentiality has never been the basis of Public Interest Immunity certificates alone. What has been required is damage to the public interest.
Leit:	What damages the public interest is the disclosure of a whole process as regards to ministers.
Scott:	Regardless of the contents?
Leit:	Yes.
Scott:	That is a very difficult proposition to justify, is it not?
Leit:	These certificates by no means are final. If the judge considers the documents ought to be disclosed, then he will order them to be disclosed.
Bax:	The judge is meant to receive assistance from the minister, is he not?

Leit:	Yes.
Bax:	And if the judge is told that this is a case where it is in the public interest that these discussions, once revealed, would be injurious to the public good, the judge is likely to believe that?
Leit:	Yes.
Bax:	He has no yardstick to know that, in fact, these discussions between the officials really would not injure a flea, and it is just because it is inconvenient?
Leit:	That is right.
Scott:	Would not every certificate have this in common – that it constitutes a representation to the judge by the person making the certificate, usually a minister, that material will be damaging to the public interest?
Leit:	Yes.
Scott:	Is it an unfair impression that there was a desire to keep the knowledge of the existence of these documents from the defence?
Leit:	Well, the prosecution obviously thought so.
Bax:	What the minister has to do, is it not, is make a judgement on the facts? Is that not what he is meant to be doing?
Leit:	He has to make a judgment as to whether the document is within the class or not.
Scott:	Why does he not have to make a judgment as to whether disclosure is going to be contrary to the public interest?
Leit:	Well –
Scott:	Why is that not the point?
Leit:	The point is that any disclosure of documents within this class is contrary to the public interest.
Bax:	You are saying that.
Scott:	Who says so Mr Leithead? The minister may say so, but if the minister does not say so, then who is it to correct him?
Leit:	It is open to challenge in court, of course.
Scott:	Mr Leithead, it is not the Attorney-General's job, let alone that of prosecuting counsel, to decide whether disclosure of a particular document would be contrary to the public interest. That is for the minister, is it not?
Leit:	Yes, I suppose it is. But, on the other hand, the minister is constrained

by what has happened in past cases –

Bax: Why?

Leit: Because of the policy.

Scott: Do you have draft Public Interest Immunity certificates in your department on the word processor?

Leit: No. We use the Xerox machine quite a bit. The minister either agrees or is brought to agree with the policy and he has formed a view.

Bax: He either agrees or is brought to agree, he is told he jolly well has to.

Leit: We, he is advised, as ministers are.

Bax: He is told he has no choice.

Leit: Not really.

Bax: Let us take the background documents of the meeting of the Machine Tools Technologies Association. I think we should actually look at them. They are briefings for the meeting with Alan Clark.

Leit: Yes.

Bax: It is Mr Steadman's note. I entirely understand there may be parts of this that one would not want disclosed, but what I cannot immediately see is why is this document not relevant to the case?

Leit: It does not exactly say what happened at the meeting.

Bax: It is before the meeting. It is saying what the Government's knowledge is.

Leit: Yes.

Bax: Why would that not be relevant, remembering what you know about defence?

Leit: That is certainly what the prosecution counsel thought, otherwise he would have not settled the certificate.

Bax: He did not settle it. You settled it. You approved it. Who wrote those words? Who thought up, saying: "It is improbable that such documents can have any significant relevance"? Or was it just put on the Xerox copy?

Leit: Certainly not.

Scott: Do you, sitting there now, regard it as a document of no significant relevance?

Leit: Yes, I do not, no. I think that is probably wrong.

Scott: I am sorry, what is your present view?

Leit: My present view is that it is relevant, but that is with the benefit of hindsight.

Bax: A minister is entitled to have a view that disclosure would not be injurious?

Leit: Well, I am not sure about that.

Scott: Your stance, as I understand it, is that once it is established that the documents fall within the requisite class, the minister has no discretion?

Leit: In effect, yes. As I say, it is damaging to the public interest to have the decision-making process exposed.

Bax: You are saying: "any decision-making process"?

Leit: To have any decision-making process exposed.

sc vi

Scene between Alan Moses and Geoffrey Robertson

An argument between Alan Moses QC, counsel for the prosecution, and Geoffrey Robertson QC, counsel for Henderson, before the trial judge, his honour Judge Smedley QC, at the Old Bailey on September 30, 1992.

Moses: My Lord, the issue before the court today is whether documents, in respect of which public interest immunity is claimed, should be disclosed to the defence.

My Lord, there are before the court a number of certificates from different ministers. In the green bundle, your Lordship sees the certificate from the Foreign Office Minister of State, Mr Garel-Jones. In the red bundle, your Lordship will find a certificate from Mr Rifkind, Secretary of State for Defence. In the purple bundle, a certificate from Mr Heseltine, president of the Board of Trade. And my Lord, finally, there are certificates from Kenneth Clarke, the Secretary of State for the Home Department.

They concern – your Lordship will be able to read them for yourself – consideration and application of policy relating to the export of machine tools to Iraq; the state of mind of those considering the policy; and consideration of whether to forbid export of the machines.

I have read those documents, so has my learned junior. We do not consider they assist the defence in relation to any foreseeable issue, still less assist the defence in relation to whether the Department of Trade and Industry connived at concealment by the defendants of the true purpose for which the machines were to be used.

The documents do not in any sense help the defence.

Robert: In looking at the certificates, to begin with the certificate of Mr Garel-Jones, he notes that these documents relate to the formation of policy of Her Majesty's Government, in particular with regard to relations with, and the export of, military and quasi-military products.

Mr Garel-Jones forms an opinion that the requirement of witnesses to give oral evidence as to meetings, discussions, and deliberations would be injurious to the public interest. We do not know what meetings he is talking about, because we have not seen the documents, but we have a most disquieting note sounding there that this minister seems to think that he can limit the scope of evidence. His reasoning is: all these documents fall into a class of documents relating to the formation of government policy and the internal dealings of government departments.

Well, the answer to that is that ministers are being called by the prosecution in this case and it is fundamental that they are going to give a version of policy which may be contested by the defence as not being the true or correct policy. The defence must be entitled to know what the real policy was.

(Reads)   *"It would be against the public interest if Category B documents revealed the process of providing ministers with honest and candid advice."*

This is, of course, a long way from the position today where ministers within a couple of years of leaving public office publish their memoirs or diaries. Indeed, a central prosecution witness, Mr Alan Clark – the publication of his diaries is about to happen.

So then we come to the documents in category C – that the security and intelligence services require secrecy.

Here we have the central claim which needs care and scrutiny.

(Reads)   *"Evidence about the identity of members of the security and intelligence services could put their lives at risk and substantially impair their capability to perform the tasks assigned to them."*

The first point to be made about that it that the only person whose life is at risk is Mr Paul Henderson, who has assisted the security and intelligence services in relation to matters with which he is charged.

sc vii
Evidence of Tristan Garel-Jones

Scott: Good morning, Mr Garel-Jones.
G-Jones: Good morning.
Bax: Mr Garel-Jones, you were Minister of State at the Foreign Office from 1990 to 1993 and I would like to ask you about Public Interest Immunity certificates you signed in that capacity. Can we go to FCO 114/2, page 186. It is a submission to you of September 3, 1992 from Mr Nixon that went through Mr Gore-Booth. What you need out is the questionnaire, your statement and the bundle.
G-Jones: I have them.
Bax: It says: "Problem: Should the minister sign the attached PII certificate?" It was recommended you should sign it "today". "Background: Customs and Excise are prosecuting three British directors of Matrix Churchill in respect of illegal export of equipment to Iraq in 1988 to 1990. At the time, Matrix Churchill was a largely Iraqi-owned British company. Leading counsel for the prosecution has examined Foreign Office files relating to Matrix Churchill licence applications, and has identified those papers likely to be relevant and potentially disclosable to the defence. They are all of a type which it would be normal for the Government to refuse to disclose. They fall into three categories: Category A, which is the informant category; Category B, which includes the minutes, notes and letters between ministers and/or officials. All these documents relate to the formulation of policy of the Government, in particular with regard to relations with and the export of military and quasi-military equipment to foreign countries. And Category C has documents which include material relating to secret intelligence.
Then paragraph 4 continues: "The Crown can seek to prevent the disclosure of documents in legal proceedings on the basis that

	disclosure would not be in the public interest. A certificate to this effect has to be given by a minister, but it is not conclusive. Whether PII can be claimed is a matter for the court to decide." Prior to receiving this submission, had you been concerned at all about signing a PII certificate?
G-Jones:	No.
Bax:	Were you satisfied that the classes referred to need to be protected from disclosure?
G-Jones:	I have no doubts about that. Curiously enough, I had a letter two weeks ago, a friendly letter on another matter, from a constituent, who clearly believes that arms exports to Iraq were agreed by the Government in secret, deceiving Parliament and so on. I believe that to be wholly unfounded.
Bax:	The public disquiet is because the public perceives that the PII claims were too broad.
Scott:	The minister signs a PII certificate. But there are degrees of damage. If the degree of damage is going to be trivial, it is almost inevitable that the judge is going to come down in favour of disclosure.
G-Jones:	As he did in this case.
Scott:	The minister has to certify that the documents, if disclosed, will cause significant public damage.
G-Jones:	"Unquantifiable" – is that not the word?
Scott:	"Unquantifiable" was the word you used. The question that troubles me is whether the nature of that damage to the public interest, which is no more than a fear that the Government might be exposed to what has been described as "captious and ill-informed criticism" is enough to justify non-disclosure?
G-Jones:	You say, "No more" dismissively. I regard that as quite important. I regard all advice to ministers as being, in principle, confidential. The trial judge took the view that the interests of justice override. If I may add this. The general view is that, because these documents were made public, the trial collapsed. The trial collapsed because Mr Alan Clark changed his evidence, not because of anything to do with these documents.
Scott:	That is a point of view. It is not the only point of view.

G-Jones: What is the other point of view?

Scott: It has also been argued that the disclosure of the documents made it inevitable that the prosecution would fail.

G-Jones: I see.

Scott: I did not want you to take it as axiomatic that everybody agreed that the prosecution collapsed because of Mr Clark's evidence.

Bax: I would like to go to a document to the Foreign Secretary copied to your private secretary, page 249 of the bundle. It refers to the fact that documents were going to be redacted, and that there might be other documents that would have to be disclosed; and they were considering whether there needed to be further PII certificates.

In fact, when the trial judge ordered that the Category C documents with the redactions should be revealed to the defendants, did you suggest that the national interest still required that the documents should not be disclosed, even if this led to the case being dropped?

G-Jones: No.

Bax: Did you ever consider doing that?

G-Jones: No.

Bax: Do you think that it is surprising in the light of the strong language in your PII certificate?

G-Jones: No.

Bax: Why not?

G-Jones: Because I think the word "unquantifiable" can mean unquantifiably large or unquantifiably small.

Scott: So when the text of your certificates reads: "The disclosure of any sources or alleged sources of intelligence information would cause unquantifiable damage to the functions of security and intelligence in relation to the United Kingdom and abroad", the trial judge should have read that as covering both unquantifiably great and also *minuscule?*

G-Jones: Yes.

Bax: I am sorry to depress you, but can we look at one or two documents. It is the comments of the Foreign Secretary on November 16, 1992: "PII certificates. The Secretary of State is not

G-Jones: at all happy about the procedure as it has affected Mr Garel-Jones and finds the role which is expected of ministers to be baffling."

G-Jones: I think I made it clear I was irked at being given an important decision of this kind at such short notice. I felt it rather strongly that I should have it in my weekend box.

Scott: The Foreign Secretary is not, here, talking about the time constraints that may apply to ministers, is he?

G-Jones: I think it could be directed to a whole range of things. In principle, it is baffling that quite an important decision – I said earlier on, although it meets with derision amongst the press – that no minister in a democracy would regard it as a light thing to withhold information from the public.

Scott: This is not withholding from the public. It is withholding it from defence.

Jones: Or indeed from a court. Therefore it is "baffling" that a decision of this kind turns up in my box at 2.00 in the morning and I have to spit out an answer by 9.00 the next day. That is one aspect of the case that is baffling.

Scott: Apart from whatever time constraints there may be, do you not find the role of ministers in the PII procedure baffling at all?

Jones: No.

SC viii
Evidence of Michael Heseltine

Scott: Mr Heseltine, good morning. Thank you very much indeed for coming here this morning to help us, and thank you for sending us the statement in answer to the questionnaire, which we have carefully read.

Bax: I would like to move to the question of Public Interest Immunity. It's page 10 of your statement to the inquiry. I would like to pick it up on September 2, 1992, when you received a submission from Mr Meadway, one of your officials. There are comments in the top-right hand corner: "This is potentially troublesome. In the short-term, it appears we have no choice but to claim immunity but, it if comes to court, the press will have a field day." Was that you?

Hesel: No, that was Peter Smith, who is my private secretary. All the hieroglyphics on this document are me.

Bax: Then in paragraph 11 it refers to the involvement of Mr Henderson and how he was providing information to the Security Service. Then in paragraph 12, it refers to an informant letter from a Matrix Churchill employee, and the fact that no action had been taken following that letter. Against that paragraph you have put lots of lines, you have put five lines. Were you very concerned about what paragraph 12 said?

Hesel: Miss Baxendale has actually rightly gone through the rolling sense of concern and the way in which I recorded it at the time, not very articulately but nevertheless graphically. I had come across paragraph 10 where it says: "The involvement of the security services ... the case against the defendants is not that the goods were used for manufacturing military equipment, but that they had lied as to whether the machines were specially designed." So my question was, if the real crime was the export of this equipment, why were they not being prosecuted for that as opposed to just the fact that they filled in a form inaccurately? We then went on to the two question marks which are here: "The case for the prosecution is a good one, but unfortunately it may appear to the uninformed reader that the Government did not and does not care that Matrix Churchill was selling equipment for manufacturing weapons of war, and only that lies were told." That is exactly what people would say.
We then go on: "It is also true that, when the security services man called upon Matrix Churchill, the defendant had told the reception that the visitor was from the Department of Trade and Industry, and so the cover was maintained. Parliamentary questions were tabled at the time this information became public, but were given a suitably uncommunicative blocking answer." Here we have a line and a question mark, because what this was telling me was that the security services at that time were in touch with Matrix Churchill. If they were in touch with Matrix

Churchill, and we were prosecuting them for lying about forms and not for the manufacture, I began to be preoccupied that we knew more than the superficialities of this official submission would indicate.

Then we go to paragraph 12. This is where it really became rather serious: "A further consideration is that in 1988, a Matrix Churchill employee wrote to Sir Geoffrey Howe telling him that Matrix Churchill were making machine tools to produce mortar shells."

That got three lines under it, because we knew, apparently. It then goes on: "No action appears to have been taken on this letter by the Ministry of Defence, to whom it was sent, or by the DTI's export licensing branch, or the Security Service, who also received a copy."

By that time you have two or three lines, because it told me that *everybody* knew. Then it goes on: "Assuming the writer retains his public-spirited interest, it may well be that, as the details of the case get into the public domain, he may well feel moved to write again, but possibly to the press."

This attracted five lines, and the reason it attracted five lines is because it became apparent to me that I would have to go and try and indulge in the process of – what is the word – "uncommunicative" answers, and I was not prepared to do that. So that was where we were when I first read the submission. I said: "Up with this, I will not put."

Scott:	How would you describe the "this"?
Hesel:	That I was being asked to sign a document which would deny these documents to the proper trial.

The upshot was I said I would not sign the PII certificate that was put in front of me. I simply said, 'I am not signing it.' It could not be right to suggest that the documents were not relevant to the defence.

Bax:	Did you consider that the timescale that you had been given, which was from 3rd September to 4th September, was too short to consider what you were meant to be doing?
Hesel:	Yes, but I think that about most of the documents on my desk.

Bax:	So you see it as inevitable –
Hesel:	I happen to know the figures. Five hundred documents come into my private office a day. One hundred of them come through to me. There is always a foot of paper waiting to be dealt with, and it is always urgent. The whole psychology of Whitehall is at 6 o'clock they close their desk, send it to me, asking for a reply by first thing tomorrow morning. That is the way the system works.
Bax:	In a note, a lawyer in your department says: "The papers Mr Heseltine had seen suggested that Whitehall departments had been well aware of the intended military use, yet the defendants seemed to be being prosecuted for concealing it ... It would look as though Mr Heseltine had been engaged in a cover-up.
	You were concerned that you thought these documents should be disclosed and if you put in a certificate "seeking to support public interest immunity" it would look as though you had not thought that?
Hesel:	My interest was not whether the case proceeded. My interest was whether I could in any way do anything to damage the defence prospects. That was my interest in the matter.
	My view was that the documents should be released. If there was injury to the public interest, for the reasons that would flow from the class category of documents that, in my view, should be overwhelmed by the justice argument.
	The Attorney-General's letter to me of September 7, 1992, makes clear his understanding of my concern. I was reassured by the following passage in his letter. It says: "The drafting of the certificate is unusual, and the judge and defendants will be alert to its limited scope which can, if necessary, be emphasised by counsel for the Crown orally." It was on that basis that I signed the certificate. I defend absolutely the system of public interest immunity. I believe that it is a system which has been justified but it is a special privilege, of course it is.
Bax:	Kenneth Clarke, the Home Secretary, Tristan Garel-Jones at the Foreign Office, and Malcolm Rifkind, the Defence Secretary, also signed PII certificates. Did they know you had signed a different certificate?

Hesel: They did ... I just did not want them to be in a position where they discovered I had done this without being told.

Bax: I want to pick up a point. It is a DTI document, page 16742. The second page says: "Mr Heseltine said that in the Matrix Churchill case, no rational person who had looked at the files could have said that the documents should not have been disclosed. It would have been terrible if a defendant had gone to jail as a result of non-disclosure." Right?

Hesel: That was the whole basis of what I was doing.

Bax: I would like to look at another prosecution involving the DTI in November 1992, shortly after the collapse of the Matrix Churchill trial, where the question of PII certificates also arose. Your private secretary says in a letter to Miss Wheldon of the Attorney-General's office: "Mr Heseltine commented that he found this incredible. In the Matrix Churchill case, he was told he had a duty to sign a PII certificate. Now, however, he was told that the prosecuting counsel had a discretion denied to ministers." Pausing here, did you find it strange that the discretion could lie with prosecution counsel and not with yourself?

Hesel: Yes.

Bax: Then it was decided the best thing was to have a meeting between yourself and the Attorney-General. We find a note of that at page 16742 – "Mr Heseltine said that no one had explained to him in the context of Matrix Churchill that there was a discretion as to whether PII should be claimed or not. He was told he had a duty."
Then: "Mr Heseltine queried whether Mr Moses, the leading prosecuting counsel, had, in fact, been aware of the difference in position between ministers on their PII certificates on the Matrix Churchill case." He quoted from the note which Mr Moses had subsequently prepared, in which he said that neither he, nor the judge, understood that other ministers were taking a different line to that taken by Mr Heseltine.

Hesel: There is a note by Mr Moses.

Bax: That is right. It says: "In the event, I argued, and the judge accepted, that all ministers were adopting the same stance, and were not intending to make any comments as to how the balancing exercise should be carried out. I was never instructed to the contrary."

Hesel: Here you have counsel for the prosecution saying that he did not understand it and neither did the judge, that there was any difference between what I had done and other ministers.

Bax: Having now looked at the passages we have drawn to your attention to in the submissions that were made to the judge, do you think a clear message of the kind you were intending was sent to the judge?

Hes: No, and it should have been.

Bax: Does that concern you?

Hes: Of course. I thought I had done all I properly could to indicate to the judge what I thought the position to be and I find it difficult to explain the way in which events worked out.

sc ix
Evidence of Sir Nicholas Lyell

Bax: Sir Nicholas, what I would like to do is to come to what happened to Mr Heseltine.

Scott: The courts have made it clear on many, many occasions, that the judge of what the public interest requires, and what is going to damage the public interest, is primarily the minister. If Mr Heseltine is running his eye down the list of documents and he concludes it is clear that these documents must be disclosed, he does not sign the certificate?

Lyell: His view deserves respect.

Scott: It is more than that. He conscientiously thinks it is clear that these documents must be disclosed, and it is a sort of instinct for justice ... knowing the purpose for which the documents are wanted ... He has had advice and he still thinks it is a clear case. He happens not to agree with the advice he has had. In such a situation, the conscientious refusal would apply, would it not?

Lyell: It could do.

Bax:　　I would like to go to Mr Kenneth Clarke's certificate for a moment. On what basis do you understand Mr Clarke authorised the giving of prosecution evidence by members of the security and intelligence services?

Lyell:　　You have suggested he is exercising his discretion to allow disclosure of information normally covered by PII certificates. I do not think it is correct. A minister does not have discretion.

Scott:　　It was said Kenneth Clarke had to conclude that evidence from the security and intelligence services was necessary for the prosecution?

Lyell:　　Yes.

Scott:　　You must of course accept that the other side of that coin is that if other information is necessary for the defence, they should also be disclosed?

　　　　In the Matrix Churchill case, you do not think that the material about civil servants advice to ministers was just as necessary to the defence as this evidence about the security services was necessary to the prosecution?

Lyell:　　No, I do not. And I could not have exercised a personal judgment in the Matrix Churchill case because I had never seen the documents.

Scott:　　I have to look at your personal involvement, and there are questions about that. I also have to look at the case overall and about whether the overall conduct of it was fair to the defence. The prosecution does not seem bound by the PII rigours in the same way as the defence does?

Lyell:　　Not necessarily so.

Bax:　　Were you aware that Mr Henderson had been in contact with the intelligence agencies?

Lyell:　　I do not believe I learnt anything about Mr Henderson being an agent until the trial.

Bax:　　Is it not strange that a minister – and it is particularly a minister because of his knowledge of the public interest – is not allowed to say in the certificate: "In my view, these documents should be disclosed"?

Scott:　　I suppose this was probably not considered, but it would not have been the clearest way of pointing out Mr Heseltine's views to add a sentence to the certificate to say: "I wish to raise no argument against disclosure of these documents"?

Lyell: Yes.

Bax: The letter was not copied to Mr Moses, counsel for the Crown?

Lyell: No, but I certainly expected Mr Moses to see it. I am very surprised that it was not shown to him through the Treasury solicitors.

Bax: Did you expect Mr Moses to see it via the Treasury solicitors?

Lyell: Yes.

Bax: Did you take any steps to make sure that Mr Moses did know about what you said?

Lyell: I did not take any extra steps and I was not aware until certainly long after the trial had collapsed that he had not seen it.

Bax: Was it not reasonable of Mr Heseltine to take the view, having seen the correspondence passing between the two of you, that Mr Moses, the prosecution counsel, was going to be instructed as to Mr Heseltine's view?

Lyell: The way that his view was going to be conveyed was by the points made in those letters. There was no other way that his view was going to be conveyed.

Bax: There could have been, could there not? You could have rung up, lots of things could have happened?

Lyell: Miss Baxendale, masses of things *could* have happened.

Scott: Sir Nicholas, to what extent do you think you have a responsibility for this lack of instructions to Mr Moses?

Lyell: I am a minister of the Crown. The Treasury Solicitor's Department is one of four departments that fall under my responsibility, and, therefore, I have ministerial responsibility.

Scott: Do you think you should have taken steps to ensure that instructions were sent, which adequately reflected the concerns of Mr Heseltine?

Lyell: No.

Scott: Did you give any instructions to the Treasury Solicitor's Department as to how they were to approach the briefing of counsel in regard to the PII matter?

Lyell:	No.
Scott:	Do you think you should have done?
Lyell:	No.
Scott:	Is there any more to be said than just "no".

SC X

Leithead, Higson, Thatcher, Clark, Heseltine, Gore-Booth, Garel-Jones, Major and Waldegrave reappear:

Leit:	It is damaging to the public interest to have decision-making process exposed.
Hig:	The Iraqi market, after the end of the Iran-Iraq war, was summed up as being "the big prize".
Thatch:	They are exactly what they say – guidelines – they are not law. They are guidelines.
Bax:	Did the have to be followed?
Thatch:	I beg your pardon?
Clark:	There was an implied invitation to them to participate in a fiction.
Hesel:	The upshot was I said I would not sign the PII certificate that was put in front of me. I simply said, "I'm not signing it."
Thatch:	Remember, they are guidelines. It is not like interpreting law ... They are guidelines.
G-Booth:	Questions should be answered so as to give the maximum degree of satisfaction.
Leit:	When one is dealing with PII claims, one tends to take a rather generous view of the –
Scott:	Take what sort of view?
Leit:	Generous.
Scott:	Generous to whom?
G-Jones:	I think the word "unquantifiable" can mean unquantifiably large or unquantifiably small.
Leit:	Yes, I do not, no. I think that is probably wrong.
Hesel:	I thought I had done all I properly could to indicate to the judge what I thought the position to be and I find it difficult to explain the way in which events worked out.

Clark: My former colleague, Mr Waldegrave, said, "Because something was not announced, it had not happened." He was arguing that because it had not been announced, it could not have happened, a sort of Berkeleyan philosophy.

Major: One of the charges at the time, of course, was that, in some way, I must have known, because I had been the Chancellor, because I had been Foreign Secretary, because I had been Prime Minister, that, therefore, I must have known what was going on ... I was asking precisely what I had known.

Lyell: Miss Baxendale, masses of things could have happened.

Walde: You have to believe that Whitehall is basically honest, which is what I believe.

Scott: Is there any more to be said than just "no"?

Thatch: I fear there will be much grammar to be corrected.

The End

Index